REAPING THE
WHIRLWIND

REAPING THE
WHIRLWIND

The Civil Rights Movement in Tuskegee

with a new concluding chapter by the author

ROBERT J. NORRELL

The University of North Carolina Press

Chapel Hill and London

Originally published by Alfred A. Knopf, Inc.,
New York, in 1985; reprinted by arrangement with
Alfred A. Knopf, Inc.

The paper in this book meets the guidelines
for permanence and durability of the Committee on
Production Guidelines for Book Longevity of the
Council on Library Resources.

Portions of Chapter 1 were originally published as
"Perfect Quiet, Peace, and Harmony: Another Look at
the Founding of Tuskegee Institute," in *The Alabama
Review*, April 1983. Copyright © 1983 by the
University of Alabama Press.

Library of Congress Cataloging-in-Publication Data
Norrell, Robert J. (Robert Jefferson)
Reaping the whirlwind: the civil rights movement in
Tuskegee, with a new concluding chapter by the author /
Robert J. Norrell.
p.   cm.
Originally published: New York: Knopf, 1985.
Includes bibliographical references and index.
ISBN 0-8078-4740-2 (alk. paper)
1. Afro-Americans—Civil rights—Alabama—Tuskegee.
2. Afro-Americans—Alabama—Tuskegee—Politics and
government.   3. Tuskegee (Ala.)—Race relations.
4. Civil rights movements—Alabama—Tuskegee—
History—20th century.   I. Title.
F334.T96N67 1999 305.896'073'09761—dc21 98-29257 CIP

09 08 07 06 05   6 5 4 3 2

Contents

A section of illustrations will be found following page 116.

Acknowledgments

My greatest debt in the writing of this book is to Paul M. Gaston of the University of Virginia, who inspired me, as an undergraduate, to want to be a historian; who suggested a set of values and concerns that are central to American history; and who directed the doctoral dissertation of which this is a revision. As mentor, friend, and editor, he has provided the precise admixture of criticism, prodding, and praise to get me to the end of a long project. Professor Gaston deserves much of the credit for whatever merits this work may have.

I am indebted to several historians who have read drafts of this manuscript. J. Mills Thornton III of the University of Michigan brought his vast knowledge of Alabama history and his keen analytical abilities to the subject and significantly improved my understanding of it. John T. Kneebone of Harvard University raised several important questions about interpretation. Robert D. Cross, David Levin, and Edward L. Ayers, all of the University of Virginia, subjected the manuscript to careful editing. I am also grateful to Professor Cross for supporting my career in other ways over the years. Howard R. Lamar of Yale University made several useful observations about social relations in Tuskegee, of which he is a native.

A number of persons assisted me in research. William P. Mitchell provided access to the files of the Tuskegee Civic Association and patiently responded to my hundreds of questions about Tuskegee and its people. Daniel T. Williams and the late Helen Dibble of the Hollis Burke Frissell Library at Tuskegee Institute gave me access to the many useful documents in their collections. Charles G. Gomillion, Ennis Sellers, Robert D. Miller, and Alice Lee Wadsworth lent me valuable personal papers. Florida Broward Segrest answered many questions about the history of Macon County. David J. Garrow of the University of North Carolina at Chapel Hill advised me on the use of the Freedom of Information Act.

I am happy to acknowledge several personal debts incurred during the completion of this book. W. Edmund Moomaw of Birmingham-Southern College has given me encouragement and professional support. Vonda W. Fulton has tolerated with good humor my bad handwriting and bad temper through many typings of the manuscript. Ashbel Green and Peter Hayes at Alfred A. Knopf, Inc., have been patient and supportive. Dan O. Dowe made several pertinent criticisms of the manuscript and endured many long discussions about Tuskegee. My wife, Kelly Dowe, has been an unswerving supporter of this project since the beginning, despite the intrusions it has made on her life. A fine editor and a sensitive interpreter of human relations, she has influenced significantly the character of this book.

It is a pleasure to dedicate this book to my parents, Robert D. and Mary Ann Norrell, who have given me unfailing support in this, and all other endeavors.

April 1984 R.J.N.

Foreword

The civil rights movement of the 1950s and 1960s made its way to every community in the South. In Montgomery, Albany, Birmingham, Selma, and a few others, it arrived with fanfare and occupied the limelight for much of its stay. It slipped into other towns and lay low for a while before making its presence known. It had a different experience in each place, and no place was the same after it left. Each community now has a story to tell about the movement, and only when many of those stories are told will the South's great social upheaval be well understood.

What follows is one of those stories. This is about Tuskegee, Alabama, and it focuses mainly on the efforts of blacks to gain the right to vote. It dwells on politics because much of the change and conflict in the county was manifested first and most fully in competition for control of political offices. But it also examines related changes in other institutions—particularly families, churches, and schools. It tries to reveal the many fears that the changes caused among whites. It is about power: whites trying to keep control of their society and blacks seeking more autonomy. In a larger sense, it is the story of two communities, one white and one black, in the painful process of merging into a single, if very different, community.

This study has particular significance for the place of Booker Washington in American history. Washington's experiment, which promised that blacks would realize full equality once they had made themselves useful to society, ultimately succeeded in Tuskegee. Well-educated, economically secure Institute professors successfully challenged white conservative control of Tuskegee after Washington's hands-off policy toward politics was forsaken in the late 1930s. Middle-class blacks in Tuskegee demonstrated after 1940 that political rights would indeed follow from economic power. The Washington philosophy was vindicated, at least in its place of birth.

There was a pattern of conflict and change for scores of Black Belt communities across the South. Tuskegee is hardly a microcosm of the region; Macon County, for which Tuskegee is the seat of government, had a higher percentage of black population—about eighty-four percent—than any other county in the United States in the 1960s. But the concerns of its people resembled those in the many southern rural communities where blacks held a large majority. The experience of blacks and whites in Tuskegee in the 1960s shared important similarities with what happened to people in the South Carolina low country, the Mississippi delta, and southern Georgia at about the same time. Sweeping political changes, the intervention of federal power, and the rejection by whites of the public school system characterized the history of Tuskegee and most predominantly black communities in the South in the 1960s.

This study fixes the beginning of the civil rights movement in Tuskegee at 1941. Most considerations of the history of the movement have put the starting date later—at the *Brown* decision in 1954 or at the sit-in movement of 1960—though they usually recognized foreshadowing events of earlier years. Historians have begun to examine the 1930s and 1940s and have found not just a few tantalizing moments of protest but a widespread, if not yet mature, struggle to overthrow segregation and institutionalized racism. Here I have focused at length on the events and circumstances that led to the rapid and dramatic changes of the 1960s. Indeed, the story of the civil rights movement in Tuskegee begins with events that took place in and around the town in 1870.

REAPING THE
WHIRLWIND

1

Perfect Quiet, Peace, and Harmony

JAMES ALSTON returned to his home in Tuskegee, Alabama, late on a Saturday night in early June 1870 from a meeting of the Republican party at the Zion Negro Church. The leader of the local black Republicans, Alston represented Macon County in the Alabama state legislature. Just as he and his wife were going to bed, a hail of gunfire blasted the house, part of it striking him in the back and hip. Mrs. Alston, who was pregnant, was hit in the foot. Alston counted more than three hundred buckshot holes in his house. Remarkably, neither he nor his wife was seriously injured. He had not seen his assailants but he had a good idea of who they were. The next morning he sent word to his fellow Macon County freedmen to come to Tuskegee. Several hundred armed blacks arrived that afternoon to offer protection against Alston's enemies, the local white Democrats.[1]

Greatly alarmed by the black response, Tuskegee whites quickly met to organize a party of forty armed men to patrol the town. General Cullen Battle, a local lawyer and planter who nine years before had raised the Tuskegee Light Infantry for the Confederacy, was appointed by the county sheriff, a white Republican currying Democratic favor, to lead the patrol. Beyond his command experience in the Confederate Army, Battle's qualifications for the task included his special relationship with James Alston: Alston had once been his slave and, as Battle later testified, was his drummer "at the commencement of our difficulties" in 1861. On Sunday night Battle and his men watched the freedmen assemble at Alston's home. At sunrise the next morning the general and the county probate judge, J. T.

Menifee, another Republican aligned with the Democrats, consulted with the injured man. Battle promised Alston that there
would be no further attacks on him, whereupon the hundreds of
freedmen dispersed, leaving only a small protective force. But Menifee delivered a stern warning to make the lesson of Saturday night's
events absolutely clear: "a nigger couldn't hold no office in that
county no longer," Alston later said Menifee told him, "and he knew
that I was going to be shot; . . . a nigger wasn't fit for nothing else
than to drive oxen, and drive the carriage of white folks."[2]

Alston's problems had hardly ended. Later that morning Thomas
Dryer, a prominent white merchant and Democrat who lived next
door, sent Alston a message threatening his life. That night Alston's
home was fired on again. The following morning a conciliatory General Battle appeared once more. According to Alston, who suspected
that his former master was behind the most recent attack, Battle had
said, "Jim, I have found that blacks will fight. I come now to you to
make a compromise. . . . The county is big enough for all of us to
live, and if you will quiet your men, I will quiet mine." Alston replied that "the colored men in Macon" were already "law-abiding
and quiet."[3]

Shortly after Battle left, eight local Democrats came to tell Alston
that if he wished to live he had to leave Macon County. Among
those in the group were his neighbor Dryer; Robert Johnson, whom
he believed to be the father of his mulatto wife and who had once
offered him three thousand dollars to campaign for the Democratic
cause, a proposition Alston thought designed to "use me as a Ten-
nessee man would use a gray horse among mules"; George Washington Campbell, a prominent merchant; and Colonel Robert
Abercrombie, a leading lawyer and planter. Alston was persuaded,
but found even leaving dangerous. He spent ten days in nearby
swamps avoiding would-be assassins—hired by Abercrombie, he believed—before he made his way to Montgomery, forty miles to the
west.[4]

Alston's troubles were only the beginning of several months of intimidation and violence aimed at controlling the November state
and local elections. Several of the freedmen who had protected Alston were soon arrested, convicted of inciting to riot, and sentenced
to a railroad work gang. General Battle and a party of armed horse-
men patrolled the county at night throughout the summer and fall,
monitoring the activities of blacks, especially their political gather-
ings. Several black churches and schools were burned during the
summer. Intimidated black ministers, fearing the arsonists, stopped
allowing Republican meetings in their churches.[5]

William Dougherty and William B. Bowen, two white Republicans who were apparently more sincere in their radicalism than the sheriff and probate judge, were hanged in effigy in the Tuskegee town square. Dougherty was shot, but not seriously injured, by a white man who he believed was also partly responsible for the Alston shooting. He identified the man as an employee of Jesse Adams's livery stable in Tuskegee, noting the violent anti-Republican feeling of both the alleged assassin and Adams. Like Alston, Dougherty soon left Macon County.[6]

A month before the election the violence reached its high point. Local Democrats brandished pistols and heckled Republican speakers at a political meeting at the county courthouse in early October. Later that night the Reverend John Butler, minister of the Zion Negro Church, convened a meeting of the congregation's official board to discuss the church's finances. Several white men rode up to the church during the meeting. Butler warned his board members to stay calm, but suddenly whites charged in and began shooting. "Shoot the damned niggers," Butler heard one of the attackers shout. "Kill them every one." They would have done just that, he believed, had he not quickly put out the only light inside the church. Two members were killed and three others wounded. Butler escaped injury by crawling under his pulpit. The attackers had heard rumors, whites later told Butler, that James Alston had slipped back into the county and had called the meeting at the Zion Church. These unfounded rumors reportedly led to the attack.[7]

Democrats explained the violence as the work of dissident black Republicans upset over the tyranny of Alston, Dougherty, and other Radical leaders. The local authorities arrested five black men who, they alleged, had fired on Alston's home after a factional dispute at the Republican meeting that Alston had just attended. John Adams, a black employee of Jesse Adams's livery, was reported by whites to be Alston's primary antagonist and one of the attackers, though neither he nor any of the other four was ever convicted of assault on Alston. General Battle later testified that Alston was known to be overbearing to blacks and insolent to whites, but he admitted that his former slave had never shown him any disrespect. White conservatives contended that angry black Republicans had committed the murders at the Zion Church despite the fact that the group had assembled for nonpolitical reasons and notwithstanding evidence found near the church implicating two young Tuskegee white men known for their violent anti-Republican feelings.[8]

Dougherty, the leading local scalawag at the time, put the blame elsewhere. He attributed the violent acts to a group of young white men who had the tacit approval of older, respected conservatives. He would later argue that violence against himself, Alston, and the men at the Zion Church could have been prevented had leading Democrats denounced such lawlessness publicly. Dougherty pointed an accusing finger at Jesse Adams, saying that much of the violence originated in his stables. He noted the failure of local law-enforcement authorities to punish the men who white conservatives claimed were responsible for the violence. He believed, as no doubt did most Republicans in Macon County, that the violence was aimed specifically at crippling Republican strength in the fall election.[9]

In the aftermath of the violence the Macon County Republican party held its majority but lost more than 600 voters among the 2,327 who had voted for President Grant in 1868. Another black replaced Alston in the legislature. Dougherty attributed part of the party's decline to Arthur L. Brooks, a Tuskegee lawyer and ardent Democrat. As the county voting registrar, Brooks had recorded the names of some Republicans in handwriting so difficult to read that many of their ballots were thrown out. Terrorism and fraud had not retrieved conservative power in 1870, but the invalidation of Republican ballots had set a precedent for a kind of action that would ultimately succeed.*

The violence had frightened the black population of the county. Butler testified in 1871 that the blacks of his acquaintance were more timid and insecure than they had been before 1870. "A great many are leaving the county, or speaking of leaving it," he noted, a result that whites had not intended. In exile in Montgomery that same year, James Alston stated that he would return to Macon County only when "I am protected by the thirteenth and fourteenth and fifteenth amendments as a man amongst men."[10]

At the same time white conservatives were pointing proudly to the growing number of blacks who were voting Democratic. Colonel Abercrombie, the man whom Alston believed responsible for assassins pursuing him through the swamps of Macon County, claimed that blacks had had promises from Republicans of "great good that they never realized, and [they] think that the course they have pur-

---

* Testimony of William Dougherty, in United States Senate Reports, No. 22, 42nd Cong., 2nd Sess., vol. IX, 1041. Dougherty added that he did not believe Brooks did "anything of the sort intentionally." He identified the voting registrar only as Mr. Brooks, but the manuscript census record reveals only one white man named Brooks in the county in 1870 and that was Arthur L. Brooks, a lawyer in Tuskegee. (*The Ninth Census of the United States: 1870*, Population Schedule, Macon County, p. 6 [Tuskegee beat, second part].)

sued has kept them estranged from the whites who are their best friends." In the fall of 1871 Abercrombie noted the absence of violence since the previous year's election. "Perfect quiet, peace, and harmony now prevail between the whites and blacks—that is Macon County."[11]

The events of 1870 in Macon County can best be understood in the context of evolving white anxieties. In the 1850s many white Alabamians had feared losing their independence and autonomy, which they felt were being threatened by abolitionism and northern opposition to slavery's expansion. Their insecurity about their inability to control their society had in 1861 led them to secede and then to go to war. Losing the war affirmed for many white southerners the legitimacy of their earlier fears. The subsequent uncertainty about the nature of the postwar society aggravated their fear, and Radical Reconstruction only exacerbated anxieties that were firmly embedded in the minds of many. In Macon County and throughout Alabama, Democrats responded tentatively to the advent of Radical Reconstruction in 1867 and 1868, but by 1870 they had determined to make an all-out effort to regain political control.[12]

The case of General Battle is instructive about the tribulations of white conservatives. The son of a North Carolina–born physician and planter, Cullen Battle had been raised in Eufaula, an antebellum trade center on the Chattahoochee River in southeastern Alabama. He was reading law in the office of his brother-in-law, John Gill Shorter, a leading Eufaula Fire-Eater and future governor, during the sectional crisis of 1850. One imagines that Battle as an impressionable young law clerk imbibed freely the Fire-Eater rhetoric of racial fear and an unwarranted northern usurpation of southern rights; the Fire-Eaters agitated for a southern withdrawal from the Union to protect the South's interests. In 1852, at the age of twenty-three, he set up a law practice in Tuskegee but devoted much of his time to politics. Like many young Fire-Eaters, he canvassed for James Buchanan in 1856. He was on the John Breckinridge electoral ticket in 1860 and toured the North on the vice-president's behalf with William Lowndes Yancey, the leading light of Alabama Fire-Eaters.[13]

Battle's war experience is noteworthy. As commander of the Tuskegee Light Infantry and lieutenant colonel of the Third Alabama Infantry Regiment, he fought at Seven Pines, Drewry's Bluff, and Richmond, where he was made a full colonel. He was injured slightly at Boonsboro and much more seriously at Fredericksburg, when his horse fell on him. He was at Chancellorsville and was promoted to general on the battlefield at Gettysburg. He encountered General Grant at the Wilderness and subsequently served at Spotsylvania and Winchester before withdrawing from active duty because of a severe knee injury sustained at the Battle of Cedar Bluff in October 1864. After such a valiant effort, defeat must have been especially hard for him to accept.[14]

At war's end, Battle could only have felt that the most foreboding predictions of Fire-Eater rhetoric had come to pass. Northern victory in a long, bloody conflict had finally denied the existence of "southern rights." The once-imagined fear of a mass of liberated blacks now had to be confronted in the flesh. He faced the uncertainty of an economic system stripped of slave labor—the crucial institution that he believed had made it viable. In politics he saw first chaos and then the emergence of a coalition of native white Unionists, Yankees, and blacks—each obnoxious in his view—that gained control of most county and state offices. He witnessed the political cooperation of respected local white men with former slaves: W. B. Bowen was a prominent lawyer and William Dougherty was the son of the county's popular circuit judge of the 1850s. He watched James Alston, a man he had once owned, become *his* representative in the Alabama legislature. He saw hundreds of armed blacks come to the defense of Alston when whites attempted to retrieve power that, in Battle's mind, rightly belonged to them. Old fears of slave insurrection and race war were, in a county that was almost four-fifths black, probably more acute in 1870 than they had ever been before.

General Battle's experience of fear and insecurity in these trying years would inform his political behavior for the rest of his life. Furthermore, the memory of secession, war, and Reconstruction would go beyond his lifetime to influence—indeed, at times to dictate—the actions of subsequent generations of white conservatives who faced similar challenges to their power and control. In later years, when white men in Macon County confronted black demands for rights, they also had to cope with the memory, and especially the myths built on it, of defeat and disorder in the 1860s. They would be no less afraid than General Battle and the men of his time.

Conservative fears were intense in the early 1870s, despite Colonel Abercrombie's proclamation of harmony. Both black and white Republicans continued to hold county offices. The party replaced Probate Judge Menifee—the man whom James Alston considered a wolf in Republican clothing—with a true Radical, Benjamin

Thompson.* In the mid-1870s whites became concerned about black emigration because a diminution in the black labor supply was seen as a threat to the local plantation economy. Some dispirited black Republicans urged a migration to the West at an "Emigration Society" convention in Montgomery in late 1874. The Tuskegee *Macon Mail,* a local Democratic paper, reported in 1876 that one party of forty blacks had just left the county, having been preceded by another group only days before, and that an emigration agent was working secretly in Tuskegee. Every train going westward was "a black cloud that pours [Negroes] down on the alluvial bottoms" of Mississippi, wrote Arthur L. Brooks, owner and editor of the *Mail* and the voter registrar reportedly responsible for the disqualification of some Republican votes in 1870. He counseled his readers to be firm in the face of this emigration: "Whenever you hear a Negro lately returned from the Mississippi bottom talk about having to walk all the way from Vicksburg and what a hard time he had, swear out a warrant against him on general principals [sic]. He is trying to entice [other blacks] off your land." The county's black population would in fact remain fairly constant at about 13,000 throughout the 1870s and 1880s, but the frequent migration of blacks caused much concern among white conservatives.[15]

National events contributed to continued white insecurity. Shortly after the Civil Rights Act of 1875 passed, the editor of the Democratic Tuskegee *News* reported that the legislation had made local blacks disrespectful and arrogant. But in a subsequent editorial, he argued that blacks had too much respect for whites to invoke the civil rights bill's equal accommodations provisions. "CUFFEE will never take advantage of the law made for his benefit, and [will] satisfy himself with accommodations heretofore enjoyed," he wrote. The editor explained what he believed to be the true purpose of the bill: "The white people of the South know full well that the measure was passed to aggravate them, and to cause trouble and dissention [sic] between the races and furnish capital for the next Presidential campaign." But white southerners would respond intelligently. "The people fully understand its design, will thwart the purpose of those hot-headed politicians who would degrade our social standing to carry their point . . . [will] submit to every indignity for a season

---

* The offices of county sheriff, tax assessor, tax collector, representative to the state House and Senate, and probate judge were all occupied by Republicans until 1875, and some were thereafter. (Tuskegee *News,* January 14, March 11, 25, April 22, June 3, 1875.)

. . . knowing that victory will be theirs." Written for an audience of local white conservatives, this editorial aimed less to persuade the undecided than to bolster the faithful. Its strained, defensive tone suggests that the editorialist may actually have been less sure about black attitudes and conservative power than his words indicate.[16]

The harmony that Colonel Abercrombie had proclaimed in 1871 finally came about—on the surface of society—in the mid-1870s, when white conservatives consolidated their political control. In a campaign marked by violence, intimidation, and vote-stealing, Democrats regained their dominance of state government in 1874, with the election of George Houston as governor. Alabama Republicans were badly split in that contest, and most subsequent ones, between a native white faction and a black-carpetbagger coalition. Thereafter they ceased to offer the Democrats a serious challenge in state politics.[17]

Conservatives began to regain control in Macon County when James Edward Cobb was elected to the circuit judgeship in 1874. A Confederate colonel who had been captured at Gettysburg and spent the remainder of the war in Union prisons, Cobb quickly asserted Democratic power when he took office. Macon County's two state representatives, both black Republicans, were charged with and convicted of felonies—adultery and grand larceny—in Cobb's court in early 1875, and were sentenced to chain gangs. At the same time the white Republican state senator apparently was charged with perjury, but avoided prosecution by resigning his office. The county's white Republican probate judge, Benjamin Thompson, though just reelected, had failed, in Cobb's eyes, to fix adequate bond to hold his office; Cobb declared the judgeship vacant and looked to his fellow Democrat, Governor Houston, to appoint a suitable replacement. P. S. Holt, the unsuccessful Democratic challenger to Thompson in the 1874 election, soon became Macon County's new probate judge. After Democrats had been elected in 1876 to fill the legislative places made available by Judge Cobb, the editor of the *News* announced with "proud satisfaction" that now for "the first time since the war" all county officials had been "selected by the white people."[18]

The development of new ways of controlling blacks also eased white anxiety. The crop lien system had evolved to a point in the mid-1870s at which most blacks, and many poor whites, were firmly lodged in a position of peonage under white planters and merchants. Black sharecroppers who were perennially in debt had to follow closely the dictates of their landlords or risk eviction, loss of credit at the local store, and perhaps a beating. Most blacks in this situation saw no alternative but to accept white dominance. The law, when administered by white conservatives like Judge Cobb, dealt severely with blacks who challenged white control. Recalcitrant blacks often drew long jail terms on charges of vagrancy or petit larceny. Blacks accounted for almost all of a significant increase in the state's convict population in the mid- and late 1870s. The convict lease system, initiated in the final antebellum years by parsimonious state legislators, was now being used by white conservatives as an efficient way of removing unruly blacks from their midst. A black man who ran afoul of Macon County authorities might find himself sentenced to the plantation of Colonel Abercrombie, who in 1880 was reputed to keep his chain gang of blacks well fed and happy.[19]

With some fears allayed, white conservatives turned their attention to local economic problems. Macon County had been suffering hard times for many years. Planters and slaves had rushed into the rich black bottom land of southern and western Macon County after the Creek Cession of 1832 and had made it a prosperous agricultural area for the next two decades. Tuskegee, which sits on a ridge in the north-central part of the county, became an important trading center serving the eastern end of the Alabama Black Belt. But Tuskegee and Macon County began to decline economically in the 1850s as new lands to the west offered better opportunities for plantation agriculture. Intensive cultivation had taken much of the vitality from Macon County's bottom land and had virtually exhausted the thinner soil on the long, low ridges that covered the northern third of the county. The economy was generally stagnant in the 1860s and 1870s. In 1879 the county tax collector advertised for sale 173 parcels of land—most of them farms of 80 or 160 acres—for nonpayment of the previous year's taxes, which were usually less than ten dollars. In the fall of 1880 the editor of the *News* noted that Macon was the only one of nineteen southeastern Alabama counties that had lost population since 1870.* "During the last ten years our population has fallen off and a large number of acres of land are standing idle, uncultivated," he observed.[20]

Arthur Brooks was a leader of an effort to improve the county's economic situation. As owner of the *Mail*, he devoted much of his journalistic energy in the late 1870s to boosting the local economy. The *Mail*'s "paramount desire," he wrote in 1878, was "the material and financial rehabilitation of our county." And, in the true spirit of boosterism, he simultaneously announced the achievement of that goal. "Tuskegee is evidently on the up grade again. The trade of the

---

* The decline in population was the result of whites leaving the county.

town has been greatly increased, while our magnificent schools and colleges, which have not been in so flourishing a condition at any previous time since the war, constitute a most reliable basis of prosperity." The academic institutions to which Brooks referred were Park High School, a private boys' academy, and the Alabama Methodist Female College. Both had indeed been a boon to local commerce for many years.[21]

Coincident with Brooks's boosterism were overtures of good will to the local black community. In 1879 the *Mail* complimented the work of the new minister of the Zion Negro Church: "Mr. Gomez is a young man of promise . . . capable of doing great good among his people." Neither the kind words nor the courtesy title afforded Gomez was likely to have gone unnoticed by Brooks's black readers. "Never since freedom has there been in this section a better state of feeling between whites and blacks," Brooks wrote. He was compelled, however, to make explicit the connection between the good relations and the political behavior of blacks. Whereas blacks had had "evil teaching" from men with "base and selfish" motives immediately after the war, "they had learned to respect the law, and rely on its authority." Brooks expressed confidence that Gomez would not permit blacks "to be led astray by meddlesome and designing persons." The message was clear: good race relations depended on black recognition of the inevitability of white conservative political control.[22]

The Tuskegee black community apparently saw in the white desire for interracial cooperation a chance to advance its own cause. In July 1878 the *Mail* published a letter to the editor from Gomez and five other men telling of the establishment of an "Educational Treasury" to benefit "the colored youths of Tuskegee" and soliciting "the aid of our white friends, who are lovers of education and intelligence." A similar but more detailed letter appeared a year later setting forth proposed means for establishing "a colored high school." Blacks would organize "educational societies" to raise money among themselves and would solicit "the aid of every one with whom they meet . . . all our white friends especially." They also intended to petition county and state authorities for aid. The letter was signed by the nine-man Board of Managers, at least six of whom were ministers. Later events would suggest that the leader of the group was a local tinsmith named Lewis Adams.[23]

The generally accepted explanation for the founding of Tuskegee Institute emphasizes the political ability of Adams. Brooks and Colonel Wilbur Foster, a local merchant and planter and the former partner of Brooks in the *Mail*, approached Adams asking for his aid in obtaining black support for their candidacies for the state legislature in 1880. Adams reputedly offered to deliver black votes to the two men in exchange for their promise to seek a state appropriation for a black normal school in Tuskegee. The bargain was struck, both sides delivered, and the school opened in July 1881. The conventional wisdom implies that Brooks and Foster made their way to the legislature by horse-trading with a shrewd black man who bargained into existence what would become a major black institution.[24]

While political motives undoubtedly played a central role in the founding of the school, Tuskegee Institute was the product of more than a simple quid pro quo. It is important to know that both Brooks and Foster had first been elected to the legislature in 1878. They may well have received black support at that time. After conservative control was reestablished in 1876, blacks may have begun to coalesce with conservatives because they sensed the inevitability of white dominance. Or perhaps black political power was already insignificant in 1878. Some evidence suggests that fraud in that election may have denied many blacks their votes. Either way—or, more likely, through a combination of both—black political independence had been severely undermined before 1880. With the loss of independence went the ability to make political deals of substantive value.*

This is not to deny, however, that Brooks and Foster approached Lewis Adams soliciting his support. They probably did. But they may have intended the action more as an effort to reinforce interracial harmony than as a scheme to secure electoral success. In view of the county's economic problems, the feared loss of black population, and the talk of even more black emigration, it made good sense to court the favor of the black leaders. Despite the continued misgivings of many whites about educating blacks, a school would be a good investment if it kept blacks in the county. Elsewhere in the Alabama Black Belt, planters had established schools for blacks to keep them from migrating westward.[25] Moreover, boosters like Arthur Brooks knew well what the economic benefits of another school might be. The two local white academic institutions had pro-

---

* The *Macon Mail* of February 12, 1879, reported that a United States marshal had recently arrested Macon County sheriff J. C. Abercrombie on charges of vote fraud, the action apparently stemming from the sheriff's refusal to receive voting boxes from two heavily black precincts during the 1878 election. Arthur Brooks contended that the arrest grew out of "an infamous spirit of revenge on the part of Negro wretches and their white allies."

vided commercial activity when the cotton economy was lifeless, and there was no reason to believe that one for "colored youth" would not do the same—or more, since there were so many blacks in the area lacking education.

Politics certainly entered into the decision of whites to support the school. Some conservatives wanted to establish a pattern of political accommodation with blacks. The events of 1870 and 1874 had demonstrated where power ultimately rested in Macon County; now rational men in quieter times could use the carrot rather than the stick to maintain control of society. "Independentism"—a local reflection of the national Greenbacker movement—had surfaced in Macon County in 1878, and while it was no real challenge to Democratic control then, it reminded conservatives of their vulnerability and of the potential political power of blacks. Moreover, in 1880 they did not know that blacks would be ushered out of Alabama politics just after the turn of the century. For those taking the long view, détente with the black community was a rational policy.*

Beyond the material and political motives, some whites probably felt a genuine desire to ease the long-standing racial tension in the community. In a county with a large black majority, most whites had regular dealings with blacks, and both races doubtless had been uncomfortable with the adversarial posture that had characterized black-white relations for so long. Now that conservatives had regained control, their paternalistic feelings toward blacks—nurtured by antebellum circumstances and attitudes—no longer had to be repressed out of fear and insecurity. They took considerable psychic satisfaction from this change in race relations. A peaceful community reinforced their belief that their view of how society should operate was correct. Perhaps most important, benevolent paternalism toward blacks made whites feel good about themselves. In discussing master-slave relations in his history of slavery, Eugene D. Genovese describes a "doctrine of reciprocity" by which white planters showed slaves kindness in exchange for black submissiveness. White benevolence to slaves also bolstered the planters' egos, Genovese explains, "because in no other way could they see themselves as morally responsible beings who were doing their duty." White conservatives in Tuskegee supported the black request for a normal school in the late 1870s for much the same reasons.[26]

The new attitude was evident in conservative support for the

---

* A *Macon Mail* editorial on December 4, 1878, alludes to a third-party effort in the recent county elections. An "independent" ticket was unsuccessful in the 1880 election. (Tuskegee *News,* July 15, August 5, 12, 1880.)

school. Thomas Dryer, the local merchant who had threatened the life of his neighbor James Alston in 1870, became one of the school's first three trustees, along with Lewis Adams and another white merchant, M. B. Swanson. When Dryer suddenly died just before the school opened, he was replaced on the Board of Trustees by George Washington Campbell, the businessman who had probably accompanied Dryer and other Democrats to warn Alston to leave the county. Campbell would for almost a quarter of a century be a friend and close adviser to Booker Washington. Colonel Abercrombie was not an immediate supporter, but in a few years Washington would consider him a friend to the school. Dryer, Campbell, and Abercrombie all managed to compromise their formerly harsh positions in order to support Tuskegee Institute.[27]

When Booker T. Washington arrived in Tuskegee in 1881, he most certainly learned about the recent compromises. His closest friend in the black community was Lewis Adams, who knew the background of the school's founding. Adams no doubt explained to Washington the poor economic conditions, the decline of black political potency, and the recent white overtures of good will. He probably told how these circumstances had worked in favor of the black community's desire for an educational institution. It is also probably safe to assume that Adams related to Washington the events of 1870. Adams was the mulatto son of Jesse Adams, the white livery stable owner who some Republicans thought was the instigator of much of the violence against Republicans in 1870. The younger Adams was in a position to know how vulnerable black efforts toward self-improvement were. He surely had no difficulty imagining what men like his father would do if the normal school was perceived as a threat to conservative control.[28]

Washington's personal experience had in some ways prepared him for the Tuskegee situation. The child of a West Virginia slave woman and a white man unknown to him, he struggled to get an education while holding numerous jobs, helped by Viola Ruffner, a white employer of Yankee origins who impressed upon him her puritan attitudes about discipline, work, and education. His quest for education led him to Hampton Institute, where he came under the strong influence of General Samuel Chapman Armstrong, the white founder of the school who believed that economic and moral uplift was the first step for blacks in their evolutionary climb toward full equality. Washington was his outstanding student, the man he suggested when George Campbell of Tuskegee asked him to recommend someone to be principal of the new normal school, even though Campbell specifically requested a white man. Armstrong knew that Washington willingly accepted the counsel of white men, clearly a prerequisite for success in Tuskegee. A realistic person, Washington no doubt recognized that he had little choice but to follow the advice of powerful whites. But his experience had taught that white friends could greatly facilitate a Negro's achievement of more personal freedom. To build an institution that would help other blacks improve themselves, he would readily solicit the advice and aid of whites.[29]

White conservatives did indeed lend significant help to the school, especially in the formative years. In his autobiography, Washington states that George Campbell "was never appealed to when he was not willing to extend all the aid in his power." Campbell guided Washington in financial affairs from his position as school trustee. A banker, he lent money to the Institute and vouched for Washington at banks in Montgomery when he needed loans larger than Campbell could handle. Robert R. Varner, a building contractor, gave the school the equipment necessary for setting up its original brickworks and then bought most of the bricks not used in campus buildings. Varner helped Washington to show whites the value of the Institute: brickmaking, which was done successfully only after several failures, suggested both the perseverance of the school's teachers and students and its potential as an economic bridge between the black and white communities.[30]

In turn, the school benefited the conservatives as its original white supporters had imagined it would. Campbell, who owned along with the bank a local railroad line, an insurance brokerage, and a large dry goods store, no doubt derived considerable income from rendering various goods and services to the Institute. Varner must have profited from construction work around the Institute. Also, he and his family owned much of the land surrounding the original hundred-acre campus that Washington purchased in 1881, and the Varners had a ready buyer for property in Washington, who regularly added to the Institute's landholdings.[31]

Later, when he had become nationally prominent, Washington would help local whites politically, something that they most certainly had not foreseen in 1881. He aided particularly the large and wealthy Thompson family of Tuskegee. When President William McKinley visited the Institute in 1898, Washington arranged for him to stay at the home of Charles W. Thompson, the local Democratic leader, and then reminded the president of Thompson's hospitality when the Tuskegee man was elected to Congress in 1900. Also, Washington helped to secure for Thompson's Republican brother

Joseph the Tuskegee postmastership and later the office of internal revenue collector for Alabama.[32]

Perhaps the greatest benefit that white conservatives received was the peace of mind resulting from Washington's pronouncements on race relations. As early as 1884 he set forth the approach that he would maintain for the remainder of his career. Any successful movement "for the elevation of the Southern Negro," he said, "must have to a certain extent the cooperation of Southern whites." He predicted that such help would indeed come because "Southern people have a good deal of human nature. They like to receive the praise of doing good deeds." Good race relations would grow out of economic interdependence between the races and better educational opportunities for blacks. "Harmony will come in proportion as the black man gets something that the white man wants, whether it be of brains or material," he said. "Good school teachers and plenty of money to pay them will be more potent in settling the race question than many civil rights bills and investigating committees." In an effort to reassure southern planters worried about the supply of labor, Washington promised that the Negro's home is "permanently in the south."[33]

Washington saw that his success at Tuskegee Institute depended on his keeping the fears of white conservatives assuaged. If acknowledging the fact of white dominance would accomplish that, then Washington the realist would oblige. He could not know that his conciliatory posture would make him the therapist for a whole generation of anxious white southerners, but he was aware that it was necessary for the survival of his institution in Tuskegee.

The founding of Tuskegee Institute precipitated a fundamental change in the nature of race relations in Macon County. To improve their economic condition, to achieve some enduring political stability, and to establish some peace in their community, conservatives had consciously accommodated a desire of the local black community. They had compromised their policy of denying the legitimacy of any black interest or concern. Whites had now actively supported black education—something that in the past they had either opposed violently or accepted very reluctantly. Given the nineteenth-century faith in the power of education, white support for the school was implicit recognition that blacks could rise above the status of peon. Many whites could certainly have denied that implication, but most blacks, fully aware of how whites had kept education from them, embraced it enthusiastically. Few conservatives ever realized that their accommodation and compromise would help to demonstrate one of history's truisms: change, however innocuous it may seem initially, is very often difficult to stop once set in motion. But two generations later, white conservatives caught in a social and political whirlwind would know all too well that their grandfathers had sown the wind of racial change.

2

The Model Community

ONE WHITE conservative not sympathetic to the accommodationist approach was James Edward Cobb, the Democratic circuit judge who had rid the county of Republican officials after 1874. Judge Cobb viewed Tuskegee Institute as a threat to white power. As a delegate to the Alabama Constitutional Convention of 1901, he called for the removal of tax-exempt status for land owned by private colleges. "There are private institutions chartered in this State that have vast amounts of money coming to them year after year, and they are buying every acre of land they can put their hands on." Cobb was no doubt referring to Booker Washington's successful fund-raising among northern philanthropists and his aggressive accumulation of property in Tuskegee. He withdrew his motion, however, after several pro-education delegates objected.[1]

Cobb may have been especially sensitive to challenges to conservative control because of his own experiences in the 1890s. He had been elected to Congress in 1884 and apparently had had no serious opposition for his seat until 1892, when a white Populist ran against him. In that race and a subsequent one in 1894, the Populists scored heavy majorities in the six predominantly white counties of the district, but lost by even greater numbers in the three Black Belt counties, of which Macon was one. Albert Goodwyn, the Populist candidate in 1894, charged that Cobb supporters had stolen both elections, claiming that in 1894 Cobb received "false and fraudulent" votes in three beats in Macon County. Several blacks and some white Republicans in Macon County testified that they had not voted in that election because they believed that the Democrats who controlled the county election apparatus—the probate judge, the sheriff, and the voting clerk—would not count their votes in the column in which they were cast. Their misgivings were well founded: the election officials did indeed "vote" men who had studiously avoided going to the polls. A congressional investigating committee recognized Goodwyn's claim in 1894 and gave him the seat, but the Democrats regained it in 1896 in an election marred also by accusations of Democratic fraud. Here again, Cobb and the local Democrats demonstrated what they had first shown in 1870: that they would take whatever steps were necessary to maintain, or reclaim, white conservative power.[2]

The 1901 constitutional convention was the triumphal moment for conservative power in Alabama. In advocating ratification of the new constitution to his fellow Macon Countians, Cobb argued that it would "tend to the purification of politics, . . . the advancement and growth of all the material interests of the state, and . . . the intellectual and moral uplifting of its people." It actually accomplished none of those things, but it did disfranchise several hundred thousand black and white Alabamians, which is what Cobb and other conservatives meant it to do.[3]

Under the new constitution an applicant for voter registration had to prove either that he was literate and employed or that he had three hundred dollars' worth of taxable property. Conservatives enacted a poll tax which ultimately disfranchised more potential voters than any of the other measures. A county board of registrars was given enormous discretionary authority to determine whether an applicant had met the requirements. The three-person board was to be appointed by state rather than local officials—a conservative attempt to prevent any maverick democratic county from expanding its electorate to the point of threatening conservative control. Conservatives believed they could more nearly control politicians with statewide ambitions than they could county politicians outside the Black Belt. They had insured Black Belt dominance of the state legislature when they insisted on basing apportionment in both houses on total population, a device that at the time favored the Black Belt. Once dominance was established, they would successfully resist all efforts for reapportionment, even though the Black Belt steadily declined in its proportional significance in the state's population.*

* Malcolm C. McMillan, *Constitutional Development in Alabama, 1798–1901* (University of North Carolina Press, 1955), 296–307. It should be noted that the 1901

In Macon County the constitution was ratified by a large majority, a result in all likelihood of vote fraud. Booker T. Washington
had lobbied against the disfranchising measures at the convention,
but did not publicly oppose the constitution thereafter. George
Campbell and former governor Thomas Goode Jones, also a friend
to Washington, counseled the Tuskegee principal against taking a
public stand on the constitution. The suffrage restrictions "will not
in the end operate harshly on the Negro race," Jones wrote to him.
Washington did, however, arrange a court test of the constitution's
suffrage limitations. Jones, who in the meantime had been appointed to a federal judgeship on Washington's recommendation to
Theodore Roosevelt, threw the challenge out of court. The United
States Supreme Court subsequently sustained Jones's action and upheld the Alabama suffrage law. Washington finally accepted the
futility of challenging disfranchisement in Alabama.*

Macon County had only sixty-five black voters after the required
reregistration of all voters under the new constitution. By contrast,
more than two thousand blacks had registered under Radical Reconstruction in the late 1860s. The number of white voters also
dropped substantially. Thus the constitution removed most of the
grounds for conservative fears about maintaining political control.
The turmoil of the 1890s was replaced in 1901 by a tentative
peace—at least on the surface of society—between blacks and
whites. With one notable exception, the apparent harmony would
last for forty years.[4]

After 1901 black and white leaders in Tuskegee often portrayed
their community as a model of good race relations. The notion
seems to have originated with the founding of Tuskegee Institute.
Whites liked the idea because it helped them to believe that their
community was harmonious. They proudly cited their role in the

---

constitution provides for an appeal of the registrars' decision to circuit court and
then to the Alabama Supreme Court if necessary.

* Louis R. Harlan, *Booker T. Washington: The Making of a Black Leader, 1856–1901*
(Oxford University Press, 1972), 300–302, and *Booker T. Washington: The Wizard of
Tuskegee, 1901–1915* (Oxford University Press, 1983), 245–47. The suit that first
tested the constitutionality of the Alabama suffrage law was *Giles v. Harris*
(1903). The Supreme Court ruled that the plaintiff had raised a political, not a
constitutional, issue and refused to overturn the law. In a second suit, *Giles v.
Teasley* (1905), the Court rejected a similar plea from Giles because he had not
claimed in state courts that his citizenship rights had been denied, though that
was the basis of his appeal in federal court. Washington wanted to try again, but
his lawyer, Wilford Smith of Washington, dispirited after losing on technicalities,
did not wish to go on. He and other legal advisers persuaded Washington to
give up.

building of the Institute. They praised Washington and called the school "the greatest institution of its kind in the world." Washington in turn emphasized the support and encouragement that he received from local whites. The model-community idea furthered Washington's goal of making Tuskegee Institute a demonstration of the industry and good character of blacks, an example of what they could do when given opportunity and good leadership. "I have found . . . that it is the visible, the tangible, that goes a long way in softening prejudices," Washington wrote in his autobiography. Robert R. Moton, Washington's successor as principal, would also advance the model-community idea in the 1920s and 1930s. It was so widely embraced that in the 1940s and 1950s some whites perceived challenges to their control as the very first instances of racial conflict in the county's history.[5]

Washington and his successors directed much of their energy toward achieving the economic and educational uplift that they believed to be a prerequisite for full equality for blacks. At Tuskegee Institute, which drew heavily on the local community for its students, they taught industrial arts, particularly agriculture and building. Every year they held the "Negro Conference," a one-day meeting begun by Washington in 1892, in which black farmers came to the Institute campus to discuss their problems and to receive advice from faculty members about dealing with them. George Washington Carver, the head of the school's agriculture department, frequently gave demonstrations on scientific agriculture in rural areas, a practice that was institutionalized with the Jesup Agricultural Wagon, sometimes called the "Farmer's College on Wheels." This work would lead in 1906 to the establishment of a regional black farm extension service based at Tuskegee Institute. After Washington had interested him in black education, the Chicago philanthropist Julius Rosenwald funded a program to build black schools in the rural South, the first of which was erected in Macon County. There would eventually be fifteen Rosenwald schools in the county.[6]

For all its energy and commitment to community improvement, however, Tuskegee Institute had only limited success in its educational effort. Black public education in Macon County remained very poorly funded, despite the generosity of the Rosenwald Fund. Indeed, the presence of the Institute and northern philanthropy appear to have resulted in reduced county funding. The contrast between funding for black and white schools was striking. In 1934 the expenditure for each white pupil in Macon County was $65.18 and for each black student $6.58. White teachers' salaries averaged $867

in 1934, as compared with $348 for blacks. ˙.
ment averaged twenty-two students; black schools ו.
pupils in each class. County buses transported sixty pɐ
white students to school, but no black children. Nearly seע
percent of black schools in the county in 1934 had only one teaᴗ

The Institute's efforts to improve farming practices apparenι.
benefited black farmers in Macon County only marginally. Charles
S. Johnson, the prominent sociologist at Fisk University, surveyed
612 black farm families in the county in the early 1930s and found
that little had changed for the better for black farmers since the end
of slavery. Indeed, many things had gotten worse: Land ownership
had declined relentlessly. More and more black farmers had become
sharecroppers, deepening their dependence on white landlords;
ninety percent of those Johnson surveyed were tenants. They all told
him the same thing: sharecropping allowed almost no room for
blacks to improve themselves. "They manage to live on advances,"
Johnson wrote, "or by borrowing for food and clothing and permit-
ting their crop to be taken in satisfaction of the debt." For the black
tenant, there was very little of the independence that Booker Washington had envisioned. "When you working on a white man's
place," one man told Johnson, "you have to do what he says, or
treat, trade or travel." The tenant system belied the earlier faith in
the curative power of education for blacks: Johnson discovered that
black men with more than an elementary education were likely to
quit farming altogether. The most successful tenant farmers were
those with a bare minimum of education—the ones literate enough
to make the best of the situation, but not so well educated as to view
it as intolerable.[8]

Johnson's research in Macon County was part of a Rosenwald
Fund project to study the effects of syphilis among the county's
black population. Physicians working for the United States Public
Health Service discovered in 1930 that thirty-six percent of fourteen
hundred black men examined had the disease. They also found that
health conditions for rural blacks in Macon County were miserable
generally. Their diet consisted largely of salt pork, hominy grits,
cornbread, and molasses; fresh meat, fresh vegetables, fruit, and
milk were rarely included. Malnutrition was chronic, and they were
afflicted by many diet-related illnesses. Most of the county's poor
blacks could not afford medical care.*

* In what now seems to be an example of official neglect, the subjects in the syphilis study received minimal treatment, despite the fact that the Public Health
Service continued its research until 1972. For an excellent account of this situa-

A compelling indictment of the tenant system in Macon County as later made by Ned Cobb, a black farmer, in his oral autobiography, *All God's Dangers*. An ambitious and forthright man, Cobb was succeeding despite the obstacles the tenant system put in his way; he had acquired mules, farm equipment, even an automobile. But in 1931 Walter Parker, a furnishing merchant, tried to halt Cobb's rise by entrapping him in a credit contract. Cobb was plain about Parker's intentions: "he had it in for me. . . . He just aimed to use his power and break me down; he'd been doing to people that way before then." Nothing could keep Parker from exploiting black tenants, Cobb believed. "They was his niggers and he could do with em like he wanted to and nobody else wouldn't fool with em. I figured this, and I might have been a fool to think it, me being a colored fellow and knowin the rules of the state of Alabama, partly, if I didn't know em all."[9]

Parker may have been motivated in part by Cobb's participation in a sharecroppers' union. Many hard-pressed black farmers in east-central Alabama had responded to a call to unionize in 1931 from organizers sent by the American Communist party. Whites reacted to the presence of "Reds" among local blacks with a brief reign of terror in Tallapoosa County, just north of Macon, in July 1931.

Ned Cobb took his stand against white power when Walter Parker foreclosed on a neighbor, a leader of the union, in December 1932. After pleading unsuccessfully for mercy from a sheriff's deputy—asking that the neighbor not be left unable to feed his family—Cobb defied the deputy to take the man's property. "If you take it, I'll be damned if you don't take it over my dead body." The deputy left, but returned soon with the sheriff and a group of armed men. Alone, Cobb watched them silently until one of the men seized him. When he pushed the man away, another fired three times with a shotgun, hitting Cobb in the hips and legs. Cobb then blasted away with a pistol and the men fled.

His injuries not serious, Cobb hid in southern Macon County until his family, under threat of death, told authorities where he was. They captured him and in the process killed his brother-in-law, who had also been at the shoot-out. Cobb later served twelve years in state prison on an assault charge. Most whites blamed the violence on Communist agitation for the sharecroppers' union. Cobb said simply that the local whites would do anything to maintain control over black farmers. He later explained why he had acted in

---

tion, see James H. Jones, *Bad Blood: The Tuskegee Syphilis Experiment* (The Free Press, 1981).

1932. "Somebody got to stand up. If we don't we niggers in this country are easy prey. Niggers had anything a white man wanted, the white man took it; made no difference how the cut might have come, he took it."[10]

Federal agricultural programs posed a potentially greater threat to the traditional repositories of power in Macon County than did the sharecroppers' union. Owners of large farms quickly acted to gain control of the local administration of the New Deal's agricultural relief programs. At least one Macon County landlord ordered all his tenants to sign their government farm-relief checks over to him. A tenant asked this landlord for $10 out of his $275 check to buy himself a new pair of overalls. "No, you can't get a nickel," the landlord replied; "bring it to me." When the tenant cashed the check anyway and fled to Montgomery, the angry landlord sent word that he still resided too close to Macon County.[11]

Notwithstanding its failure to combat the evils of cotton tenantry, Tuskegee Institute lived up to Washington's goal of establishing a model of black progress. By 1940 the town of Tuskegee had in its midst more than one thousand middle-class black professionals. Washington and his successors had maintained a policy that all Institute employees who lived in Tuskegee—and this was everyone except the occasional fundraiser or public relations person—had to be black. This strategy dictated that blacks would enjoy the few benefits as well as the numerous hardships of the Jim Crow system. Physically, Tuskegee Institute was a showplace of black achievement. On the neat, rolling campus were imposing red brick buildings bearing the names of Washington's industrialist friends. On nearby streets stood rows of large, comfortable homes with well-kept lawns. Most of the Institute staff lived in Greenwood, the "Model Negro Village" laid out in 1904 on land owned by the Institute. Some of the tree-lined streets in Greenwood were lighted and paved. The children of the Institute community attended Children's House, the model public grammar school. Greenwood and Tuskegee Institute were proof that when blacks were given the opportunity to embrace the American values of materialism and success, they did so with enthusiasm and efficiency.[12]

The Institute community had local heroes who personified the success ideal. Washington was beloved—a friend of the rich and powerful, a champion of his people, a great man. He had played the white man's game and won. Robert R. Moton, Washington's successor, continued the founder's heroic tradition. Also, having been born with very dark skin, Moton gave the lie to racist theories of black advancement that emphasized the mixed blood of successful blacks like Washington. George Washington Carver was viewed as a scientific genius, one who had demonstrated that blacks could succeed at intellectually rigorous pursuits. All three men, so familiar to the Institute community, were proof that talented blacks could overcome the obstacles of the caste system and gain the respect of blacks and whites alike.

Washington, Moton, and Carver established in the Institute community a pattern of warm, happy relations with "white" Tuskegee. Foy Thompson, a descendant of a wealthy white family, enjoyed warm personal friendships with various Institute staff members, especially Carver, as a boy growing up in Tuskegee in the 1920s and 1930s. William Varner, Jr., a contemporary, recalls that it was hardly unusual to see Carver, or another respected Institute personage, drinking tea on the front porches of the homes of prominent white Tuskegeeans, though he also remembers that black visitors were careful to call initially at the back door. Whites from town regularly attended religious and cultural events at the Institute, which provided a reserved section for them near the front of the chapel. Whites did not reciprocate—they did not include the Institute elite in their own social and religious occasions—but they did welcome them courteously to the various shops and stores in downtown Tuskegee.[13]

The warm relations with the Institute affirmed for whites a sense that Tuskegee was no ordinary southern town. Many whites believed that it greatly surpassed places of comparable size in its social and cultural life. The Institute lent an aura of refinement that benefited whites as well as blacks. The wealthier families—the Campbells, the Varners, the Thompsons, the Cobbs, and others—traveled regularly and thought of themselves as worldly and cultured. They also believed, with some justification, that Tuskegee was an unusually pretty town. Situated on a heavily forested ridge, Tuskegee had long, shaded streets lined with large Greek Revival houses. In contrast, architectural simplicity marked the business district. Low, unadorned shops and a curious Victorian courthouse of yellow brick fronted the town square, a grassy yard occupied by azaleas and a statue of an armed Confederate soldier looking northward. In the view of the leading whites, Tuskegee's physical beauty complemented its cultural sophistication and its excellent race relations.[14]

These peaceful relations probably owed less to the happy social interaction of the black and white elites than to a careful effort to keep the Institute community insulated. School administrators discouraged students from going downtown, and at times prohibited them from doing so. If a student complained about being demeaned at the segregated theater, he was reminded that the Institute sponsored a movie each Saturday. The administration emphasized to students that the Institute community was a self-sufficient entity—down to having its own water and electrical supply. Probably the most important aspect of the insulation was an informal arrangement between Institute presidents and local police about breaches of the peace. If a student was caught breaking the law, the local authorities usually turned him over to the school for punishment. A townsman disturbing the Institute's peace was, conversely, delivered to the local police. In effect from the Institute's earliest days, this arrangement largely prevented conflict over police action.[15]

The truce that the black and white elites imposed in Tuskegee after 1901 was interrupted only once. But that breach of Macon County's "perfect peace," in 1923, revealed that both white anxieties over their controlling position and black desires for change were still powerful forces in the county.

In the summer of 1921, Mayor William Varner brought to the attention of Dr. Moton a newspaper story announcing plans for a Veterans Administration hospital for black veterans of the recent war. The son of Robert Varner, the Tuskegee builder who had given Washington his brickworks and who had sold the Institute and its employees considerable amounts of nearby property, the mayor was thinking in the same way that some white Tuskegeeans had in 1880 when considering the possible economic benefits of Tuskegee Institute. He asked Moton to use his influence with President Warren Harding to locate the hospital in Tuskegee. Moton liked the idea; the hospital would afford much professional opportunity for blacks in Macon County, thus strengthening the economic base of the local black community. The Tuskegee Institute trustees, led by George Campbell's son Wright, voted to give a portion of the school's land to the VA, an act of generosity subsequently matched by a few white landowners who similarly anticipated economic benefits from the hospital. Mayor Varner also made it known that he had adjacent property available for the VA to purchase. Dr. Moton's influence in Washington and the town's enthusiasm persuaded the VA to place the hospital in Tuskegee. With the assistance of local merchants, contractors, and workmen, the hospital complex—comprising twenty-seven buildings and costing $2 million—was ready for opening in February 1923. In a dedication ceremony on Abraham Lincoln's birthday, Vice-President Calvin Coolidge lauded the valor of black soldiers in the recent war and reaffirmed the Great Emancipator's quest for freedom for all. But Coolidge added a cautionary note to this momentous occasion: "It takes time and patience and perseverance to put into practice our theory of human rights."[16]

The matter of staffing the hospital proved a serious test of that theory. A VA officer had in the early planning stages assured Tuskegee whites that the hospital would be white-run, though the staff would include some black doctors, social workers, and nurses. Moton had wanted an all-black administration but settled for a white chief administrator, provided he was of northern origin. But when the hospital opened, the man the VA appointed chief was Dr. Robert Stanley, a native Alabamian who brooked no exceptions to segregation. Stanley informed Moton that, except for laborers, all his staff would be white—even the nurses, despite the Alabama law prohibiting white nurses from ministering to blacks. Moton told Harding of Stanley's betrayal of the original purpose and then went to see the President on February 23. He explained the damage the change could do to both of them when word of it reached the black press. He probably did not need to remind the President that black voters were among the most loyal supporters of the Republican party. Harding responded by freezing appointments to the hospital until black staff could be located.[17]

Anger arose among whites in Tuskegee when they heard that Stanley's plans for a white staff were being thwarted. Moton's home had to be placed under guard in April because of threats against him, and he soon began an extended vacation out of the state. Tension in the white community continued to build in May and June. Wright Campbell warned the Institute trustees of the problems that might be caused by having blacks in authority at the hospital: "It is possible for a few Negroes in army uniforms, glorying in a little chief authority, to kindle conflagrations that would destroy the friendships that it has taken half a century to develop." Macon County's state senator, Richard Holmes Powell, sounded a similar theme in an open letter in the Montgomery *Advertiser:* "Where peace and harmony once reigned supreme, rumors of strife, open threats, and impending friction are now present"—all this in a town where whites had lived quietly "with their black-skin brothers and had watched and assisted in the growth and development of the greatest institution of its kind in the world." In the face of this challenge, Senator Powell felt the need to remind his readers where power had historically rested in Tuskegee: "The very best representatives of the white race, from its first beginnings until now, have controlled the destinies of this town. Those who live here now, true to the traditions and heritage of a noble ancestry, by the grace of God, will continue that white control to the end."[18]

Blacks understood that money and power were the issues in the VA hospital controversy. Albon L. Holsey, Moton's secretary and the man who apparently ran the Institute in the principal's absence, wrote to James Weldon Johnson, secretary of the National Association for the Advancement of Colored People, that "the whites are making a desperate effort to hold on to the Tuskegee Hospital because when it is fully staffed there will be a payroll of $75,000 per month, and it is this money which they want to get into the hands of white people." There was also, Holsey believed, a significant degree of white resentment at the very idea of blacks having charge of such a handsome institution: "The Officers Quarters and the Nurses Quarters are most beautifully equipped and appointed, and it is this situation which is a source of irritation." In letters to leading newspapers and magazines, Walter White, assistant secretary of the NAACP, pointed out the hypocrisy of Tuskegee whites wanting to run a hospital that ministered to blacks. Just a few years earlier Alabama had passed a law prohibiting whites from "nursing Negroes." Now, White wrote, "race prejudice falls with a bang before the almighty dollar." White quoted an Alabama white man about the other crucial concern in the controversy: "If niggers are put at the head of this hospital, they'll be responsible *only* to the United States government and we don't want any niggers in Alabama we can't control."[19]

Whites appeared ready by early July to use violence to gain control of the hospital. The local Ku Klux Klan ordered the hospital's first black employee to leave town immediately upon his arrival. A procession of Klansmen drove through the Tuskegee Institute campus, but no violence resulted. In an unprecedented move, the commander of the Institute's cadet corps organized an armed defense of the school.[20]

But in this case white power would not be reclaimed. Two days after the Klan demonstration Frank Hines, the head of the VA, came to Tuskegee to settle the matter. Hines, a former military officer, stood firm against arguments by Wright Campbell, Senator Powell, and other officials to amend his order to staff the hospital with blacks. Increased pressure from the NAACP probably strengthened the VA's resolve. The position of Tuskegee whites was also undermined when other southern whites, concerned with maintaining segregation, began to question the idea of having white doctors and nurses attending black patients. Gradually the tension eased. There was little public response from the white community when Hines sent six black doctors to Tuskegee in mid-August. Even when the VA removed all white staff members from the hospital the next year, white Tuskegee reacted more with indifference than with anger.[21]

For conservative whites, the controversy was a moment of disturbing revelation. Powell voiced feelings of betrayal in a letter to Hines after the VA's policy had been made clear: "This situation demonstrates clearly and conclusively how rapidly a Negro grows in presumption, courage and the attempted assertion of power, when he is dealt with on the basis of a white man, and treated with consideration and courtesy." The two decades of communal peace since 1901 apparently had persuaded many local whites that the black appetite for change had been sated. Indeed, the accommodationist posture of Washington and Moton was easily interpreted as acceptance of the status quo. But the realization in 1923 that blacks would aggressively pursue further improvement in their status—and that the federal government would, when pushed, act on their behalf—revived the old anxiety about white control. "The Negroes are gradually taking things away from us by contesting every inch of the ground, refusing all compromise, and fighting to a finish," Powell concluded a few weeks after the controversy.[22]

Powell here overstated the combativeness of blacks, but he was quite right in his assertion that the blacks had been taking "things"—that is, power—from whites. Ever since Booker Washington's arrival in 1881, blacks had been reacquiring power in small, almost imperceptible increments. True, much of the power Washington accumulated was only useful outside Tuskegee; he was strongest in Washington, D.C. But the nation's capital was precisely where Moton, who inherited much of the founder's influence, needed to be heard during the VA controversy. That power had led to black control of an institution that ultimately would provide fifteen hundred blacks with high-paying federal jobs. In that base of economic independence lay the potential for challenging conservative control of Macon County.

3

Keep Everlastingly At It

CHARLES GOMILLION discovered that he needed a pair of shoes when he arrived in Tuskegee in the fall of 1928 to begin teaching at the Institute. At his first opportunity he went to one of the shoe stores on the town square. "What can I do for you today, Preacher?" a white salesman asked as he approached Gomillion. "Not a damn thing," Gomillion replied, angry at the man's assumption that any black man in a suit must be a clergyman. He walked out of the store and resolved then and there that whatever items he could not purchase at stores in the Institute community, or get from the Sears, Roebuck mail-order catalogue, he would do without. It was a resolution that, with rare exceptions, he would keep.*

This refusal to tolerate a white man's casual condescension was perhaps an augury of Gomillion's later leadership in challenging the racial status quo in Macon County. At twenty-eight, however, he

---

* Interviews with Charles G. Gomillion, March 13, 1978, and December 6, 1979. Unless otherwise cited, the personal information on Gomillion given here comes from these interviews.

Gomillion's recollections about his life and work have been considered critically. His explanations of his motives are sometimes self-serving; he is, however, an excellent interview subject. He wants to explain his life. He freely admits when he does not remember. He does not guess about the dates of events; if he does not know, he says so. Gomillion's credibility is supported by the fact that no significant discrepancy exists between my interviews and two other sources: a feature on Gomillion in *Southern Patriot* XVIII (October 1960); and an interview with Charles G. Gomillion, March 29, 1972, Alabama Center for Higher Education interviews.

was not yet ready to lead—though he already looked determined. He wore rimless glasses and had a slightly furrowed brow that suggested thoughtfulness. A colleague would later observe that Gomillion often failed to say hello as he walked past friends on the Institute campus, an indication, the colleague believed, of his deep concentration on serious matters. He was five feet eight inches tall, weighed about 165 pounds, and was a medium-brown color. He spoke slowly and correctly, but when amused he giggled in a high pitch. An FBI informant reporting on Gomillion's personal "peculiarities" in 1943 would note that he "always wears a black or dark blue suit and walks very fast."[1]

He was born in 1900 in the town of Johnston in Edgefield County, South Carolina, the oldest child of Charles and Flora Gomillion. His father, who was illiterate, worked as a custodian and janitor and was regarded as a good colored man by his white employers, though he was known to have a temper. Late one night during his early boyhood Charles and his family were awakened by a man beating on the kitchen window of their home. Charles's father demanded that the man identify himself, but there was no reply. Gomillion then fired his shotgun through the window and killed the intruder, a drunken white man from a nearby town. Gomillion was jailed, but at the trial his white employers testified to his good character and persuaded the court that his action was justifiable homicide.

Charles inherited much of his father's temperament, but his mother had more influence on his values. He was, by his own admission, something of a "Mama's boy." Flora Gomillion taught her children to be frugal. She encouraged them not to ask for help in any task they could do themselves. She emphasized the individual's moral responsibility not only to do good, but also to avoid doing evil, and constantly reminded Charles in particular that, as the oldest child, he must set a good example for his siblings. She stressed the various responsibilities that go with being a good citizen, and insisted that the children be especially kind to the elderly and the handicapped. Flora combined this conservative moral code with a religious ethic that encouraged her children to work to bring the Kingdom of God on earth. "What kind of world would this be," she asked Charles, "if every person were just like [you]?" He responded in good faith. "By the time I left home," he wrote later, "I had learned much about one's personal indebtedness to his society, and his responsibility to contribute to its well-being."[2]

She also educated Charles about the peculiar racial mores of his hometown. One day when he was about seven, he visited with a white neighbor who offered him a piece of watermelon of which part had already been eaten. Charles had been taught the previous year in school that it was unsanitary to eat after someone else, and he politely refused the melon. The woman became angry and, turning away from him, said, "I don't know what's coming over these young niggers. They think they're as good as white folks." Her harshness surprised Charles, and he ran home and told his mother about it. Flora explained that the white woman was a good person, but that he had broken an important rule of racial etiquette. In small towns like Johnston, she said, if blacks wanted to get along with whites, they never refused anything a white person offered them; if they did not want it, they simply waited until they were out of sight and threw it away. In later years, Gomillion would cite this watermelon incident as his first awareness of the difference in status between whites and blacks. It was also the beginning of his education in the ways that whites controlled the behavior of blacks.

Only marginally literate herself, Flora encouraged her children's education. She borrowed magazines—particularly the *Ladies' Home Journal, Pictorial Review,* and *Woman's Home Companion*—from white neighbors for them to read. She and her husband encouraged Charles, his brother, and his two sisters to ask questions, and they always attempted an answer. When the children complained that the Sunday school teachers at their Baptist church refused to answer questions—advising them not to question but to believe—Flora allowed them to attend the local Colored Methodist Episcopal Church, where the teachers were more enlightened. Charles became active in the Epworth League, the Methodist youth organization. He was inspired by the league's motto, "Keep Everlastingly At It," and adopted it as his personal credo.

Charles's formal education in Johnston was limited, though it probably surpassed what most black children in the South got at the time. During his first three years in school the term lasted only three months. It was five months for the next three years, though his parents had to pay for the additional two months. In the seventh year, after a total of twenty-six months of schooling, Charles dropped out because of poor teaching, with the feeling that he had gotten all the education he could in Johnston. He worked on local farms for the next two years.

When he was sixteen he enrolled at Paine College, a small Methodist school in Augusta, Georgia. He began as a first-year high school student and worked hard to make up for the deficiencies in his earlier education. He had a particularly hard struggle with

English, but was aided by a young white teacher, Mary DeBardeleben, a Methodist missionary who believed that her church had a responsibility to educate the descendants of Negro slaves.[3] She was,
Gomillion says, the first white who "treated me as a person." De-
Bardeleben encouraged him to become a teacher, and he enrolled in
Paine College's department of teacher training. After two years,
however, he dropped out to support his parents. At the same time he
married Hermyne Jones, a Paine classmate. He worked in a post office in Philadelphia and then taught school in Milledgeville, Georgia, before returning to Paine in the fall of 1926 to finish his
education. He graduated in 1928 and had accepted a job selling insurance in South Carolina when he received the offer of a teaching
position at Tuskegee.

On the eve of his departure for Tuskegee, he told someone that
Booker Washington had taught blacks how to make a living, but
that now Gomillion was going to teach them how to live. Once in
Tuskegee, however, he lost this cockiness. Assigned to teach ancient
and medieval history in the high school department, despite the fact
that he had majored in sociology at Paine, Gomillion worked very
hard during his first years in Tuskegee at mastering the new discipline and the skills of teaching; he would later say that he was more
a student than a teacher in his early years at the Institute. He
participated in few community activities, but a public issue that
later concerned him greatly was originally brought to his attention
by a group of schoolteachers whom he taught in summer school in
1929. They explained to him in fine detail the gross inequalities between black and white public education in Alabama.

In the fall of 1933, Gomillion took a year's leave of absence to
study sociology at Fisk University. It was Bertram Doyle, who had
taught him sociology at Paine and was now on the Fisk faculty, who
originally drew him to the Nashville school. But once there he was
influenced more by Charles S. Johnson. Gomillion already knew of
Johnson as the editor of *Opportunity*, the influential Urban League
magazine which he read throughout the 1920s. Johnson would
shortly gain national attention for his studies of the effects of cotton
tenancy on rural blacks, among them the survey of black farm families discussed in Chapter 2. While Gomillion developed as a sociologist under the instruction of Doyle and E. Franklin Frazier, who was
also on the Fisk faculty at the time, he acquired a role model in
Johnson, whom he admired for being a citizen as well as a scholar.
Johnson associated comfortably with whites, an ability that Gomillion recognized as essential for an effective black leader. "I got from

him some idea about how a group would need to work to get the kinds of help necessary to improve educational opportunities for Negroes," he said of Johnson years later.

Johnson was an important link connecting Gomillion to Booker Washington. Gomillion had come to Tuskegee somewhat skeptical of the Washington philosophy. He had been reading W. E. B. DuBois's writings in *The Crisis*, the magazine of the NAACP, since he was a teenager in South Carolina, and he was sympathetic to DuBois's anti-Washington opinions. Johnson, on the other hand, had a keen appreciation for Washington; he defended the accommodationist approach in *Opportunity*. He in turn had been influenced in his views on Washington by Robert E. Park, his mentor in graduate school at the University of Chicago. Before he became a nationally renowned sociologist of race relations, Park had worked as a publicist and ghostwriter for Tuskegee Institute and admired Washington greatly. Partly as a result of the Park-Johnson connection, Gomillion began to look more kindly on Washington and the accommodationist approach. Later, when he became familiar with the character of the Macon County white community, he would come to believe that the Tuskegee environment simply did not allow Washington to be more assertive about black rights.[4]

Gomillion returned to Tuskegee in the fall of 1934 to begin what amounted to a new academic career, moving to the Institute's college department to teach sociology. He became assistant to Monroe Work, the director of the school's Department of Records and Research. It was Work who assembled the data for the Institute's annual report on lynching and for the *Negro Yearbook*. From him Gomillion learned that the collection and dissemination of information about blacks was an important task in the larger effort to uplift the race.

Gomillion became active in the Tuskegee Men's Club, a civic organization of Institute faculty and administrators formed in 1910. The Men's Club sought to improve public services—drainage, sewerage, and road surfacing—in the areas around the school. It had petitioned the local government for help, but without much success. The handsome homes and manicured lawns of Greenwood stood in stark contrast to the streets of the area, which were often unpaved and sometimes totally unimproved, and impassable in bad weather. But neither the city of Tuskegee nor the Macon County commissioners had made a real effort to improve them. The Men's Club had also criticized the local sheriff's department for arresting an inordinately high number of blacks for bringing liquor into

Macon County, which was dry. Most of the county's sheriffs, who were paid according to the number of arrests they made, had ignored such criticism.

Gomillion asked why local government was unresponsive and quickly learned that white officials had no political reason to respond to black concerns. He discovered that only thirty-two blacks in Macon County voted; administrators at the Institute and the Veterans Administration hospital and a few businessmen made up this select few. It was no coincidence that almost every black voter had significant economic power. Albert C. Bulls owned several businesses in the Institute community and had no trouble when he registered to vote in 1919. "I had done so many favors for so many crackers in the county that they couldn't turn me down," Bulls said later.[5]

The poll tax, enacted in the 1901 Alabama constitution, kept away most potential black voters in Macon County. John Hugh Reynolds, the county tax collector, estimated in 1939 that only fifteen blacks paid the poll tax, though perhaps another fifty black voters had been exempted from it by virtue of age or military service. Nearly eight hundred whites paid the tax, or had it paid for them. Reynolds further estimated that between twenty and forty percent of all poll taxes collected in the county were paid by political candidates or their supporters. It was commonplace for a man to pay the taxes for the white tenants on his farm or the clerks in his store. "[Many] of the tenants are voted," Reynolds observed when asked about the political impact of this practice. But "nobody ever goes so far as to pay a nigger's poll tax," insisted William Varner, the county probate judge. Despite these abuses the poll tax was good for the political process, claimed Watkins Johnston, chairman of the county Democratic committee and a state senator. "It keeps out a certain class of white voter who isn't really competent to vote. In this county, and in some others, it prevents those Negroes who might want to vote for the money they might get out of it, from trying to register." Here Johnston reiterated an argument that James Edward Cobb had advanced in 1901 to his fellow Macon Countians when he contended that the new constitution would "tend to the purification of politics." In fact, the constitution had not cleansed Macon County politics. It had just made the process white.[6]

A black able and willing to pay the poll tax still had to pass muster before the three-person Board of Registrars. The board exercised great discretion in deciding whether an applicant met the requirement of either property or literacy. In Macon County the board also required the applicant to have two white registered voters vouch for his suitability as a voter. Blacks in Macon County usually asked whites with whom they did business to vouch for them. Retail merchants, insurance agents, and car salesmen were likely candidates for vouching.*

Gomillion's effort to register demonstrated the difficulty of the process for blacks. Although he was convinced of the importance of voting as early as 1934, he did not make an application until 1939, because until then he had only one voucher, a dry goods merchant from whom his wife made purchases. When a white contractor approached Gomillion in 1939 about building him a house, he recognized this as his opportunity to get registered. They agreed on the terms of the building contract, but Gomillion refused to sign it until the man appeared with him at the Board of Registrars. He went with Gomillion to the courthouse and then presented the contract for Gomillion's signature. Again Gomillion refused, saying that he would wait until the board had acted on his application. The board promptly approved it—no doubt at the urging of the contractor— and Gomillion signed the agreement. Gomillion's registration resulted from his acute understanding of the realities of power. It was, however, an example of success that suggests the likelihood of failure.[7]

Gomillion had begun encouraging people to register as soon as he returned from Fisk in 1934. He believed that the solution to the problems of street and sanitation service in Greenwood lay in political participation. He also was convinced that the larger problem of discrimination in public education had to be addressed politically. He began to analyze the annual reports of the state superintendents of education, which listed separately how much was spent for black and white schools in each Alabama county during the previous year, and found that Macon County disbursed more than five times as much on a white student as it did on a black one. He prepared reports that pointed out the inequities and the resulting need for political action, and circulated them at the Men's Club and among other colleagues at the Institute.[8]

Gomillion's initial efforts for community improvement were well received partly because he commanded respect in the Institute community. He worked hard at teaching and was considered one of the

* Ralph J. Bunche, *The Political Status of the Negro in the Age of FDR* (University of Chicago Press, 1973), 283. The voucher requirement was used widely in Black Belt counties, though the 1901 constitution had not included it among the disfranchising devices. Boards of registrars initiated the vouching system to determine whether an applicant met the stringent residency requirement of two years in the state, one year in the county, and six months in the precinct.

best professors on the campus. In 1929 his wife Hermyne left him, saying, "You [are] not fun enough for me"; she meant, he later explained, "I was not active enough in social affairs, that I spent too much time with my work." Gomillion received custody of their two daughters, ages five and six, and reared them alone until he remarried in 1936. By then his sense of duty and family responsibility was widely appreciated in the Institute community. He lived frugally and incurred few debts. Whereas many Institute residents had their groceries delivered from downtown stores and were billed, usually with an interest charge added, Gomillion went to the small food stores in the Institute community and took his groceries home, a practice that earned him the nickname "Cash-and-Carry" Gomillion. He did not drink, smoke, or gamble because he did not want his children or students to have as an example his use of these vices. He rarely used superlatives or made absolute statements in conversation. He was self-effacing and, at times, reticent. Few, if any, black persons doubted that Gomillion's motives for exercising community leadership were selfless.[9]

His activism emerged at an opportune moment. Historically, the principal of the Institute had represented the entire Institute community, including the neighborhood of Greenwood, in its dealings with local whites. Washington had established this practice and Moton had continued it during his first years as president. Toward the end of his tenure, however, Moton became reluctant to speak for the whole community. Frederick Patterson, who succeeded Moton in 1935, never attempted to be the community voice. Consequently, a vacuum of community leadership resulted in about 1930. Gomillion stepped into that void in 1935.[10]

He did not go in alone. Several faculty members and administrators shared Gomillion's belief that the Institute community needed a stronger voice. The group included, among others, Hollis Price, an economics professor; William Shields, an assistant to Dr. Patterson; James Johnson, dean of the school of business; and Alonzo Davis, a psychology professor. They were approximately Gomillion's age or younger; like him, they had spent their formative years outside Tuskegee, and most of them had been educated elsewhere. They neither expected nor wanted a fatherly Institute principal to speak for them.[11]

This group's first major activity was the founding of the Tuskegee Institute Federal Credit Union in 1938. Members of the Men's Club had long recognized that Macon County blacks needed an independent credit institution. Supply merchants and landlords trapped tenant farmers in a web of credit often impossible to escape. Institute and VA employees frequently paid exorbitant interest rates to retail merchants and loan sharks. The City Bank of Tuskegee, the town's only bank, catered largely to whites. Using the business expertise of Hollis Price and James Johnson, Gomillion's group established an institution that promptly remedied the situation. The group had also demonstrated its ability to deal with and correct a serious community problem.[12]

Gomillion's emphasis on voting realized its first results in the 1938 election for tax collector. About forty additional black voters had been added to the rolls by then, at the rate of about ten a year. The tax collector's race, between the incumbent W. S. Webb and John Hugh Reynolds, promised to be close. Both men realized that, in a county where there were only two thousand registered voters, the approximately seventy black voters could determine the outcome. Both wanted the black vote but they sought it in different ways. Webb "wasn't man enough to come out here and ask for it," said one Institute voter later. "He tried to grab a man on the street and whisper in his ear." But Reynolds "came right out there and talked with us—face to face. He told us he didn't want no public endorsement and we knew why, but he did want our vote, and he promised to protect us if we gave it to him. He went to see every single Negro voter, and he got it." Reynolds won by twenty-two votes.[13]

The 1938 election alarmed white officials, some of whom were already concerned about Negro voting. The black vote "is getting to be a serious menace," Judge William Varner said in 1939. "Worrisome" was how H. N. Watson, the circuit clerk, described it. "We hold it down all we can, but we got this Veterans' Hospital and the Institute here. They're educated, and they've got property, and there's not much you can do," Watson explained. The Institute and the VA hospital could "control things here if they want to," said E. E. "Pat" Evans, the sheriff. "We ain't had no trouble yet," Evans noted, "but there might be if they turn them loose." The mere presence of the Institute and the hospital troubled him. "I think there ought to be a law about putting two big nigger things like that in one county."[14]

White officials resolved to stop, or at least to slow, black registration. Judge Varner complained that many of the recently registered blacks could have been rejected by testing for "understanding" of the United States Constitution. "They could have kept them out this way, but the registrars didn't have sense enough to do it," he said. In 1939 the registrars began asking applicants questions about the Constitution, though they had no legal authority to do so. This did not, however, prove as successful as Varner imagined it would.

"Most of the boys know a lot about the Constitution. I think they had been studying," said Mrs. Caro Wright, chairman of the board. A doctor from the veterans hospital stunned the board with his knowledge of the Constitution. "He started rattling it off from memory so fast they couldn't stop him for five minutes," a black voter reported. The board then began to require black applicants to meet both literacy and property qualifications, though the state constitution clearly made property an alternative means for qualifying. The property requirement did keep out a few veterans hospital orderlies who had recently applied.[15]

Gomillion and his group regarded Probate Judge William Varner as the major opponent of black voting. He held the most powerful office in the county; his duties included keeping the voting roll and overseeing all county elections. He had been mayor of Tuskegee and a state legislator, and by virtue of his public service alone commanded great respect in the community. He was, in addition, descended from one of Macon County's oldest and wealthiest families. His paternal grandfather—also called William Varner—had come to Tuskegee in 1850, acquired much land, and built the town's architectural masterpiece, Grey Columns, a mansion that replicated the Parthenon. His father was Robert R. Varner, the building contractor, farmer, and merchant who had been Washington's friend. Judge Varner's wife was Caro Wright's niece, and it may have been this family connection that gave Varner his strongest influence over the board. Wright acknowledged in 1939 that she was unsure about her duties there; it would have been natural for her to look to her niece's husband for advice.[16]

Varner's personal character also helped make him influential. Except for the name, he bore no resemblance to the Faulknerian Will Varner, the coarse and amoral patriarch of *The Hamlet*. This William Varner was widely considered a gentleman, and he looked the part. Six feet tall and erect of carriage, Judge Varner remained in his early fifties a very handsome man. His manners were impeccable: he tipped his hat to women and treated blacks who came into the probate office with a natural politeness. Many blacks liked Judge Varner because of the courtesy he had shown when selling them building lots near the Institute, and they later found it difficult to believe that he was the leading opponent of black voting. A reserved and private person, he never discussed the voting issue even with his oldest son during the twenty-five years that the controversy bedeviled his office. He was a devoted father to three sons, each of whom inherited his good looks and acquired his good manners, and he was very attentive to his mother, who lived with him. He served as a steward in the Methodist church and raised camellias in his spare time.*

Varner apparently never voiced his reasons for opposing black voting, but his personal background affords a basis for plausible speculation about those reasons. Only thirteen years old at the time of disfranchisement in Alabama, he had not witnessed black political activity of any consequence. What he must have heard about blacks in politics—stories of Republicans herding them to the polls during Reconstruction—was entirely negative. As a young man he probably inherited a residue of anxiety, left over from the 1870s and 1890s, about whether conservatives could keep control of Macon County. He certainly remembered the veterans hospital controversy in 1923—as mayor, he had worked to bring the hospital to Tuskegee—and the vulnerability that it exposed in the white conservative position. Now, in 1940, Varner could see clearly the threat of black voting. John Hugh Reynolds had estimated in 1939 that more than a thousand people at the Institute and the hospital were better qualified to vote than the average white voter in the county. As an incumbent, Judge Varner surely feared that new voters, especially black ones, might weaken his political standing. Thus, both his personal experience and his political interests gave him reason to oppose black voting.[17]

Gomillion also realized the potential power of blacks in Tuskegee, but he was not seeking the political revolution that some whites feared. His group's primary goals were to improve public services, to get equal opportunities in public education, and to heighten black awareness of all community concerns. In 1941 Gomillion took the next step toward achieving these goals: he led a move to change the name of the Men's Club to the "Tuskegee Civic Association" in order to include in the group several women who shared its interests and had the ability to further its purposes. He derived the new name from his commitment to the idea of "civic democracy," which he defined as a "way of life . . . in which all citizens have the opportunity to participate in societal affairs, and benefit from or enjoy public services, in keeping with their interests, abilities, and needs, without limitation or restriction based on race, color, creed, or national origin."[18]

Civic democracy was color-blind democracy, a concept that Go-

---

* William Varner, Jr., interview; Gomillion interviews. Gomillion had bought a lot from Judge Varner in the 1930s and had found him to be pleasant and accommodating. On the social graces of the Varners, interview with Florida Broward Segrest, June 14, 1978.

million took largely from his high school civics textbook. Part of the mission of the Tuskegee Civic Association would be "civic education," the process of teaching the black community how civic democracy worked, in both theory and practice. To blacks, he stressed the responsibilities of civic democracy as much as, if not more than, the rights, a reflection of both his mother's conservative moral code and the Booker Washington philosophy. Civic democracy was a radical departure for Macon County in 1941, but its full implementation was not Gomillion's immediate goal. First the TCA would try to unify and educate the black community, no easily attainable goal in itself. In its first year the TCA sponsored a Works Progress Administration school, a Boy Scout troop, and the Macon County observance of National Negro Health Week.[19]

But the goal of overall community improvement inevitably led Gomillion and the TCA back to politics. "Realizing the importance of participation in politics, the Association has encouraged its members and others to register, pay their poll taxes, and vote intelligently," Gomillion wrote near the end of the TCA's first year. "It has even sought to influence the Board of Registrars to register citizens whom the Board was reluctant to register." Gomillion and the TCA did not relish conflict with the board and Judge Varner, but their purpose demanded it. They did not know then that voting would become their overriding concern for the next twenty-five years.[20]

With the founding of the TCA, Gomillion assumed the leadership of the Tuskegee black community. He represented a break with certain traditions of black leadership. While Booker Washington had not liked disfranchisement but had accepted its inevitability, Gomillion believed that voting was the ultimate solution to many black problems. Washington was personally conciliatory toward whites; he would not have responded angrily to the shoe salesman's patronizing greeting as Gomillion did in 1928. Gomillion's departure from attitudes of the past was especially apparent to an informant for the FBI, which investigated him in 1942 on the suspicion that his civil rights activism reflected Communist sympathies. The informant quoted Gomillion telling a group at the Institute that "Education alone will not change the [Negro's] condition as long as there is prejudice, segregation and hatred . . . among his white neighbors." According to an FBI agent, the spy explained that "the old school type of negro leader such as Booker T. Washington and George Washington Carver who believed in a conservative progress . . . by achievement and meritorious service, was passing out of control at the Institute and a 'Modern' school of thought has been gradually replacing the old." Gomillion and Frederick Patterson were the leaders of "this Modern group . . . which seizes upon any and every opportunity to advance the position of the negro to that of equal rights."[21]

But there were significant continuities between "the old school type of negro leader" and the "Modern" group. Washington had paved the way for Gomillion by establishing an independent middle class at the Institute, and Moton had expanded that group when he got the veterans hospital. Gomillion believed that he was simply taking Macon County blacks up the next logical step in the climb to full equality. Gomillion and Washington agreed on one especially important point: change in Macon County was a slow process. While he was not nearly as patient as Washington, Gomillion was prepared for a long struggle. "Gomillion is a very obstinate man," an old Tuskegee friend and colleague observed years later. "He will follow anything through."[22]

4

The Voice of Jacob,
the Hand of Esau

ON SEPTEMBER 20, 1941, T. Rupert Broady bought a fifty-dollar radio at Price's Jewelry Store on the Tuskegee town square. Broady, a twenty-four-year-old sociology instructor at the Institute, arranged to pay for the radio in installments. He intended by the purchase to induce John Price, the jeweler, to vouch for him before the Macon County Board of Registrars. The credit arrangement was meant to reinforce Price's motivation to help Broady. A former student and now a colleague of Charles Gomillion, Broady understood that blacks in Tuskegee commonly used this kind of economic coaxing to get whites to vouch.[1]

On October 7 he went to the board to apply for registration and gave the names of Price and Rivers Rush, a haberdasher with whom he had also done business, as his vouchers. Caro Wright asked Broady if he had three hundred dollars' worth of taxable property. Broady replied that he did not but that he understood the property qualification to be merely an alternative to the literacy requirement, which he was sure he met. "No, you will have to have three hundred dollars' worth of property or forty acres of land," Wright said. Only if he could meet the property requirement, she told Broady, should he have Rush or Price come before the board on his behalf.[2]

Convinced that Wright was wrong about the necessity of both property and literacy qualifications, Broady decided to secure his vouchers. Price agreed to vouch but broke several appointments to go to the board. Broady gave up on him and asked Rush, who accompanied Broady to the courthouse on November 12. Wright told

Rush that Broady could not register because he lacked the necessary property. Broady again contended that property was only an alternative requirement. Rush tried to interpret the board's policy for the young sociologist. "It doesn't make any difference whether you graduated from Harvard, if you don't have the property you can't register," he explained. As they left the courthouse Rush said to Broady, "Well, you got to get you $300 worth of property or 40 acres of land somewhere." But Broady insisted: property was an *alternative* qualification, and the Alabama constitution provided a means for appealing the board's ruling. The idea of a Negro taking the registrars to court astonished Rivers Rush, Broady later reported.[3]

Broady returned to the courthouse the next day with Gomillion and William Shields. The three men asked Wright to read the property provision for voting in the Alabama constitution. She did, and then they asked her to read the literacy provision, which she also did. They asked her how she interpreted the "or" between the two provisions. She replied that the board got its interpretation from the state attorney general. Gomillion asked if the registrars knew that the constitution provided for an appeal of the board's decision. Wright said they did. Where else could we get an opinion? Shields asked. Troup Cunningham, another board member, suggested that Probate Judge Varner might offer one.[4]

Judge Varner received Gomillion and Shields cordially. In answer to their query, however, he told them that both property and literacy were necessary qualifications. Gomillion then asked: Do all registered voters in the state of Alabama have three hundred dollars' worth of property? Varner pleaded ignorance. Shields pushed further: What steps should they take to get an opinion on the disputed passage of the constitution? Apparently this was one question more than Judge Varner's geniality could tolerate, for he jumped up from behind his desk, knocking over his telephone, and shouted angrily, "Find out for yourself!" He stormed from his office. On his way out of the courthouse, Gomillion went to the registrars and issued a warning. "If Broady is not registered by Monday, we'll file suit against you."[5]

Gomillion had resolved to sue the board when a registrar called Broady and asked him to return to the courthouse. He was registered the next morning. Sensing that the board might be softening its position, Gomillion and Shields took two Institute faculty members to the courthouse and challenged the white voucher requirement. Gomillion argued that it, too, was unconstitutional, and he added, "we will test it in court if necessary." The board stood firm then, but when Gomillion and Shields returned the next day Troup

Cunningham asked the whereabouts of the two faculty members, implying that he was prepared to register them. Shields quickly offered to vouch for them, but Cunningham refused, saying that he did not know Shields—though Shields and Gomillion's running battle with the board was now in its fourth day. The blacks countered that they had no intention of getting white vouchers. Clearly afraid of a lawsuit, the registrars accepted as vouchers G. W. A. Johnston and Lloyd Isaacs, two older Institute administrators well known to Tuskegee whites.[6]

The sequence of events that began with Broady's purchase of a radio had ended in two victories for Gomillion and his group: they had forced the board to acknowledge at least tacitly that it could not make black applicants meet both property and literacy requirements, and they had compelled the registrars to accept black vouchers. But these were minor victories; the voucher system continued, and the board decided *which* blacks could vouch. It was still free to devise new means to obstruct black registration—as Gomillion and company would soon see.

Broady's persistence marked the start of a new era in Macon County history. The seemingly peaceful, insulated coexistence of the black and white communities had ended. No longer would black leaders refrain from open confrontation with whites about voting. Judge Varner's anger at the black challenge to the board and Gomillion's subsequent threat of a lawsuit had, in a matter of moments, torn away the veneer of harmony that had obscured almost all conflict for forty years. Now fully exposed once again was the historic white anxiety about control of society.

Important though it was, the conflict over voting no doubt commanded less attention from Macon Countians in the fall of 1941 than did the war in Europe and the threat of war in the Far East. The bombing of Pearl Harbor, just three weeks after Gomillion confronted Judge Varner, further separated the present from what had preceded it. The war would change society dramatically, even in a relatively isolated place like Macon County.

The county had felt the impact of war even before Pearl Harbor. President Franklin Roosevelt announced during the 1940 presidential campaign that the army would train blacks as aviators—a decision that was partly a response to demands from black journalists that black soldiers be treated more equitably in the coming war effort than they had been during World War I. When Frederick Patterson inquired about where the black airmen would be trained, the War Department told him that a separate facility would be built. He suggested Tuskegee as the site, noting the warm climate and the existence of a civilian training program for pilots at the Institute. His suggestion was accepted: the army announced in January 1941 the establishment of a training program for black pilots at Tuskegee.[7]

Patterson's pursuit of the aviation program continued the Tuskegee tradition of seeking new opportunities for blacks. Patterson knew that the aviation program would create civilian jobs in Tuskegee, and he intended for blacks to get them. He encouraged the War Department to use a black-owned construction firm to build the Tuskegee Army Air Field, explaining that when the VA hospital was constructed the government set the precedent that blacks "of professional ability should, as a matter of fairness and common decency, be given a chance to render the professional services in connection therewith." The black contractor got the job—the traditional strategy of the Institute prevailed again.[8]

But his maintenance of the Tuskegee tradition earned Patterson scorn from black activists working to end segregation in the military. Walter White, now executive director of the NAACP, had told Patterson before the War Department's decision that he opposed segregated training. White and his organization were pushing the department to integrate the aviation training program as the initial step in the desegregation of the armed forces. NAACP leaders believed that Patterson, by enthusiastically offering Tuskegee as the site for segregated training, had helped to thwart their efforts, and they were angry with him. In July 1941 White blamed Patterson for the fact that only thirty-three blacks were among the estimated fifty thousand fliers then being trained: "This is what comes about because a Negro asked for segregation." William Hastie, the Howard University law dean whom President Roosevelt appointed as a civilian aide to the War Department to monitor the treatment of blacks in the armed forces, called Patterson's action "an object lesson of selfish and short-sighted scheming for immediate personal advantage with cynical disregard for the larger interests of the Negro and of the nation." When he resigned from the department in 1943 in protest against continued segregation in the army, Hastie blamed Patterson's early complicity in segregation for much of the discrimination that persisted in later years. In Tuskegee Institute, he wrote, the army had "a willing and useful accomplice in their design of keeping the Negro strictly segregated."[9]

The dispute over the Tuskegee airfield continued the debate over strategy that W. E. B. DuBois and other black intellectuals had begun a generation earlier when they challenged Booker Washington's accommodationist approach. The airfield had revived an old controversy, NAACP assistant secretary Roy Wilkins explained, over "whether a militant and uncompromising adherence to certain principles should be the philosophy of an entire racial group of thirteen million persons, or whether a policy of taking what you can get and submerging principles for the time being is the best philosophy." In Patterson's mind, his action had not been a matter of principle; the War Department had told him unequivocally that the airmen's training program would be segregated. On that basis he acted practically—or, from the NAACP viewpoint, selfishly—to secure the training base for Tuskegee. If blacks were to receive a new opportunity, then he wanted it to be given at Tuskegee, the symbol of black progress for so many Americans. The NAACP activists objected so strongly to Patterson's action precisely because they believed that Tuskegee's national prestige on the side of segregation hindered their efforts to integrate the armed forces. The army's impulse to segregate may well have been so strong that a policy of separation was inevitable, but Patterson's action probably kept the NAACP from putting maximum pressure on the War Department at the start of the military buildup for World War II.[10]

Conceived in controversy, the Tuskegee Army Air Field (TAAF) remained a source of conflict for the remainder of its existence. Relations between black soldiers and white civilians in Tuskegee were always uneasy. The presence of three thousand young black men in uniform heightened the racial anxieties of the one thousand white Tuskegeeans. Many black soldiers were well-educated northerners unaccustomed to the naked prejudice of a small Alabama town. An initial misunderstanding about police authority exacerbated the tension. Many soldiers and some local whites at first did not recognize that the airmen were subject to civil authority when they were off the base. This ignorance led to some disrespect among soldiers for the local police and to great fear among whites. To make matters worse, armed military policemen patrolled the town during the TAAF's first year. Some white townsmen established arsenals of shotguns and got commitments from whites in nearby towns to help defend Tuskegee in case of attack by black soldiers. Not long after the airfield opened, local policemen forcibly took from a black MP a soldier he had arrested. They also disarmed and arrested a black sentry when he challenged a white civilian. Foreseeing the potential for disaster, Patterson asked the War Department in August 1941 to make an effort "to educate white citizens . . . particularly law enforcement bodies, regarding the rights of Negro soldiers . . . who are very apt to innocently violate certain customs, yet when they are abruptly and unceremoniously dealt with, are not inclined to submit to such coercive tactics." The army did not heed Patterson's advice until it was almost too late.[11]

On the night of April 1, 1942, a payday at the TAAF, a policeman in Tuskegee arrested a black soldier for public drunkenness. A black MP saw the arrest and, drawing his gun, demanded custody of the soldier; several other MPs backed him up. The policeman handed over the soldier but quickly called his chief for help. Several city policemen and a state highway patrolman soon arrived, disarmed the MPs, and retrieved the prisoner. In the process they beat one of the MPs seriously enough to require hospitalization. When a somewhat distorted version of these events reached the base, a party of airmen armed themselves and set out to Tuskegee to free the captured soldiers. A black officer on the base, recognizing the potential for serious violence, called Colonel Noel Parrish, the white director of training at the TAAF who lived with a civilian family in Tuskegee, and explained the situation. Parrish intercepted the angry soldiers and persuaded them to return to the base, thus averting a crisis.[12]

This incident alarmed white Tuskegeeans and high-ranking officers in the War Department. The action of the black MPs intensified the fear of whites who already had serious misgivings about the presence of uniformed blacks carrying guns. Local officials complained to Colonel Frederick Kimble, the commander at the TAAF, that black soldiers did not believe they were responsible to local authority. The War Department fixed blame on the black MPs for interfering with civil authority, and Kimble "plainly and emphatically impressed upon" his troops that they must be obedient to local police. After weeding out the black MPs involved in the incident, Kimble sent the remainder of the force to conferences with city and county officials at Tuskegee City Hall. Henceforth white MPs would patrol the white areas of the town; black MPs would confine their activities to black Tuskegee and the base itself. "A small minority of personnel on duty at Tuskegee are radically inclined," a War Department adjutant concluded, ignoring the actions of the Tuskegee police before the April 1 incident. The radicals "are participating in agitation to keep alive race questions and questions of social equality." The real question, of course, was not social equality, but who controlled Tuskegee.[13]

Immediately after the April 1 incident, Tuskegee whites withdrew their support from the army's plans to build yet another training base for black fliers near Tuskegee. The Tuskegee City Council and the Macon County Board of Revenue, the county governing body, publicly opposed another army facility. State politicians added vociferous opposition to the proposal. "The establishment of such a

camp anywhere in the South in times like these," Governor Frank
Dixon argued, would create "an absolutely impossible situation so
far as our own social structure is concerned." Senator John Bankhead asked General George C. Marshall, army chief of staff, to remove all black troops from the South, because he believed their
presence would lead to a race war. "Locating troops in the South . . .
at a time when race feeling among the Negroes has been aroused,
will result in conflict at a time when all the energies of both the
whites and the blacks should be devoted to the war effort," Bankhead said. At least part of the opposition to another army base resulted from fear of labor shortages. White planters in Macon County
"who watched their cheap help skitter off the fields to get better jobs
at the Army post," *Time* magazine reported in August 1942, spoke
contemptuously of "that nigger airport." The TAAF had provided
several hundred civilian jobs that no doubt attracted the keen interest of local blacks accustomed to the deprivation of sharecropping.
Another airfield would only have threatened further the supply of
cheap farm labor.*

When the army scrapped its plans for the second Tuskegee base in
November 1942, conservative whites were relieved but still anxious.
State Senator Richard Holmes Powell of Tuskegee thanked Governor Dixon for his help "in killing out what was a pretty well arranged plan to put this additional burden upon the white people of
Macon County." Dixon could consider himself the leader of "this
great movement for the protection of our white people," Powell
wrote, against "the determined encroachment of our colored population." Powell knew that the outcome could have been different; he
no doubt remembered the less successful end—from the white conservative perspective—to the VA controversy of 1923, when he had
concluded that "the Negroes are gradually taking things from us."
For his part, Dixon worried less about the black challenge than the
threat posed by the Roosevelt Administration. "We are facing a
really serious situation in this country unless we can in some way
persuade the present National administration to abandon their
crackpot efforts at social reform during this emergency," Dixon
wrote to Powell. "We can handle the situation if let alone; to save
our souls, we can't handle it in the long run unless some wisdom is
shown in Washington."[14]

* Birmingham *News*, December 1, 1942; Pittsburgh *Courier*, May 30, August 8,
1942; *Time*, August 3, 1942. General Marshall denied Bankhead's request that he
remove all black troops from the South, an act for which Frederick Patterson
commended him. (Patterson to Marshall, August 14, 1942, Patterson Papers,
President's Vault, Tuskegee Institute.)

One of the "crackpot efforts" to which Dixon referred was the federal Fair Employment Practices Committee, which had held hearings on racial discrimination in defense industries in Birmingham in June 1942. Mark Ethridge, the committee chairman, tried to assure Alabamians that the FEPC had no intention of challenging segregation. "There is no power in the world—not even in all the mechanized armies of the earth, Allied and Axis—which could now force the Southern white people to the abandonment of the principle of social segregation," Ethridge had said. Entirely unconvinced, Dixon sent copies of the FEPC proceedings in Birmingham to dozens of his fellow Alabama conservatives. "The protestation throughout," he wrote to Senator Powell in October 1942, "is that no remotest thought is being given to any attempts to abolish segregation in the South, but the practical effect is to bring about exactly that result." To drive home his point, the governor referred to the story of deception in the book of Genesis in which Jacob put on goatskins to make his blind father Isaac believe that he was his hirsute older brother Esau, in order that he, not Esau, might receive Isaac's blessing and, thus, the leadership of the Israelites. "The voice is the voice of Jacob," Dixon wrote about the FEPC proceedings, paraphrasing Isaac, "but the hand is that of Esau."[15]

The tension at Tuskegee Army Air Field in 1942 probably surpassed even the anxiety among Alabama conservatives. The black soldiers and officers disliked Colonel Kimble intensely, and stories of his discrimination frequently appeared in black newspapers. A native Georgian, Kimble rigidly enforced Jim Crow on the air base. He complained to his commanding officer about an air base in Illinois—at which many Tuskegee airmen had previously trained—that did not segregate its mess hall. He placed signs reading "For White Officers" and "For Colored Officers" over toilets on the base, in direct violation of new army regulations. When black MPs twice removed the signs, he replaced them. He reportedly ordered white officers to stay away from the post officers' club in an effort to stop all interracial fraternization. Black officers accused him of discrimination in making assignments and of preventing the post finance officer, a black captain, from performing his duties.[16]

Kimble's determination to enforce segregation, and the resulting hostility of black soldiers toward him, persuaded the army to remove him from command in December 1942. Colonel Parrish, the popular young director of training, took over and improved race relations significantly, though he, too, was a southerner. He removed the Jim Crow signs once and for all, integrated the officers' mess, and dealt fairly with black officers on assignments. Parrish "will volunteer a

discussion of racial issues when a discussion is pertinent without getting emotionally excited," the Pittsburgh *Courier* reported. But Parrish did not change the living arrangements for white personnel. All
150 white officers lived off base, at least partly because of housing
shortages at the TAAF. This remained a source of bitterness among
some black airmen, who saw it as favored treatment for whites.
"Every morning there is a long line of automobiles bringing the
white lords to this plantation," a Tuskegee soldier told the *Courier* in
October 1944. "All day long they shove us around and run the field.
Late in the afternoon there is another long line of automobiles carrying the white lords away. Their day's work is done."[17]

Parrish witnessed the troubled racial climate of Tuskegee from a
uniquely revealing perspective. White women were dating black soldiers, local whites told him. "Which was really true," he later wrote,
"although the women either 'claimed' or 'acknowledged' Negro ancestors." Parrish found a corresponding fascination with whites' sexual behavior among the black soldiers. A false rumor about white
men attacking black women in Tuskegee persisted at the TAAF for
many months. "Hundreds of individuals amused themselves, for
hours in speculating about the sexual tendencies of the 'other
race.'" During the five years that the TAAF operated, Parrish wrote
in 1947, "almost every conceivable inter-racial complication arose
except one—sex. It appears that the so-called 'sex problem' as connected with the problems of race is the most entertaining, the most
fascinating, for many people, the most frightening, and in the end
the least important of all."*

At the moment in 1942 when Tuskegee whites were most anxious
about the presence of black soldiers, another potential threat to conservative power arose over the conduct of the county sheriff, Edwin
E. "Pat" Evans. The Tuskegee Civic Association began to collect
evidence of Evans's brutality after the death of Walter Gunn, a Tuskegee black, in June 1942. Evans and his deputy, Henry Faucett, attempted to arrest Gunn—for public drunkenness, they later said—at
a country revival meeting. Gunn reportedly resisted, perhaps because he knew the hazards of being in the sheriff's custody: Evans, a
220-pound former high school football star, had beaten him with a
blackjack and a walking stick in the course of an arrest the previous
October. When Gunn tried to break away from the sheriff at the re-

---

* Noel F. Parrish, "The Segregation of Negroes in the Army Air Forces" (thesis,
Air University at Maxwell Air Base, May 1947), 7, 22–26. In a moment of comic
relief for Parrish, the writer Carson McCullers, who was visiting in Tuskegee,
asked him if it were not true that Negroes could fly *better* than whites "because
they're closer to nature."

vival meeting, Evans hit him with handcuffs, a blackjack, and the butt of a pistol. Gunn escaped momentarily, whereupon Faucett shot him in the leg. Gunn died, the coroner later testified, not from the gunshot but from a blow to the head.[18]

Gunn's death was the worst example of a pattern of violence during Evans's tenure as sheriff. Louis James Hatcher, a black Tuskegeean, testified that Evans had handcuffed him to cell bars in the Tuskegee jail in May 1940 with his feet only partially touching the floor and then hit him repeatedly with a rubber hose and a walking stick. Eugene Brown stated that Evans and Faucett had handcuffed him to a tree in a secluded woods in March 1942 and then beat him with tree limbs and blackjacks. Just three days after they killed Gunn, Evans and Faucett beat Readie Glenn Huguley, a mentally retarded white man, on the head and body. They whipped Lillie May Hendon with blackjacks and walking sticks in August. They used, in addition to the usual instruments, an automobile fan belt on Edgar Cullen Bryant in November.[19]

Evans's exploitation of Macon County's prohibition law had earned him almost as much contempt among blacks as his brutality. He had informants in state liquor stores in adjacent "wet" counties who would notify him when blacks from Macon bought alcohol. Evans would then arrest them as soon as they reentered the county and extract from them a stiff fine, out of which the sheriff received a fee. Evans would confiscate the liquor, but blacks suspected that he was not pouring it down a drain. A black man whose Christmas spirits Evans had confiscated resorted to emergency measures on Christmas Eve and went to one of several bootleggers who flourished in Macon County. There the man, who had written his name on his bottles before they were confiscated, was sold the same liquor that Evans had recently taken from him. To blacks, Evans's corruption appeared total.[20]

Gomillion and the TCA started raising money in August 1942 to bring a lawsuit against Evans. "Have you contributed to the WALTER GUNN FUND?" Gomillion asked in a letter to Tuskegee blacks. "A contribution will mean a protest against police brutality and an expression of faith in the efficacy of intelligent group action." Some money was collected, but the TCA discovered that many blacks doubted that a suit would be successful. The organization then took its information on Evans to the United States attorney in Montgomery, who in April 1943 procured an indictment against Evans and Faucett for brutality. The Justice Department made a point of announcing the indictment in Washington, an action that the Montgomery *Advertiser* interpreted as an effort "to combat Japanese propaganda . . . about alleged racial discrimination."[21]

Evans's conduct had also disturbed some leading whites, including Tuskegee mayor Frank Carr and state representative Henry Neill Segrest, who had asked Governor Dixon in 1942 to consider removing him from office. Dixon sent an investigator to Tuskegee, but did not act on the situation after Evans was renominated in the Democratic primary in May 1942. The death of Gunn and the beating of Readie Huguley in June reinforced Carr and Segrest's determination to get rid of Evans. When Segrest heard that Evans had beaten Lillie May Hendon, he arranged to examine her at his law office. Segrest, his wife Florida, and two local businessmen were appalled at Hendon's condition. "Her hips looked like battered liver," Florida Segrest said later. Representative Segrest and Mayor Carr decided to cooperate with the United States attorney in the suit against Evans, though they did so at some risk. Soon after the indictments were handed down, the FBI learned that Evans's friends were threatening potential witnesses and saying that, if he was convicted, "the white people of Macon County, Alabama will have to move."[22]

Lillie May Hendon was the center of attention when Evans and Deputy Faucett went on trial in June 1943 in Opelika, twenty-five miles northeast of Tuskegee. "A glamor negress" was how Atticus Mullin of the Montgomery *Advertiser* characterized her. Carr and Segrest described the condition of Hendon's back, hips, and legs after the alleged beating. Evans boasted that he "had slapped the hell out of Lillie May," the Tuskegee police chief testified. After the victim told how Evans and Faucett had beaten her, defense attorneys attacked her character. "Pull down your skirt, Lillie May," ordered one lawyer in the midst of his cross-examination. Several black defense witnesses testified to her bad character, and some suggested that her boyfriend, not Evans, had beaten her.[23]

Defense lawyers successfully made the origin of the prosecution the main issue in the trial. Is the Tuskegee Civic Association paying for the prosecution? the defense counsel asked the United States attorney. Are Eleanor Roosevelt and the NAACP behind it? Of course not, the prosecutors replied, but a conspiracy between blacks and the federal government had been suggested to the twelve white male jurors, most of whom came from small towns in southeastern Alabama. Sheriffs from all over the state attended the trial, because, the partisan Mullin explained, "they feared that if Sheriff Evans was convicted, it would mean that the federal government had laid its heavy hand upon local law enforcement in the counties and cities." After a short deliberation the jury acquitted Evans and Faucett.[24]

Despite the victory, Tuskegee conservatives were left with a sharp sense of uneasiness about the whole matter. "The old carpetbagger instincts still cling to some who hold high official positions," the editor of the Tuskegee *News* asserted a few days later. They worried also about the possible reemergence of the old scalawag instincts. When they testified against Pat Evans, Representative Segrest and Mayor Carr went against the conservative majority who believed that the sheriff must be defended against challenges from blacks and the federal government—regardless of what he had done. Most whites saw the issue as control of the community, not Evans's inhumane treatment of prisoners. In their view Segrest and Carr had committed a kind of treason.[25]

Carr's testimony may have been an anomalous act—he later was a bitter opponent of Gomillion and the TCA—but Henry Neill Segrest presented a genuine threat to conservative power. He staunchly supported the New Deal, something that must have been known when he was elected to represent Macon County in the Alabama legislature in 1938 and then reelected in 1942. That a man of Segrest's views could twice win a majority among county voters no doubt worried conservatives. Segrest was less susceptible to conformist pressure from conservatives than were other Tuskegeeans—perhaps including Mayor Carr. The tall, spindly lawyer remained outside the town's white social elite, though he was a member of one of the county's oldest families. His law practice was only marginally successful, apparently because he lacked a strong materialistic impulse. A devout Presbyterian, he believed in the idea of the brotherhood of all men.[26]

A new surge of conservative insecurity swept across Alabama and the South in April 1944, when the United States Supreme Court struck down the white primary in the case of *Smith v. Allwright.* Although the few black voters in Macon County had been allowed to vote in the Democratic primary all along, this decision removed a potential obstacle to blacks' gaining significant political power. The decision heightened the concern that Alabama conservatives already had felt about their ability to dominate the Democratic party. Men like Frank Dixon had become alienated from the national party when the New Deal's program of governmental activism emerged in the early 1930s. By the early 1940s they were bitter opponents of Franklin Roosevelt and were openly talking of revolt against the party. In late 1942 Dixon accused the Democratic party of betraying white southerners. "It is their party which is dynamiting their social structure, which is arousing bitterness and recrimination, which is attempting to force crackpot reforms on them in a time of national crisis." Dixon was particularly incensed about a recent effort in Congress to outlaw the poll tax—"childish casuistry"—and about the Fair Employment Practices Committee—"an illustration of stupid tampering with the delicate question" of race relations. "Suggestions are rife as to the formation of a Southern Democratic party," Dixon warned.[27]

The Alabama Democratic primary in May 1944 gave conservatives even more cause for worry. They enthusiastically backed James Simpson, a conservative corporate lawyer from Birmingham, in his challenge of Lister Hill, the incumbent junior United States Senator who had frequently voted with the Roosevelt Administration. Simpson tried to make race the issue in the campaign, suggesting that Hill's New Deal connections kept him from defending white supremacy, but the effort failed. Hill won and showed conservatives that most Alabama Democrats liked the New Deal programs.[28]

Conservatives moved to build new obstacles to political participation when the Alabama legislature went into session in May 1945. The white primary decision had torn down one of the barriers that assured conservatives of a limited electorate. The property and literacy requirements for voter registration now kept away fewer blacks than they had in 1901. State Representative Edward Calhoun Boswell offered an amendment to the Alabama constitution that gave boards of registrars the authority to test whether an applicant "understood" the United States Constitution—something that the Macon County board had done as early as 1939. "A smart parrot could be taught to recite a section of our Constitution," wrote Gessner McCorvey, the chairman of the Alabama Democratic party and the leader of the movement for new voting restrictions. The Boswell amendment "would give certain discretion to the Board of Registrars and enable them to prevent from registering those elements in our community which have not yet fitted themselves for self government." McCorvey contended that the amendment would prevent "the average Negro who owned a car," and who thereby met the three-hundred-dollar property qualification, from becoming a voter. To the relief of conservatives who had felt the flow of political events go against them for several years, the Boswell amendment passed both houses. A statewide referendum to ratify the amendment was to be held the next year.[29]

Despite this apparent victory, Alabama conservatives looked apprehensively to the future as the war's end seemed near. Almost since Pearl Harbor they had assumed that the war would change their society in ways they did not want. They drew a parallel between this war and the one eighty years earlier, which had altered their grandfathers' world in unwanted ways. Judge Walter B. Jones of Montgomery, son of Governor Thomas Goode Jones and a well-known conservative in his own right, had demanded in 1943 that black groups, Communists, and the Roosevelt Administration "cease the attempted reformation of the South, their second reconstruction." Senator Powell of Tuskegee used the same analogy. "True Southerners," he wrote to Frank Dixon the same year, are "manning the ramparts and keeping close watch as they did in the days following the War between the States." The real challenge for white southerners would come after the war, another conservative wrote to Dixon. "We in the South face a condition which, when the war is won, will bring problems only less grave than those our forebears overcame during the decade following Appomattox." Their romantic view of the first Reconstruction—which suggested that white control was regained through courage and honor—comforted Alabama conservatives, because it seemed to promise that power would likewise be retrieved in the postwar period just ahead. In reality, however, events during the war years pointed to a different outcome this time, and many conservatives knew it.[30]

Blacks in Tuskegee looked ahead in 1945 with more optimism. They had broken with the past in 1941 to pursue more forthrightly a greater share of the political power in the county. Their progress since then had been minimal; only a handful of blacks were registered to vote during the war years. But national and world events had worked in their favor. The war had set off a sequence of changes that redounded to their benefit—the airfield, most notably—and it had promoted an ideology of freedom that furthered their cause.

That ideology provided part of the impetus for the founding of a local branch of the NAACP in Tuskegee in the summer of 1944. Two men had written independently of each other to the national headquarters requesting assistance in forming a branch. Detroit Lee, a civilian employee at the TAAF and a Texas native, explained that the many blacks who had come to Tuskegee "from various parts of the United States" would support a local branch. Robert Spiceley, manager of the Tuskegee Institute cafeteria, cited among his reasons for activism the recent murder of his brother, a soldier, by policemen in Durham, North Carolina. His brother's death was a challenge "to all of us who claim to believe in democracy," Ella Baker, the NAACP's director of branches, wrote to Spiceley. "The fight for the citizenship rights of Negro Americans is as vital to the survival of

American Democracy as are the battles now being waged on foreign soil." The desire for democratic rights was so strong that Lee, Spiceley, and others simply ignored Tuskegee Institute's historic antipathy to the NAACP. The war had worked a remarkable change on people and society.[31]

Charles Gomillion and other TCA members fully supported the new organization. They had noted the significant victory that NAACP lawyers had just won in the white primary decision. They expected that their conflict with the Board of Registrars would eventually end in litigation, and they hoped that the NAACP would help them when that time came. Indeed, even before the Japanese surrendered, they were on their way to court.

5

Something Good
from Nazareth

CARO WRIGHT must have felt harried during the first week in July 1945. It was hot in the Macon County Courthouse, where she had to go each day to convene the Board of Registrars. A short, prim woman in her sixties, Wright had recently been widowed and had, of necessity, taken over her husband's insurance business. It was hardly a convenient time to spend a whole week at the courthouse. To make things worse, the tension at the board's office fairly crackled. More than two hundred blacks stood outside waiting to apply. Wright had never seen such a clamor to register. There was only one other registrar—Virgil Guthrie, a farmer—to help her cope with the onslaught. In five days she and Guthrie accepted ninety-seven applications, ninety of them from blacks. More than half of the blacks who came to register, however, went away angry when they did not get to apply. Everyone could have applied, the disgruntled blacks no doubt recognized, had Wright and Guthrie worked more diligently. They kept the office open only four-and-a-half hours each day and accepted but two applications at a time. Wright, whose aristocratic family had long supported Tuskegee Institute and who was known to be kind to her black friends and employees, resented the anger directed at the board and at her personally.[1]

The anger increased in a few weeks when blacks realized that the board had approved only ten of their applications. The board never notified the other eighty applicants that they had failed, but TCA leaders knew the registrars typically did not inform black applicants that they had been rejected. The voucher system appeared to be the stumbling block once again. Wright and Guthrie told several applicants not to bring their vouchers to the courthouse; one of the registrars would contact the person designated. But in fact neither ever did and the applications were not approved. The registrars refused to accept most black vouchers, usually saying that they did not know the person suggested. The board always refused Gomillion's offer to vouch. Of the ten successful applicants, three had white vouchers and seven had the supporting signature of G. W. A. Johnston, the Institute's purchasing agent. No other black had vouched successfully.[2]

Gomillion and the TCA decided that the time had come to challenge the Board of Registrars in court. On August 1, twenty-five of the rejected applicants filed a suit in state circuit court charging that the board had unfairly denied them the right to vote. This suit appealed the board's decision through the channels prescribed by the Alabama constitution, which allowed an initial challenge in circuit court and then, if necessary, an appeal of the lower court's decision to the Alabama Supreme Court. But the chances of a state court's providing relief were slim, TCA leaders believed, so they organized a similar, simultaneous challenge in federal district court in Montgomery. William P. Mitchell, a VA employee who, TCA leaders believed, could withstand any pressure put on him by whites, was chosen as the plaintiff in the federal suit. Wright and Guthrie were named as defendants. The new NAACP branch raised money to pay for the litigation, and Arthur Shores, a Birmingham attorney who handled NAACP cases in Alabama, represented all the plaintiffs.[3]

The suits revealed a surge of support for the TCA's challenge of the Board of Registrars. The first objections to the board's procedures in 1941 had been raised by a small group of Institute professors and administrators, but now larger numbers of VA and TAAF employees were escalating the conflict. Most of the applicants rejected at the July meeting worked at either the airfield or the hospital. Half of the plaintiffs in the state court suit were VA employees. Among them, Daniel L. Beasley typified the attitude and experience of those who were expanding the challenge. A Macon County native and Institute graduate, Beasley was stationed at the TAAF when the army discharged him in 1945. He went to work at the VA hospital and began trying to register. "When I came out of the army I was determined to register to vote," Beasley explained later. "I was born here. I was a college graduate. I had been in the army . . . I had never been in jail. . . . I just figured I ought to be registered." Beasley immediately took a leading role in the voter registration battle. Pressure also came from black war veterans like Otis Pinkard, who returned to his native Macon County in April 1945. "A lot of guys . . . didn't expect to find the same situation that we left," Pinkard said later. "Which was not the case at all. . . . After having been overseas fighting for democracy, I thought that when we got back here we should enjoy a little of it." Pinkard also joined in the TCA's registration efforts.[4]

William P. Mitchell, the plaintiff in the federal suit, yielded to no one in his determination to become a voter. He had been trying to register since the late 1930s, and his numerous rejections had only hardened his resolve to force some changes on the Board of Registrars. A tall, lean, dark-brown man in his early thirties, Mitchell had a combative personality, probably acquired during his youth in the rough industrial town of Bessemer, Alabama. He had left school at thirteen to become a laborer in a Bessemer brickyard, where he worked until he was nineteen. At that time his mother persuaded him to return to school. Mitchell chose to go to Tuskegee Institute because he understood that persons of all ages attended the high school there. He finished high school but could not afford college. He took a job as an orderly at the VA hospital in 1935 and was soon trained to be a physical therapist, a position he would keep for the next thirty-three years. But his job never provided Mitchell with the personal challenge he wanted. By 1945 he had found an avocation—the voting rights conflict—that would provide the major interest and challenge of his life. He became executive secretary of the TCA—in effect, the "chief operating officer" to Gomillion's "chairman of the board." He managed the daily affairs of the TCA and kept meticulous records of black voting applicants. Quick-witted and well-spoken, Mitchell was better at personal confrontation with whites than Gomillion, who tended to avoid direct contact with conservative whites after the early 1940s. But on nearly all decisions of policy and strategy, Mitchell deferred to Gomillion, who had taught him world history in the high school department at Tuskegee Institute.[5]

The accelerated voting challenge must be put in the context of demographic changes taking place in Macon County during the 1940s. Between 1940 and 1950, the number of blacks occupying white-collar positions increased by 172 percent. The number holding skilled jobs more than doubled. Blacks filled almost fifteen hundred new, middle-income jobs. The VA hospital provided most of the new employment; its staff grew rapidly to accommodate the influx of disabled black veterans from the war. The Institute staff expanded substantially to handle returning servicemen and to provide several new graduate programs. This growth in employment more than doubled the size of the black middle class in Tuskegee, giving the TCA additional manpower and financial support with which to fight the Board of Registrars. The fifteen hundred people who worked at the VA hospital were especially important because, as federal employees, they were immune to pressure from local whites in a way that public-school teachers and Tuskegee Institute administrators were not.[6]

The population changes were a mixed blessing to whites. The growth of the black middle class resulted in substantial business expansion for the white merchants who provided goods and services to the Institute, the hospital, and their employees. The number of white sales and clerical workers almost doubled during the 1940s; professionals and proprietors increased about thirty percent. But despite this growth, the white middle class had lost ground to the black middle class. In 1940 whites had a slight majority of the white-collar positions in the county, but by 1950 there were sixty-eight percent more blacks in white-collar jobs. This change was probably less apparent to whites than the physical presence of more blacks in Tuskegee. The population in and near the town increased by 6,217 persons, or sixty-three percent, during the 1940s. Nine of every ten new Tuskegee residents were black. The town had become much more crowded, and now blacks held a greater numerical majority than ever before. The presence of more blacks—especially when so many of them were well-to-do—only exacerbated the insecurity that white residents already had about their ability to control Tuskegee.*

Farmers moving to town accounted for much of the increase. The rural population of the county declined about nineteen percent during the 1940s, the first significant decrease since the decade 1910–20 when it had fallen about eleven percent. Almost four of every ten black farmers and farm workers left their cotton fields, though by no means all of them moved to Tuskegee. The departure of black farmers, most of them sharecroppers, must have worried the many white landowners who still depended on black farm families to produce crops on their lands. Moreover, migration away from the farm un-

* Because the boundaries of the city of Tuskegee did not include many black residential areas that were contiguous to the town, I have used the population figures for the entire Tuskegee beat to estimate urban population growth. While there was some rural population in the Tuskegee beat, it was much smaller than the number of town-dwellers who were classified as rural because they lived outside the city limits of Tuskegee. Using the Tuskegee city population figures would have greatly underestimated the urban population of the Tuskegee area. As it is, I have slightly underestimated the rural population.

dermined white control of blacks. A landlord could virtually dictate a sharecropper's behavior by controlling his access to credit with the furnishing merchant. A sharecropper who moved to Tuskegee was likely to be a poor wage-earner, but his well-being did not always depend on staying in the good graces of a single white man.*

The TCA soon learned that its battle with the Board of Registrars would require patience. As expected, no relief was forthcoming in the state courts; and it was February 1947 before the Alabama Supreme Court ruled that the voucher requirement was "fair, just and reasonable." The twenty-five plaintiffs' "failure to comply therewith justifies a denial of registration," the judges declared. The TCA put the most attention, and hope, into *Mitchell v. Wright,* which moved more quickly in the federal courts. In October 1945 Judge Charles B. Kennamer of Montgomery dismissed the suit, without hearing evidence, on the grounds that Mitchell had not exhausted his remedies in the state courts. But the Fifth Circuit Court of Appeals soon overturned Kennamer's decision: The state itself was implicated in the discrimination against Mitchell, and it could hardly be expected to redress the grievance, the judges declared. The registrars were "acting under color of state authority . . . to deprive Negroes of the right to vote in Alabama," they stated in their order remanding the case to Kennamer for a full hearing. The registrars appealed the Fifth Circuit's decision to the United States Supreme Court, but in October 1946 the high court refused to hear their plea. Judge Kennamer rescheduled the case for early December.[7]

Many Alabama conservatives viewed the Macon County suits as the realization of their worst fears. Their anxiety was reflected in wild charges about the origin and intent of the suits. "The suit filed in Macon County," the Montgomery *Advertiser* reported just after the Mitchell case was entered, "is but a part of the campaign of the CIO to break down Alabama's election laws and qualifications in a long range effort to secure race fraternization and the destruction of white supremacy." The Congress of Industrial Organizations, one of the country's two major labor federations, actually had no part in the Mitchell case, but many conservatives could not admit to themselves that native blacks were responsible for such a challenge. The CIO served as a convenient object onto which conservatives could

---

* *The Sixteenth Census of the United States: 1940, Census of the Population, Alabama; The Seventeenth Census of the United States: 1950, Census of the Population, Alabama.* I have derived the nineteen percent figure by counting all the population of the Tuskegee beat as urban and all of the population of the other nine county beats as rural. There is a small error in this because a few rural people in the Tuskegee beat are counted as town-dwellers.

displace the anger resulting from their insecurity about black voting. Such accusations were also meant to help conservative candidates in the approaching Democratic primary. In their unsuccessful effort to defeat Senator Lister Hill in 1944, conservatives had tried to make the CIO's support of Hill an issue by portraying the labor group as an alien force bent on subverting Alabama politics. While some conservatives undoubtedly knew that the CIO threat was a red herring, many others believed quite sincerely, if irrationally, that a conspiracy of unions and blacks was plotting against them.[8]

The 1946 primary showed that powerful political forces really were working simultaneously, if not in collusion, against conservatives. Joe Poole, the conservatives' choice for governor, finished third behind two more liberal candidates, Handy Ellis and James E. "Big Jim" Folsom. In the runoff Ellis appropriated the conservatives' CIO bugbear. He accused Folsom of being the tool of Sidney Hillman, the head of the CIO's political action committee. "The principle involved in this campaign," Ellis shouted, "is whether a political agitator and rabble rouser, a man who was born and reared in Russia, can fasten his greedy clutches on the free Americans in the State of Alabama, slap a ring in their noses and tell them what they must do in a local Democratic primary."[9]

But again the tactic failed. The six-foot-eight-inch Folsom, who campaigned as the "Little Man's Big Friend," used his folksy manner and a liberal platform to win the race. The CIO helped Folsom significantly, but his majority was broadly based. A newspaper editor wrote that Folsom was "a genius at knowing the people's mind and [had] diagnosed, as none of the other candidates could, the hopes and aspirations of the small farmers, the country storekeepers, the rural school teachers, the thousands of workers who labor in overalls and white collars." Folsom promised Alabamians expanded governmental services, including greatly increased spending on education; a monthly pension for the aged; and a larger network of paved farm-to-market roads. He advocated repeal of Alabama's right-to-work law. And if these positions were not enough to instill fear into conservatives, he called for an end to the poll tax and for reapportionment of the Alabama legislature. Folsom stood squarely against virtually every important conservative position.[10]

Conservatives in Macon County had watched the primary nervously. Harold Fisher, the editor of the Tuskegee *News*, raised an alarm on the eve of the runoff election. "Perhaps not since Reconstruction days," he wrote, "has Alabama faced a more serious threat to local self government than is presented by the determination of the radical C.I.O. to elect James E. Folsom governor of Alabama."

The specter of Sidney Hillman hung over the election, Fisher warned. "Macon County, as an agricultural community . . . can have nothing in common with radicals of Hillman's stripe." It was true that Macon Countians shared few interests with Sidney Hillman—probably only a handful of them knew who he was—but most of them liked Big Jim Folsom. He received fifty-five percent of the county vote, running especially well among small farmers in the northern part of the county near the village of Notasulga. Conservatives were more successful in local races. Sheriff Pat Evans won a big victory—and perhaps in his view further vindication of his conduct in office—over weak opposition. Henry Neill Segrest lost his race for state representative to G. O. Bush, a Notasulga farmer. Segrest's testimony against Evans had apparently hurt him, though Bush benefited from an intense village loyalty among Notasulgans.[11]

The Macon County voting conflict received more public attention in the fall of 1946 when conservatives campaigned for ratification of the Boswell amendment, the measure that would give registrars the power to test whether a voting applicant "understood" the United States Constitution. If the amendment did not pass, the prominent Wilcox County conservative J. Miller Bonner told the Montgomery Civitan Club, "within four years the Negroes will take over every public office in Macon County." For the Civitans who did not know instinctively the danger of such an outcome, Bonner provided a short history lesson. "During post Civil War years, it was clearly demonstrated that Negroes, if allowed to vote in large numbers would elect only carpetbaggers, scalawags and other disreputable persons." In a kind of apocalyptic musing that would become characteristic of many conservatives in the postwar years, Bonner asserted that whites had only three choices if the Boswell amendment failed. They could "leave their homes, submit to Negro domination, or engage in inter-racial conflict resulting in extermination of one or the other races."[12]

The outgoing governor, Chauncey Sparks, lent a hand to the pro-Boswell forces when he reported in September 1946 that he had received a request from the TCA to appoint a Negro registrar in Macon County. Caro Wright and Virgil Guthrie had resigned from the board immediately after the suits were filed. New registrars were appointed, but all soon resigned; there was no board at all after June 1946. The registrar position was a "hot potato," one of the appointees told the Montgomery *Advertiser;* no white would risk ending up in court. The state constitution required that the governor, the state commissioner of agriculture, and the state auditor act together as an appointing board to select the registrars in every county, but Sparks had no intention of doing this duty in Macon if he could not find a willing white. "Never while I am governor," he announced, "will I consent to the appointment of a Negro to such a position." Sparks said that "around 2,000" blacks had crowded about the Macon County Courthouse on registration days. The governor grossly exaggerated the registration effort of July 1945, but those mob scenes were described vividly in pro-Boswell advertisements in the Birmingham *News*. Such tactics helped conservatives to dull the luster on the previous spring's liberal triumph. Despite Folsom's opposition, the Boswell amendment passed by a slim margin.[13]

The hearing for *Mitchell v. Wright* began in Judge Kennamer's Montgomery courtroom on December 6. Kennamer, a Republican appointed by Herbert Hoover, immediately denied Mitchell's request that the suit be considered a class action on behalf of every Macon County black who might try to register. Each person would have to petition individually, he declared. Caro Wright, the first witness, was understandably nervous. Robert Carter, an attorney from the national office of the NAACP, asked if she thought blacks had a right to vote under the laws of Alabama. "If I hadn't felt that way I wouldn't have recommended so many of them to be registered," she replied indignantly. At one point in his questioning Carter put his foot on the witness stand and pointed his finger at the elderly white woman, whereupon Judge Kennamer ordered the bailiff to move the black lawyer a suitable distance away from Wright. Richard Rives, the defendants' attorney and, ironically, the leader of the unsuccessful effort to defeat the Boswell amendment, then elicited from her the information that ten of the seventeen persons registered in July 1945 were black. Are all applicants, including whites, required to have vouchers? Rives asked. They are, she replied. Virgil Guthrie followed Wright to the witness stand and reiterated that point. William Mitchell's problem was that he failed to get vouchers, Guthrie said.[14]

Mitchell testified that he had given the board the names of G. W. A. Johnston and William Campbell, a white building materials salesman, as his vouchers. Johnston had vouched for him in his earlier registration attempts, Mitchell explained. Just before he went to the board on July 5, 1945, he had asked Johnston to vouch again and Johnston agreed to do so. Guthrie had promised to contact Campbell personally, Mitchell said. Campbell testified, however, that he had gone to the courthouse to vouch for Mitchell but was unable to get inside the board's office and left without signing Mitchell's application.[15]

George Washington Albert Johnston came to the witness stand with divided loyalties. He believed in black voting; he had helped many of Tuskegee's black voters to register. Johnston knew that the suit had broad support among Tuskegee blacks. But this small, black-skinned man in his seventies had been brought up to believe that blacks and whites in Tuskegee avoided such conflict. A favorite nephew and confidant of Booker Washington, he was part of the Institute aristocracy that enjoyed warm relations with Tuskegee's leading white families; Caro Wright was a friend of long standing. As the Institute's purchasing agent, he did business with many local white merchants, who had included Wright's late husband. The Wrights had entertained Johnston in their home. Mitchell had once seen Johnston put his arm around Wright in the Macon County Courthouse and tell her how well she looked that day—an act of familiarity by a black man toward a white woman that astonished Mitchell. When Wright's attorney asked him whether he had vouched for Mitchell, Johnston revealed his ultimate allegiance. No, he had not, Johnston told the court. He did not remember Mitchell's even asking. Furthermore, he had never vouched for Mitchell.[16]

Wright returned to the witness stand in a final effort to counter the charge of discrimination. Do you have any prejudice against Negroes voting? Rives asked. "No, I think if they can qualify they are entitled to register and that was what I tried to help them do," she answered. You have no prejudice against Tuskegee Institute? her attorney pressed further. "I would hate to live where they didn't have Tuskegee Institute," she responded passionately. "My husband's people . . . were the ones that first started the school. My own father was the one that got the appropriation for the school." Wright did not exaggerate greatly her family's involvement with the Institute. Her late husband, George Campbell Wright, was the nephew of George Washington Campbell, the white Institute trustee who had hired Booker Washington and then become the young principal's friend and adviser. Her father, William Thomas, had headed the appropriations committee in the state senate in 1880 and helped Wilbur Foster, the senator from Tuskegee, get the original funding for the school. Her family's support of Tuskegee Institute did not really pertain to the matter at hand, but it formed the context for the sense of betrayal Wright now felt: The people for whom she and her family had done so much were subjecting her to the indignity of a lawsuit. In the Tuskegee that she loved—the Tuskegee of George Campbell and Booker Washington—blacks and whites rarely aired their differences openly and never took them to court.

Unfortunately for Wright and her friend Albert Johnston, that Tuskegee existed no longer.[17]

Judge Kennamer heard closing arguments and immediately ruled in favor of the registrars. The board registered all blacks and whites who had vouchers, he declared. Mitchell had simply failed to get vouchers, the judge said, citing Johnston's testimony. The decision did not surprise TCA leaders.[18]

Real disappointment came when they appealed Kennamer's ruling to the Fifth Circuit Court of Appeals. In May 1947 Judge Varner informed Richard Rives that he had "discovered" that the board had already registered Mitchell. He produced a registration certificate dated January 29, 1943, and explained that, had Mitchell paid his poll tax, he could have been voting all along. Although he must have been chagrined by his clients' deviousness, Rives dutifully filed a motion to dismiss the appeal on the grounds that the issue was now moot. The Fifth Circuit granted the motion, thus ending the suit.[19]

The registrars' trickery infuriated the TCA. Gomillion and Mitchell believed that Judge Varner and the registrars, knowing that the Fifth Circuit might rule against them, had retrieved one of several applications Mitchell had made in years past and signed it. They allowed Mitchell to vote, many blacks speculated, to forestall the possibility of the appeals court making a strong order against voting discrimination. In their disappointment the TCA leadership considered whether to take action against Johnston, who they believed had perjured himself at the hearing when he said he had never vouched for Mitchell. Johnston's friends on the Board of Registrars had exposed him to a possible perjury charge when they "discovered" Mitchell's 1943 application, which Johnston had signed as voucher. But Gomillion decided that embarrassing Johnston would serve no good purpose and would unnecessarily divide Tuskegee blacks. They might well go to court again and would need the support of the whole community, he reasoned. The litigation had proved to be very expensive. They had spent seventeen thousand dollars—to get one man registered to vote.[20]

The Mitchell case and the larger conflict over blacks voting put Frederick Patterson in a precarious position. Facing a decline in philanthropic support for the Institute—especially the end of the Rosenwald Fund's generous assistance—Patterson in 1943 had requested and received a large increase in the state's contribution to the Institute budget. Governor Chauncey Sparks, aware of the United States Supreme Court's dictate on equal educational opportunities in the *Gaines* decision, had helped Patterson to get state support for three new professional degree programs at the Institute. In return the Institute accepted six additional state-appointed trustees on its board, a concession for which Patterson was roundly criticized by Walter White and the NAACP. Although Patterson viewed the concession as necessary for the Institute's financial well-being, it made him and the Institute more vulnerable to pressure from state politicians.[21]

These circumstances formed the context for state senator Forrest Bridges's visit to Dr. Patterson's office one day in 1948. Bridges, a Notasulga poultryman, had known Patterson, a veterinarian, since he had consulted with the Institute president about diseases common among chickens. A short, light-skinned man with a mustache and a hearty laugh, Patterson no doubt had gotten on well with Bridges, as he did with most southern whites. But Bridges came this day to talk not about chickens but about Negroes, and one Negro in particular. This man Gomillion is causing a lot of trouble, Bridges told Patterson. "I think you should call off this voting rights activity," he advised. "You can do it, with your prestige." Patterson knew that Bridges was threatening implicitly the Institute's state appropriation, which as a senator he could influence directly. But Patterson also knew he could not accommodate Bridges's request. "Senator Bridges, I think you are wrong," he said. "I cannot call that off, and if I tried, I'd lose what little prestige you think I have. Furthermore, I believe that black citizens *ought* to vote."[22]

Bridges left angry, and he subsequently refused to help Patterson in the legislature with the Institute appropriation, though he did not oppose it actively. In the early 1950s Patterson would have a similar discussion about Gomillion with Governor Gordon Persons. When Persons complained about Gomillion's voting activities, Patterson responded that Gomillion was acting as a private citizen and as president he could not interfere with a faculty member's personal life. "Yes," Persons replied, "but you and I know that you can't separate his citizenship activities from his role at Tuskegee Institute." Still, Persons did not try to punish the Institute for Gomillion's civil rights work. By then Patterson had recognized that the Institute's prestige was high enough, even among many conservative white Alabamians, so that he could withstand the pressure about Gomillion's voting rights activity. "I did not openly advocate what he was doing," Patterson later said of Gomillion, "but I was his silent supporter. He didn't lose his job."[23]

The resolution of *Mitchell v. Wright* did nothing to ease the tension in Tuskegee. By December 1947 the Board of Registrars had been inactive for eighteen months, and some leading whites clearly preferred that it stay inactive. They expected blacks to try to register en masse when a board was constituted. "If we had an open registration," Judge Varner told a reporter soon after the Mitchell case was dismissed, "every Negro at the Institute and everyone who works at the Veterans Hospital would come down here, along with a few others who live out in the country." Another reporter told Varner of Henry Neill Segrest's prediction that relatively few blacks would try to register. "What's the use of saying that," Varner asked in reply, "when [NAACP members] are holding the meetings they are to see what crowd they can stir up?" To this same reporter Gomillion himself expressed doubt that any mass black registration would develop soon. "My guess is that there would not be more than 500 Negro voters in the next 15 years," he said, noting that 110 blacks were registered at the time.[24]

Throughout 1947 the TCA had put pressure on state officials to appoint a board of registrars. Gomillion and Mitchell wrote letters to the governor, the state auditor, and the commissioner of agriculture imploring each to name registrars. Gomillion finally asked Governor Folsom whether it was impossible to find whites to serve on the board. "Almost impossible," Folsom replied. The task must have gotten easier in early 1948, for the *Advertiser* reported the resignation of one S. Charles Parker from the chairmanship of the Macon County Board of Registrars in mid-April. Parker, a Tuskegee businessman, had been appointed the previous January, the newspaper explained. W. D. Tommie, a Notasulga pharmacist, and J. J. "Jack" Rodgers, a Tuskegee lawyer, had gone onto the board at the same time, and since then the three men had registered two hundred whites. They had registered no blacks, but that was because no blacks had applied, Tommie told the *Advertiser*. No blacks had applied, of course, because the board's existence was a secret. Only Parker's resignation exposed this underground registration effort. "He only accepted the appointment to let some servicemen register," Parker's wife said in defense of her husband's betrayal of the clandestine board.[25]

Gomillion was furious when he saw the story in the *Advertiser*. "How did it happen," he asked Folsom in an angry letter, "that only whites knew about the existence of a board unless there was a deliberate effort made to inform whites and an equally deliberate effort made to keep Negroes ignorant of the existence of a board?" Folsom should have taken it upon himself to tell the Tuskegee blacks that a board had been appointed, Gomillion believed. "The Tuskegee Civic Association had expected that in view of the situation which had existed in Macon County, you would have notified it of the appointment of a Board of Registrars for the County," he told the governor. Folsom certainly knew of the board's existence because he had appointed Parker; but the governor was often outwitted by conservative opponents, and it is possible that he had not foreseen the possibility of the board's meeting secretly.[26]

The board met only once after its existence was made public. Fifty blacks went to the courthouse on that day to try to register. Unable to locate the board, they asked Judge Varner its whereabouts. The board had "disbanded," he told them. Highly skeptical of the judge's information, the blacks sent a very light-skinned VA employee to the courthouse in search of the board. He was directed to a remote corner of the building, where he found the board registering whites behind closed doors. He alerted the others, twenty-one of whom made applications. The board did not convene for eight months after that day. W. D. Tommie would later cite his mother's illness for his numerous absences from the board meetings. Jack Rodgers offered no excuse. A short, elderly bachelor who regularly read the *Times* of London on the courthouse veranda—a literary taste acquired when he was a Rhodes Scholar—Rodgers was considered eccentric by some Macon Countians, but he stayed in the conservative mainstream politically. He participated in the Dixiecrat movement, which most Macon County conservatives supported enthusiastically in 1948.[27]

The board's deception and recalcitrance persuaded Gomillion to consider new tactics. He first thought of using economic pressure. He personally had carried on a one-man boycott of downtown businesses since the shoe salesman's insult in 1928; and he knew that nearly all white-owned businesses in Tuskegee depended on black customers for most of their trade. The TCA leadership had already discussed an economic boycott of white businesses in 1947, and Gomillion had suggested one in early 1948 when the Tuskegee *News* did not give black women courtesy titles in a list of Macon County voters. "If we Negroes keep on paying to be treated like this," he wrote to Mitchell, "we have ourselves to blame for much of our troubles. Withdrawal of economic support is our best weapon of attack." For reasons not entirely clear, however, the TCA did not begin a boycott after the secret board meetings were revealed. Gomillion would later say that the TCA leadership did not think the organization had the strength and resources in 1948 to conduct an effective boycott. Several TCA members did promote a boycott—called a "Trade with Your Friends" campaign—in late 1948 without the organization's sanction. Leaflets encouraging a boycott were distributed for many months and they apparently worried white businessmen, but most blacks continued to shop in downtown Tuskegee.[28]

Gomillion had also sought help from the federal government in early 1948, asking the civil rights section of the United States Justice Department to investigate the denial of voting rights in Macon County. A Justice Department official told Gomillion that the civil rights section would look into the situation. When he learned of the secret board meetings, Gomillion wrote the official again and related the latest trickery of the Board of Registrars. But no serious inquiry by the Justice Department followed. In May 1948 Gomillion agreed with Mitchell that the department was moving too slowly. Perhaps large numbers of complaints from unregistered black citizens might stir it to act sooner, Gomillion suggested to Mitchell. But this tactic did not elicit federal assistance either. The TCA would make regular appeals for help from the Justice Department throughout the late 1940s and early and mid-1950s without receiving any significant aid. They would, the TCA leadership realized, have to bring about change entirely on their own.[29]

For the moment, they would try to force the board to operate. Daniel Beasley, who had emerged as a leader in the TCA after serving as a plaintiff in the state court suit, tried throughout the summer of 1948 to see Folsom to discuss ways to make the board function. The governor made and broke two appointments. Gomillion, Mitchell, and Beasley finally had an audience with Ira B. Thompson, Folsom's legal adviser, in October. Was there any way to force the registrars to meet? they asked Thompson. Could their salaries be withheld? Thompson gave the men some reason for hope. The governor's office seemed to share his determination "to make democracy work in Macon County," Gomillion subsequently wrote to Thompson.[30]

When no action followed, the TCA made a stronger appeal to conscience. In "An Open Letter to the Citizens of Macon County" printed in the Tuskegee *News* in December, the organization asked whites to consider serving on the Board of Registrars. "Our political democracy," the letter concluded in phrases that were distinctly Gomillion's, "is based on the principle that all law abiding citizens who meet the qualifications of electors have the right, and should have the opportunity, to participate in self-government." An open letter to the governor, the state auditor, and the commissioner of agriculture appeared in the Montgomery *Advertiser* the next day. It used the same statement about "political democracy" and noted that the TCA had already asked "fellow-citizens" to serve on the board. "We hope that the principles of democracy and the spirit and teachings of Christ," Gomillion wrote, "will so permeate and motivate their minds and hearts that some might even volunteer to serve." Then, in a question meant for Folsom, Gomillion asked, "May we count on you to help relieve us of the embarrassment we are now experiencing and the political disfranchisement we are now suffering?"[31]

Without realizing it, Gomillion had struck the chord that the governor could not resist. Folsom was a "radical democrat," one historian has written. He had ultimate faith in the wisdom of the people to decide what was best for them. Andrew Jackson was his political hero. The Jacksonian suspicion of voting restrictions formed part of the background for his opposition to the poll tax and his support for legislative reapportionment. Gomillion had forced Folsom to consider the Macon County situation in the context of Jacksonian ideals. Although he was often tentative and even inept as a politician, Folsom always wanted to act on his democratic faith and this time he did. Four days after the open letter appeared in the *Advertiser,* Folsom appointed W. H. Bentley of Notasulga as the chairman of the Macon County Board of Registrars.[32]

Folsom appropriately had chosen a common man, in the Jacksonian sense, to be his instrument of democracy in Macon County. Herman Bentley was a farmer, and as Daniel Beasley would observe later, "he looked the part." A tall, thin man in his mid-fifties, Bentley worked his modest farm without the aid of tenants. He made a comfortable living, however, and had time for many civic and religious activities. He was a Mason and had served as president of the Notasulga Lions Club. He had represented the Notasulga beat on the county committee that advised the Agricultural Adjustment Administration. He frequently filled pulpits as a lay minister in the Methodist church, though he had only a seventh-grade education. A New Deal Democrat, Bentley was thought to have influence among his neighbors about political issues and candidates.[33]

That reputation for political influence explains why Folsom had appeared in Herman Bentley's barnyard one day in 1938. Folsom was running for Congress against a well-entrenched incumbent and he was looking for support around Notasulga. The gigantic young man must have startled Bentley, who was cleaning out his hogpen, but Folsom quickly moved to put Bentley at ease. "Old Big Jim pulled off his size-fourteen shoes," recalled Robert Bentley, who was assisting his father in the hogpen that day, "and jumped in and helped us clean it out." From then on, "Dad was a Jim Folsom man," Robert said later. When he ran for governor in 1946, Folsom carried the Notasulga ballot boxes by a large majority—a result, at least in part, of Bentley's campaigning. Although he was due some small patronage reward like jury commissioner or voting registrar, Bentley received none after the election, apparently because he did not ask for it. When Folsom appointed Bentley to the board in December 1948, the Notasulga man was accepting not a reward for campaign work but a call to public service that he knew would be controversial.[34]

Bentley changed the board's behavior profoundly. He convened it at the appointed times and accelerated its rate of taking applications. He freely accepted blacks as vouchers and allowed Gomillion and Beasley to correct minor mistakes on black applications, knowing that any error would give one of the other registrars cause to reject an application. In a thirteen-month period beginning in January 1949, he registered 449 blacks, thus quadrupling the number of black voters in the county.[35]

The TCA leadership had known nothing of Herman Bentley before Folsom appointed him and was, therefore, startled by his actions. Daniel Beasley was particularly confounded. Beasley's family had lived in Macon County for several generations, and he knew the whites around Notasulga to be the most racist people in the county. "I didn't know a good man could come out of Notasulga," Beasley said later. "Herman Bentley was like Jesus coming out of Nazareth," he observed, referring to the Disciple Nathanael's response when first told of Christ: "Can any good thing come out of Nazareth?" Bentley explained to Beasley that in good conscience he could not deny the well-educated blacks in Tuskegee the right to vote. "Beasley, them folks out there got more sense than I got. How can I fail to register them?"[36]

But such straightforward reasoning set Herman Bentley apart from everyone else who had served on the board in the past ten years. Why did he behave so differently? His background hardly distinguished him, and he was subject to the same conformist pressures other board members had felt. Bentley himself attributed his nonconformity to his reading of the Bible. "I know I'm right because of the way I was brought up, because of the Scripture I study," he told his son. "I know I'm right because all people are created equal." He was an unusually independent man. Verbal harassment from neighbors did not alter his behavior. He was unmoved when his son reported that "folks are resenting what you are doing" at the board. "If they talk about me, it's not going to hurt anybody but me, and it's not going to hurt me." He thought he was only being realistic. The educated blacks in Tuskegee inevitably will become voters, he told other whites. But he made few if any converts. "A prophet is not without honor except in his own country and in his own house,"

Christ said before being driven from Nazareth—words that Herman Bentley had no doubt read and appreciated.[37]

Bentley's effectiveness on the board, however, largely ceased in February 1950, when both Jack Rodgers and W. D. Tommie stopped attending board meetings. For applications to be accepted, the presence of at least two registrars was required. The board did not meet at all in the spring of 1950; it was, of course, no coincidence that this was the period leading up to the Democratic primary. The board did convene in June, but it would meet only ten times over the next eight months. Excuses such as "the room is to be painted" and "the door is locked" were given for not meeting. Rodgers and Tommie slowed the application process to a crawl when the board did meet. They worked only two or three hours a day and asked applicants unnecessary and unrelated questions. They refused to act on applications that Bentley had long since approved. During the last year of Bentley's tenure on the board, which would end in February 1951, only sixty-four blacks were registered.[38]

But the black registration during Bentley's year on the board dramatically changed Macon County politics. The approximately six hundred black voters made up about thirty percent of the electorate—easily enough to determine the outcome of most elections. Even Pat Evans had to recognize that. In the runoff election of the Democratic primary in 1950, he faced the formidable opposition of Preston Hornsby, a gregarious young state highway patrolman with strong support from whites in the northern part of the county. Knowing that he needed black votes to win, Evans came to William Mitchell's home to ask the TCA leadership for its support. He invited them all to his campaign rally, where free barbecue would be served, but the blacks declined his hospitality. He reminded individual TCA members of favors he had done for them. He told Clarence Dunn, a barber, that he had interceded on Dunn's behalf with state liquor agents who thought Dunn's homemade shampoo had too much alcohol in it. He informed Mitchell that he had once passed by a Ku Klux Klan meeting just as it ended and some Klansmen asked Evans where Mitchell lived. "I told them, 'don't you bother that boy,' " Evans related to Mitchell. "Sheriff, thank you for upholding the law and order of Macon County," Mitchell retorted sarcastically.[39]

Watching Evans humble himself was satisfying to the TCA leaders, but they had no intention of supporting him. For most blacks, the sheriff was the most important county official because he had power over life and death. Evans had demonstrated many years earlier that he could not be trusted with that responsibility. They voted in a bloc for Hornsby and helped to elect him. It was the first major political victory for black voters in Macon County since the early 1870s. They gave Bentley much of the credit. "Herman Bentley was the best thing to happen to black people in Macon County since Booker T. Washington," William Mitchell said later.[40]

Evans's defeat climaxed a decade of acute political anxiety among Macon County conservatives. The liberal dominance of the national Democratic party had caused them much worry throughout the 1940s. That concern had culminated in the Dixiecrat movement of 1948, which gained the spotlight in Alabama politics momentarily but in the end did not reclaim lost power. In statewide elections throughout the 1940s, liberals like Lister Hill, John Sparkman, and Jim Folsom defeated strong conservative candidates. The Boswell amendment, which conservatives had hoped would protect their power by keeping down black registration, was declared unconstitutional in 1949.

Folsom especially had worried conservatives because he opposed devices used to maintain conservative control—particularly a malapportioned legislature and a highly restricted ballot. But he did not significantly undermine conservative power; while he was governor, conservatives maintained control of the state party machinery and the legislature and largely thwarted his efforts to make the political process more democratic. The notable exception occurred in Macon County, where his appointee to the Board of Registrars redistributed political power in one year's time. That exception resulted from the TCA's persistence, but many local conservatives believed that Folsom had singled them out for political attack.[41]

By the end of the 1940s many Macon County whites felt a strong sense of alienation from the local black community. It was not only the voting challenge that was responsible for this disaffection. The black migration off local farms and the growth of the black middle class in Tuskegee increased still further the distance already imposed between the black and white communities by the Jim Crow system and Booker Washington's careful insulation of the Institute. Whites knew the black community less intimately in 1950 than they had known it in 1930. Black community leaders reinforced the separation to some extent: in their rejection of segregation and the caste system, Gomillion and others withdrew from contact with much of white Tuskegee. Frederick Patterson broke Washington's tradition of segregated seating at school events attended by whites, a decision that apparently ended much white participation in Institute activities. Blacks and whites had largely lost touch with one another.[42]

The intrusion of forces from outside Macon County heightened the conservative alienation. The war, the federal government, the national Democratic party, the NAACP, the CIO—all had undermined their society, conservatives believed. Indeed, those forces had worked against conservative interests and values, though not in the conspiratorial fashion that many of them imagined. Alabama conservatives had known a comparable alienation at least once before: the secessionist impulse of the 1850s, one perceptive student of antebellum politics in Alabama has argued, resulted partly from the belief among Alabama whites that abolitionists, the Republican party, and unknown economic forces were intruding on—and trying to change—their society. The feelings of Macon County conservatives almost a century later were remarkably similar.[43]

The alienation made the changes in their society all the more difficult to accept. Many conservatives hardened their resistance to change as the gulf between the two communities widened. The accommodationist approach that leading conservatives had taken at the time of the founding of Tuskegee Institute had now been forsaken entirely. Judge Varner, the son of one of Washington's best white friends, stood in opposition to the black community with a determination reminiscent of James Edward Cobb, Washington's chief local critic. What Varner's father had learned about getting along with blacks in the 1880s simply did not apply in the 1940s. Social change had become so rapid that the past had little relevance to current realities. Judge Varner was an intelligent and rational man, but he probably never realized that a fundamental discontinuity of history was vexing him.[44]

But the less useful the past became, the more firmly conservatives held on to it. Reconstruction, at least as they understood it, was most instructive. They could easily interpret recent events in a Reconstruction context: latter-day scalawags—Jim Folsom and Herman Bentley—were cooperating with the ambitious Negro Gomillion to march hundreds of blacks to the polls in a sleazy grab for political control. The Reconstruction myth provided psychic satisfaction because it promised that conservative control would ultimately be restored. "The more glorious the past by comparison with the present," a sociologist has observed about ruling elites, "the more firmly the dead claim the living, making them unfit for life in the here and now." By 1950 myth and history had failed Macon County conservatives, but they either did not know it or could not admit it to themselves.[45]

The conservative resistance to change was dramatized in Judge Varner's office just after the 1950 primary. Gomillion, Mitchell, and two women members of the TCA came to protest the absence of courtesy titles for black women on the voter lists published in the Tuskegee *News*. Ever the gentleman, Judge Varner politely listened to the appeal from the two women, but he kept his back turned to Gomillion and Mitchell all the while. He assured the women that he would discuss the problem with "higher authorities" to see if some change could be made in the voter list. Finally, as the blacks were leaving, Varner faced Gomillion and Mitchell. "Let me tell you one thing," he said with controlled anger in his voice, "the quicker Macon County can get rid of the two of you, the better off Macon County is going to be."[46]

But Gomillion and Mitchell were going nowhere. Had conservatives accepted in 1950 the reality of black political power and made some compromise with it, they might have known less trauma during the next two decades. But they apparently gave no thought to relinquishing any power. Instead, they fought back with a determination not seen since the last days of Reconstruction.

6

More Ways Than One
to Kill a Snake

IN THE same election in which they rejected Sheriff Pat Evans, the voters of Macon County elected Samuel Martin Engelhardt, Jr., to the state legislature. A farmer, merchant, and cotton-gin owner at Shorter, a hamlet in western Macon County, Engelhardt had entered politics out of concern about black voting. The registration of several hundred blacks in 1949 alarmed him greatly. "The niggers were just about to take us over," he said later. "They were gaining political power because Folsom was after their votes." Engelhardt believed that Herman Bentley "had illusions of becoming king of Macon County by registering all the blacks." To try to prevent that from happening, he ran for the Macon County seat in the state House of Representatives and easily defeated Henry Neill Segrest in a race in which he made white supremacy the major issue. Segrest was aligned with Folsom and the blacks, Engelhardt told white voters.[1]

Behind his concern about black voting lay economic self-interest. "Everybody has an angle when they get in [politics]. I was worried . . . about the tax assessor . . . because of all our holdings," he said later, referring to the many thousands of acres of rich agricultural land the Engelhardt family owned in Shorter. "That was my angle—to protect ourselves. Not only me, but my family. My aunts, uncles, and cousins owned land." He based his concern about who was tax assessor on a racist assumption. "If you have a nigger tax assessor," he rhetorically asked a journalist in 1956, "what would he do to you?" The obvious answer, to Engelhardt, was that a black tax assessor would try to exploit white landowners.[2]

Engelhardt defended the conservative cause very effectively. He searched for new ways to maintain conservative power and pursued every advantage in the political arena. He intentionally intimidated political opponents and unabashedly used racist arguments to achieve white solidarity. But Sam Engelhardt crusaded effectively for the conservative position partly because he was attractive personally. The descendant of two of Macon County's oldest families, he was well known and well liked among the Black Belt gentry. His father was a Montgomery city official and his father-in-law was J. Miller Bonner, the archconservative state senator from Wilcox County and former legal adviser to Governor Frank Dixon. Engelhardt had attended Virginia's prestigious Washington and Lee College and was probably more sophisticated intellectually and culturally than most whites in the county. A genial man who put on big dove hunts on his Shorter plantation, Engelhardt tempered his combative political style with a well-developed wry humor. In short, he could be a formidable opponent.[3]

Engelhardt's first act as a legislator was to arrange the removal of Herman Bentley from the Board of Registrars. He asked Gordon Persons, the newly elected governor, to fire Bentley in early 1951. To strengthen his appeal to Persons, Engelhardt enlisted the aid of Joe Edwards, a Tuskegee businessman and former college classmate of the governor. Edwards had raised money for Persons's recent campaign and had been appointed to his cabinet. Persons removed Bentley in early February—even though Bentley's term would have expired by law the following September—and replaced him with Grady Rogers, a Macon County postal worker known for his kindness to the people on his rural mail route. Over the next decade Rogers would gain a reputation among Tuskegee blacks for his obstinate resistance to black voting.[4]

Engelhardt's first legislative initiative was an effort to protect segregation in public schools. He submitted a bill in the state legislature that would end public education in Alabama should the United States Supreme Court outlaw segregated schools. The bill was prompted in part by *Briggs v. Elliott,* the NAACP's challenge to segregation in the Clarendon County, South Carolina, school system, a case that would become a companion suit to *Brown v. Board of Education.* If the court should strike down segregated schools, "there's nothing left to do but . . . shut off state appropriations for education and establish private schools," Engelhardt told the legislature. "Now is the time to see who wants to stand up for preservation of our segregation policy—and who does not," he said, drawing a distinction that left no room for debate, at least among the vast majority of white Alabamians. "I do not want to see a single brick removed from the wall of segregation."[5]

Engelhardt's concern originated partly in Tuskegee. The previous January the mother of a student at Tuskegee Institute High, the town's black secondary school, had asked the county superintendent of education to provide her son with instruction in geometry, which was not included in the curriculum. If the superintendent could not arrange that, the woman asked, then would he please allow her son to attend the geometry class at Tuskegee High, the town's white school? When her request was denied, Charles Gomillion drew up a petition which informed the school board that it was denying black children "equal protection of the laws secured by the Fourteenth Amendment to the Constitution of the United States." The board apparently did not respond, but the petition gained statewide attention and was viewed, according to one political reporter, as an "opening wedge move by Negroes to gain admittance to white schools."[6]

The Tuskegee blacks did not take the challenge to the school system any further. Because the TCA fully expected to file other voting suits in coming years, Gomillion believed that Tuskegee blacks should not expend their resources on a school desegregation suit at this time. He and other black leaders were aware of the NAACP's challenge to school segregation. Still, the absence of geometry in the black high school curriculum must have tempted Gomillion, who had originally embarked on the voting rights challenge in part out of anger over the inequities in black public education. To remind TCA members of the larger purpose of their struggle with the Board of Registrars, he had reported periodically throughout the 1940s on the gross disparities in spending between black and white schools in Alabama. He concluded in his 1951 report that the gap had narrowed significantly, but that "there is still a marked differential, which is not expected or justified in a democratic society."[7]

In Sam Engelhardt's system of values, public education ranked much lower. Since Reconstruction most Alabama conservatives had supported public education only reluctantly, and then they had beggared it. Faced with the prospect of integrated schools—the idea of which genuinely appalled him—Engelhardt could opt with few qualms for the dissolution of public education. His first concern was to maintain conservative political control. He understood, nonetheless, that most white Alabamians placed great value on public education, and that they would be terribly troubled and alarmed by any proposal to desegregate their schools. This would eventually provide an issue around which conservatives could rally most whites against racial change. But in 1951 desegregation was not yet a real enough threat to elicit white solidarity: Engelhardt's proposal authorizing the dismantling of the public schools was defeated by a margin of more than two to one.[8]

Undeterred by this defeat, Engelhardt proposed a spate of measures to diminish black political power. He submitted a bill to outlaw "single-shot" voting, the practice of voting fewer than the prescribed number of times in at-large elections. Engelhardt intended to stop blacks from voting for only the moderate or liberal candidate—and perhaps the black candidate—in city council, county commission, board of education, and state and national Democratic committeemen elections. Such a "single-shot" strategy effectively magnified the impact of the black votes for the one candidate. Engelhardt also proposed that the Alabama Democratic party be made to use its slogan, "White Supremacy for the Right," in all primary elections, hoping that blacks would find the slogan so obnoxious that they would spurn the party. He offered a bill to require the reregistration of all Alabama voters, a process which would offer the opportunity to rid the voter lists of the dead, the departed, and the Negro. He discussed publicly, but postponed submitting to the legislature, a bill to gerrymander county boundaries throughout the Black Belt in order to redistribute the black population more evenly. The gerrymander would maintain white political control in all counties, Engelhardt promised, and pointedly emphasized that the federal courts had not interfered with the states' right to fashion political boundaries. He was substantially correct in his analysis of the Supreme Court's hands-off attitude, though he would in time be instrumental in the Court's breaking with that tradition.[9]

Engelhardt's initiatives sailed through the legislature in a few days. He had quickly established himself as an aggressive advocate of conservative power. His sheer energy and determination made him a man to watch, not just for Macon Countians but for politicians throughout the state. In style and political substance he resembled the Fire-Eaters of the 1850s; like them, he would fiercely reject the prospect of racial change and offer radical alternatives to it. He would persuade many whites to follow him, just as the antebellum radicals had.

Conservatives in the 1951 legislature put their greatest hopes of limiting black political participation in a measure called the Voter Qualification Amendment. When the Boswell amendment had been overturned in 1949, registrars lost the authority to test the literacy of applicants who owned three hundred dollars' worth of property. The Voter Qualification Amendment returned this authority by allowing registrars to require any applicant to read any article of the Constitution. It also prescribed a uniform registration application, to be drawn up by the Alabama Supreme Court. The amendment was ratified in a deliberately quiet campaign with very little public mention of its racist intent—the Boswell amendment had been declared unconstitutional in part because pro-Boswell advertisements clearly showed its intent to disfranchise blacks—and the Supreme Court justices quickly designed the new questionnaire. They produced an ambiguous, legalistic form sprinkled with words and phrases like "bona fide," "priority," "secular," and "moral turpitude." It would prove to be difficult for many applicants, both black and white, though most registrars tended to help whites fill it out. The requirement to read the Constitution would disfranchise many illiterate blacks, intimidate some who were semiliterate, and slow the registration process. In many counties in Alabama in the 1950s, the United States Constitution would be the very instrument used to obstruct the Fifteenth Amendment.[10]

After Engelhardt arranged for removal of Herman Bentley from the Macon County Board of Registrars in February 1951, the registration of blacks slowed dramatically. The board certified only twenty-three during all of 1951; in 1952 there would be fifty-two new black voters and in 1953 twenty-eight. The board usually met on the prescribed days, but it accepted very few black applications. It convened for a few hours each day, took only two applicants at a time, and required each black to demonstrate at length his ability to read the Constitution. The registrars often hid from black applicants: on several occasions in 1953 TCA members found the board registering white applicants in Judge Varner's vault amid stacks of old deed books. The board rejected most of the blacks who did manage to apply; between 1951 and 1953, only eighteen percent of black applications were approved. Most were rejected because of minor mistakes made on the confusing registration application.[11]

The TCA's efforts to force the board to cooperate failed. The organization published letters in newspapers in May 1951 appealing to their fellow citizens and state officials for help in getting blacks registered. In contrast to the 1948 open letter which apparently spurred Folsom to appoint Herman Bentley, this effort yielded nothing. Regular requests to the Justice Department for an investigation of the board's practices resulted in no action until late 1952, when federal lawyers began to consider bringing a criminal suit against the registrars. But the Justice Department and Thurgood

Marshall, the chief NAACP attorney, agreed that a civil suit against the board probably stood a greater chance of success. The TCA began working with Arthur Shores, the NAACP's Alabama counsel, to prepare such a case in late 1953. At a pretrial hearing for that suit, however, Shores learned that many rejected applications contained minor errors that gave the registrars grounds for their action. He decided to drop what he now believed was a weak suit. TCA members immediately began a series of "voting schools" where William P. Mitchell, Daniel Beasley, and others taught blacks how to file a perfect registration application. The aborted suit was not a complete failure in one sense: fearing the consequences of legal action against them, the registrars started accepting and approving more black applications in early 1954.[12]

Although they had clearly been winning the battle over black voting since early 1951, local conservatives seemed just as worried in 1954 as they had been in 1950. The suit against the registrars explains some of the anxiety, but politics, particularly the impending Democratic primary, probably accounted for more. What conservatives seemed to dread most actually happened in early 1954: a black ran for public office. No doubt to the surprise of many conservatives, the challenge came at the county Board of Education.

A position on the five-person board had come open when Robert E. Varner, the judge's son, was disqualified from seeking reelection as a Democrat because he had broken the state party's "loyalty oath," an agreement that all Democratic candidates had signed promising their support to the party's presidential candidate. National party loyalists in Alabama had passed this rule in 1950 to punish the Dixiecrats and any party officeholders who subsequently strayed. Like many Black Belt conservatives, Robert Varner had at the first opportunity bolted the party and supported Dwight Eisenhower for president.*

Here was the chance to field a black political candidate, Gomillion believed. Since to him the first goal of political activity was to get equal educational opportunities for blacks, the Board of Education was the logical place for a black politician to start. He also believed that fewer whites would object to a black school board member than to a black sheriff or a black tax assessor. When a board member had died two years earlier, Gomillion wrote to the board chairman asking him to appoint a black to the vacancy. Noting that four-fifths of the students in the school system were black, he ex-

---

* Montgomery *Advertiser*, February 14, 1954. Robert Varner became a full-fledged Republican and was appointed assistant United States attorney by Eisenhower and then federal district judge by Richard Nixon.

plained that blacks believed that "through representation on the
Board of Education they could, and should, share with you, their
white fellow-citizens, the responsibility of planning and providing
public education opportunities for the educables of Macon
County." A white man was chosen to fill this position, but Gomillion
remained convinced that a black should be on the board.[13]

Jessie Parkhurst Guzman, director of the Institute's Department
of Records and Research and a former dean of women, announced
her candidacy for the Board of Education in February 1954. Guzman contradicted completely the conservatives' stereotyped image
—handed down as part of the Reconstruction myth—of the ignorant
but ambitious black politician. A small, middle-aged woman
with rimless glasses and a thoroughly professorial visage, she held
degrees from Clark, Howard, and Columbia universities. She no
doubt was the most highly educated person to try for public office in Macon County up to that time. Not surprisingly, she ran a
high-minded campaign that resurrected the idea of Tuskegee as a
model community. "In Macon County," she said in a campaign
speech, "we have a wonderful opportunity to get into the mainstream of the progressive South and to set an example for those
places that are not so far advanced in their democratic thinking as
we are." Guzman intended no irony in this comment. "A real community attempts to develop a working arrangement that will resolve
conflict and make consistent progress possible."[14]

But the reality of politics in Macon County in 1954 operated on a
much lower level. Guzman lost by more than three to one in a
strictly racial vote. Neither she nor Gomillion had realized the in-
tensity of white fear of black political activism. To most whites, no
office, not even a seat on the school board, could be trusted to a
black. Most whites apparently never imagined that Guzman's candidacy reflected a sincere hope for better educational opportunities;
they assumed that larger political motives were at work. A few who
were familiar with the NAACP's school desegregation suits perhaps
suspected that Guzman would try to integrate the public schools.
The chasm between the two communities was vast in 1954, and it
would only get wider.[15]

Sam Engelhardt fully understood the concerns of white Macon
Countians. He campaigned entirely on the race issue in opposing
Henry Neill Segrest for a state senate seat that year. "Are you a
member of the Board of Trustees of Tuskegee Institute?" Engelhardt
asked Segrest in campaign advertisements. That Engelhardt could
use Segrest's friendliness to the Institute against him revealed how
far relations between blacks and whites in Tuskegee had de-

teriorated. "Is it a fact," he asked further, "that you were a witness
. . . against Sheriff Pat Evans . . . when he was sued for damages by
Negroes who claimed that they had been mistreated while in the
Macon County jail—and isn't it a fact that Sheriff Pat Evans was
acquitted?" Engelhardt resurrected the brutality case eleven years
after the fact to demonstrate that Segrest was not a reliable defender
of white power. "I Stand for White Supremacy and Segregation," he
told the voters in a terse summary of his position. He received more
than three of every four white votes and beat Segrest soundly.[16]

Henry Neill Segrest and Jessie Parkhurst Guzman provided an
immediate challenge to conservative power in Macon County, but
the greater threat in 1954 came in the familiar and gigantic form of
Jim Folsom. Again Folsom campaigned on positions that were
anathema to conservatives. He promised an expensive school construction program that would "take the Negro schools out of the
barns and shotgun shacks and put them in buildings." He claimed
he would push harder than ever for legislative reapportionment,
saying "We're going to get [reapportionment] if I have to keep the
Legislature in session for four years." To explain the significance of
reapportionment to voters in northern Alabama, Folsom held up
two lead pipes, one three inches in diameter and the other a single
inch across, and told his listeners that the larger pipe represented
Dallas County in the Black Belt, which had three men in the legislature, while the smaller one was this very northern Alabama county,
which had only one man in the legislature. "Now, which pipe can
funnel more money back home?" Folsom asked his audience.[17]

Folsom won a big victory, defeating six opponents without a runoff. Farmers and working-class men and women simply liked him,
while recent changes in the electorate no doubt widened the margin
of his victory. At the behest of women's groups and Folsom's allies,
the legislature in 1953 removed the cumulative feature of the Alabama poll tax. Now a voter who registered long after his twenty-first
birthday did not have to pay the poll tax for the earlier years in
which he had been eligible to register. This change made the ballot
box more accessible to poor whites and blacks and accelerated a
statewide growth in black registration that was already underway.
The number of black voters in the state had increased almost tenfold
since World War II, though they still composed only a small percentage of the electorate. The vast majority of the approximately
fifty thousand black voters in Alabama, including those in Tuskegee, looked on Folsom as their best white friend in the state.[18]

Alabama conservatives took another blow just after the Folsom
triumph when the United States Supreme Court outlawed public

school segregation in the *Brown* decision. The ruling did not surprise men like Sam Engelhardt who had followed the NAACP challenge to segregated schools through the courts. The previous year the legislature had appointed a study committee to recommend legislation to protect school segregation in the event of a court ruling. Chaired by Senator Albert Boutwell of Birmingham, the committee met soon after the *Brown* decision was announced and asked outgoing Governor Persons to call a special session of the legislature to consider legislation to remove all mention of segregation and public education from the Alabama statute books. The legislation would have ended public education and replaced it with a system of state grants to private schools, a plan that Engelhardt had suggested in 1951. The Boutwell committee wanted the legislature to act before Folsom came into office in January 1955, because they believed that he would oppose their efforts. But Persons, although he had been conservative in his racial policies, refused to call the special session and, consequently, no legislation to circumvent *Brown* had been passed when Folsom's new term began. Conservatives were especially tense when he took office.[19]

Sam Engelhardt and Jim Folsom locked horns almost immediately. Folsom forces in the state senate were pushing in February 1955 for passage of a large bond issue for road construction, but were meeting strong opposition from a group of conservative senators, of whom Engelhardt was one. Through an intermediary Folsom told Engelhardt that "if you don't go along with my new highway program, I'm going to get a new board of registrars in Macon County and register every damn nigger in the county." It would have been a clumsy effort even had it been directed at someone who trembled in fear of Folsom, but it was foolhardy to use such a tactic on a hard-nosed man like Engelhardt. Checking his natural tendency to respond to Folsom in kind, Engelhardt cleverly took the high road, exuding moral indignation when he relayed Folsom's threat to the press. "I can't visualize any native Alabamian resorting to such methods which could jeopardize the good feelings that exist between the people of both races in Macon County." He portrayed Folsom as ignorant of the implications of black registration. "I do not think the Negroes of my county are ready to take an active part in politics, and if Governor Folsom should carry out his threat of registering all of them to vote, I am afraid it would not benefit either race." Folsom tried to pass off the remark as a jest, but the damage had been done. He soon accepted a compromise on the road bond issue.[20]

Folsom's threat to register "every damn nigger" in Macon County

had a lasting impact on the voting conflict in Tuskegee. It gave Engelhardt a vivid illustration of the present danger and helped him to
marshal support for his aggressive resistance to change. He later
traced his boldest acts of resistance partly to the Folsom threat.
More important, the incident appears to have weakened the governor's resolve to push for black registration. In the 1954 Democratic
primary he had helped Agnes Baggett in her race for state auditor
because she had promised to appoint voter registrars receptive to
blacks' voting. When the Democratic nominee for commissioner of
agriculture died soon after the primary, Folsom engineered his replacement by A. W. Todd, a former state senator from northern Alabama, in part because Todd also agreed to support black
registration. The governor could virtually dictate registration policies in every county through his alliances with Baggett and Todd.
He usually chose to relinquish that authority to local politicians, but
he had intended in 1954 to use it in Black Belt counties like Macon.
The unabated opposition to his programs from Black Belt conservatives, his own popularity among blacks, and the gross disregard in
those counties of the democratic principles he cherished—all gave
him reason to reverse the registration policies in the Black Belt. But
he began to lose his determination after the threat to Engelhardt
backfired. Just after the incident, he broke an appointment with
TCA leaders to discuss the Macon County Board of Registrars, and,
a month after taking office, he went on a vacation. This sort of response came to be characteristic of Folsom during the next four
years.[21]

Engelhardt had little time to enjoy his triumph. In July thirty-two
Tuskegee blacks informed the county Board of Education that they
would soon submit to it a desegregation petition. The Tuskegee
group was part of a national NAACP effort to have local branches
petition for school desegregation. Engelhardt responded fiercely: "I
regret [that] the innocent colored people will have to suffer because
of the action taken by the National Association for the Agitation of
Colored People." He quickly explained how innocent blacks would
suffer: "We will have segregation in the public schools of Macon
County or there will be no public schools." He issued a final cryptic
warning: "The National Association for the Agitation of Colored
People forgets [that] there are more ways than one to kill a snake."*

---

* Montgomery *Advertiser*, July 17, 1955. The petitioners did not carry their protest any further. The TCA leadership continued to believe that voting rights
should be their first priority. (Gomillion to Detroit Lee, November 20, 1956,
Tuskegee Civic Association Files.)

But as tough as he talked, Engelhardt actually had little recourse against the petitioners. He pushed through the legislature a bill giving the Macon County Board of Education the authority to fire any teacher advocating racial integration or belonging to any group advocating school desegregation. "We've got 190 colored teachers in Macon County and the board tells me they'll fire everyone of them that takes part in this agitation," he announced. But this patently unconstitutional bill would have no impact on the situation because no public-school teacher had signed the petition. Folsom vetoed the bill anyway, an action that Engelhardt said was designed to "garner the Negro vote." Engelhardt knew that after the *Brown* decision he was fighting a losing battle on school desegregation, though he never allowed his rhetoric to reflect that knowledge.[22]

To Engelhardt the larger conflict was over political control, and he clearly had not accepted defeat there. But he saw signs of great danger. Despite the registrars' tactics of evasion and delay for the past five years, the number of black voters in Macon County had crept slowly upward. Slightly more than one thousand blacks were registered voters by the end of 1955; they composed about one-third of the county's electorate. Approximately forty percent of the voters in the city of Tuskegee were black. A unified black vote—and at this time blacks always voted in a bloc—could determine the outcome of any county or city election in which whites were divided. Moreover, it seemed certain in the fall of 1955 that black political power would continue to increase. After dawdling over the appointment for nine months, Folsom named Herman Bentley as the new chairman of the board. Again Bentley dramatically altered the behavior of the board, which began freely accepting and approving black applications in its last few meetings in 1955.[23]

But Bentley would not have another opportunity to do what he thought was right about registering blacks. After the first of ten scheduled board meetings in January 1956, the other active registrar resigned, making the board inoperative. S. S. "Shack" Humphries, a Notasulga farmer who had served on the board since 1953, denied that the increase in black registration had anything to do with his decision. "There was no friction whatsoever" between him and Bentley, Humphries told the Montgomery *Advertiser*, "and me and the darkies got along fine." Judge Varner had in fact been pressuring Humphries to enforce the strictest possible standards on the application form. Bentley, a close friend of Humphries, was trying at the same time to make registration easier for blacks. Humphries removed himself from a difficult situation by resigning from the ooard, and in so doing also stopped the registration process, which relieved worried conservatives who remembered all too clearly what Herman Bentley had done in 1949.[24]

The board would not meet again for seventeen months. Agnes Baggett, A. W. Todd, and Jim Folsom all tried to ignore the situation, because they, like Shack Humphries, realized that there was no room for compromise between blacks and white conservatives in Tuskegee. Baggett, whose original appointee to the board had refused the job, set an impossible criterion for naming someone else: "If all the citizens of Macon County get together on a recommendation, then I will be glad to make the appointment." A. W. Todd had appointed Humphries, but said nothing publicly about replacing him. Ambitious for higher office, Todd no doubt thought it wise to stay away from the politically volatile issue of black voting. Folsom told the *Advertiser* in March that he had already made his one appointment to the board. It was up to Baggett and Todd to form a working board, he said.[25]

Folsom was using his two colleagues as scapegoats for his own irresponsibility. He had the authority to fill the other positions, and he probably had the political power to make Baggett and Todd appoint registrars. To make things easier for the governor, the TCA had found two white businessmen in Tuskegee who agreed to go on the board. Both men wrote to Folsom in the summer of 1956 volunteering to serve. When nothing happened, Gomillion sent Folsom the names of six hundred black citizens who wanted to register and reminded the governor that the board had not functioned since January. Gomillion told Folsom that he did not understand how "the citizens of Macon County and the officials of the State would permit such a situation to continue." He hoped that the state officials would "soon give relief to these citizens who desire to perform their civic responsibilities." When he finally acted in September, Folsom appointed not one of the whites committed to black registration but Grady Rogers, the former board chairman who had so effectively slowed black registration from 1951 through most of 1955. But the board still did not meet because Herman Bentley had become seriously ill; he died in December without having convened the board again. Tuskegee blacks had lost their best white friend.[26]

Folsom and his two colleagues finally formed a board in March 1957, again passing over the Tuskegee merchants willing to register blacks. E. P. Livingston, a retired Notasulga farmer and businessman who was head of the Macon County White Citizens' Council, was named chairman. Another Notasulgan, Jesse Zachary, was also appointed. Gomillion duly thanked the state officials for "having set in motion the machinery for orderly government," but he actually doubted that the situation would improve. "This does not seem to be any basis for elation," he wrote to an associate about the new board. "We shall accept the appointment, however, in good faith." Gomillion's patient determination to work within the system would, however, reach its limits very soon.[27]

Folsom's irresolute handling of the Tuskegee voting situation was part of his larger failure to counter resistance to racial change. He had taken a dim view of the efforts to circumvent the *Brown* decision but had stopped few of them. When the Montgomery bus boycott and a desegregation attempt at the University of Alabama intensified the already acute white anxiety in the winter of 1955-56, Folsom froze. He did nothing as Sam Engelhardt and other conservatives channeled the rising emotions into the White Citizens Council movement, a quasi-official effort to save segregation and white political control. By not responding, Folsom wasted the political power centered in the governor's office. But his very access to power had quickened conservatives like Engelhardt into a frenzy of resistance. The cause of racial liberalism in Alabama paid the price—in more intense conservative opposition—of having a liberal governor, but, because of Folsom's inaction, it realized few, if any, benefits.

Why did Folsom not fight back? He may have thought that he could not reverse the tide of resistance and that he should not make a futile effort. But that reasoning begs the question; Folsom never knew whether he could have successfully challenged the conservative resistance because he did not mount an all-out effort. He clearly could have implemented a policy of black registration in Macon and other counties, but did not. At least one reason for Folsom's weak response lay in his personal problems. An alcoholic, he drank more and more as his term progressed and was absent from his office most of the last two years of that term. The drinking contributed to his overall failure of political leadership, which was felt most acutely in his unwillingness to do battle with the conservatives.[28]

But Folsom's failure in no way lessened conservative anxiety. At the very moment when the governor seemed to have conceded defeat on the race issue, Sam Engelhardt was creating his masterpiece of resistance. Tuskegee officials gave him the signal in early 1956 to go ahead with a plan to gerrymander the boundaries of the city. For several years Engelhardt and Mayor Phillip Lightfoot had discussed a gerrymander as a means to assure white control of town government. The boundaries simply could be redrawn to exclude all black voters, Engelhardt believed. He knew that the federal courts traditionally had not interfered in the states' authority to fix political boundaries; thus, such a gerrymander would stand up in court. Apparently some of the town fathers had been skeptical of the idea originally, but Folsom's threat to register "every damn nigger" persuaded them to accept the gerrymander as a necessary protective move. Engelhardt had strong support from Lightfoot and Greene B. Edwards, Jr., the City Council president, both of whom could reassure any councilman who became fainthearted about this bold action. The City Council "went along in toto," Engelhardt said later, though one councilman disavowed any prior knowledge of the gerrymander. Very few others knew about it, though many Tuskegeeans were curious about all the survey work being done in town in 1956 and early 1957.[29]

Thus, most residents were startled in May 1957 when Engelhardt introduced in the Alabama legislature a bill that would change the shape of the city of Tuskegee from a perfect square to a twenty-eight-sided figure which resembled, one reporter observed, a stylized seahorse. The all-black sections were now completely excluded. What remained was the town square, the nearby streets where whites lived, and several thin arms reaching out to take in whites residing on roads leading out of Tuskegee. In a few cases, the new boundaries ran down the middle of streets to exclude the blacks on one side. All but twelve of the four hundred black voters had been removed, that dozen remaining only out of the need to keep all white voters. Sam Engelhardt, the modern-day Fire-Eater, had created what Justice Felix Frankfurter later thought was a most interesting "essay in geometry and geography." From its first public moment, Engelhardt's handiwork caused a furor.[30]

7

Sop in Your Own Damned Gravy

CHARLES GOMILLION had to park four blocks from the Butler Chapel African Methodist Episcopal Zion Church on the night of June 25. That was a good sign, he thought. He had called a meeting of all interested citizens to discuss Sam Engelhardt's bill to gerrymander the Tuskegee city boundaries. He chose Butler Chapel for the meeting because it had been the site of the founding of Tuskegee Institute in 1881. The church was a symbol of independence for Macon County blacks, and Gomillion hoped that tonight's meeting would advance the effort for black autonomy that Booker Washington had begun almost seventy-six years earlier. Indeed, Butler Chapel was an even older emblem of independence than Gomillion realized. Founded in the early days of Reconstruction by the Reverend John Butler and other freedmen, the church represented one of the first attempts by Macon County blacks to create institutions free of white control. It was where James Alston and the black Republicans had met in 1870 and where two freedmen had been killed by Democrats intent on retrieving political control. Booker Washington, who manipulated symbols extraordinarily well, perhaps had chosen Butler Chapel as the place to open his school to suggest continuity in the quest for black autonomy, even while the strategy for that quest was shifted from politics to education.[1]

Five hundred people crowded into the small brick church and twenty-five hundred more gathered outside as the meeting began. In the invocation the Reverend Kenneth L. Buford of Butler Chapel used as his text the account in Genesis of the Israelites' flight from

Egypt. Buford read about the Israelites' fear as the Egyptians pursued them toward the Red Sea and quoted God's command to Moses in the face of the danger: "Lift up your rod, and stretch out your hand over the sea and divide it, that the people of Israel may go on dry ground through the sea." He spoke rapidly as he began to relate the plight of the Israelites to Macon County. "Tonight, we the Negroes of Tuskegee and Macon County stand facing our Red Sea," Buford said, adding, "We too have our Pharaoh," without saying Engelhardt's name. "We have our Egyptian hosts that are pressing in from the rear in the person of those who would rob us of the rights, the God-given rights, that have been guaranteed to us by the Constitution of these great United States of America." Buford raised his high-pitched voice and quickened his pace as he affirmed the promise of deliverance for Macon County blacks. "We can, if we will, stretch our rod across . . . the waters of our *Red Sea* and cause them to be divided so that we can cross the narrows to safety, as even did the children of Israel."[2]

Gomillion followed Buford to the pulpit. "The Tuskegee Civic Association," he began in a powerful tenor voice, "has been diligently striving to provide for this community, Tuskegee and Macon County, the kind of civic education which is designed to promote intelligent behavior and the general welfare of all people." He spoke at a slow, steady pace in an accent that rarely betrayed his poverty-stricken origins. "We have encouraged our members to observe the law, to vote intelligently, to save and invest their earnings, to improve their educational opportunities." But the TCA's efforts were lost on local whites, Gomillion said. For years the TCA had been asking to meet with the Tuskegee City Council, but the councilmen never consented. All county officials, all city officials, all police officials, and all polling officials are white, he said; blacks have no representation in local government.[3]

Now, he continued, "our honorable senator" had thrown all black voters out of the city of Tuskegee. The TCA had asked the city council and the state legislature to stop the gerrymander, but no help had come. "We even appealed to the citizens of Alabama not to stand by and allow this injustice to be perpetrated against a people who have sought to live honorably and industriously within the law." But again no aid was forthcoming. "Our voices have been as voices crying in the wilderness," Gomillion concluded.[4]

After a spirited rendering of the hymn "Jesus, Keep Me Near the Cross," the Reverend S. T. Martin delivered the evening's sermon. "Learn to sop in your own damned gravy!" Martin exhorted at its climax, a command that finally revealed the meeting's primary purpose. Returning to the pulpit for benedictory remarks, Gomillion announced that the TCA would lead a "selective buying" campaign. "We are going to buy goods and services from those who help us, from those who make no effort to hinder us, from those who recognize us as first-class citizens." From now until further notice, he said, the motto of Macon County blacks would be "Trade with Your Friends." He and the other speakers had carefully avoided using the word "boycott," but a boycott was what had just begun. "Soon the time will come when they will have to respect us," Gomillion said in closing. "They may hate our guts, but they will respect us."[5]

The idea of a boycott was not new. It will be recalled that the TCA had considered, and rejected, such a proposal in the late 1940s. And an editorial in the TCA newsletter in February 1956 had called for a boycott if a Board of Registrars was not formed immediately, though no action in fact resulted. By then Tuskegee blacks had the example of the Montgomery bus boycott to encourage their use of the tactic. Gomillion and the TCA had begun organizing a boycott while they were making the various appeals to stop the gerrymander bill in early and mid-June 1957. When the bill passed both houses of the Alabama legislature without a dissenting vote and after Folsom told them that a veto would be futile, the TCA answered resolutely. Gomillion still had serious doubts about whether it would work, but he believed that Engelhardt's drastic act required a strong response. The three thousand people at Butler Chapel on June 25 heartened him. "I actually believed at that point that we were going to be eventually successful," he said later.[6]

In planning their protest, the TCA considered how to get the full support of the black community. The Montgomery bus boycott again influenced their thinking. The success of the Reverend Martin Luther King, Jr., suggested to some black Tuskegeeans that local ministers ought to lead a mass protest. A few persons objected to Gomillion's leading the boycott because he belonged to no local church and attended religious services only irregularly. To insure the support of those holding this view, the TCA asked the local ministers' association to lead the protest, knowing that at least two influential clergymen would urge the group to defer to the TCA. The ministers indeed refused the leadership role. But the TCA decided to use religious ritual and symbols to encourage widespread support. To have an effective boycott, the TCA needed the full participation of the thousands of poor and uneducated blacks in the county who looked first to their minister for leadership. The TCA executive committee decided to have a mass meeting every Tuesday night and to secure "a dynamic speaker," usually a minister, for each one. Buford's provocative analogy between Macon County blacks and the Israelites and Martin's admonition to "sop in your own damned gravy" suggested that the protest would indeed operate at a level accessible to all local blacks.[7]

The boycott was effective from the outset. Virtually all Tuskegee blacks withdrew their trade immediately. The rural blacks apparently participated less fully at first, but they fell into step soon after a merchant told a reporter that the "country nigger customers" still shopped at his store. Most people traded at black-owned stores in the Institute community and traveled to Montgomery or Opelika, twenty-five miles to the northeast, for the items not available there. Car pools to Montgomery and Opelika and informal shopping cooperatives formed quickly. The purchasing agents at the VA hospital and the Institute honored the boycott, though they already bought most goods from out-of-town wholesalers. A few very enthusiastic boycotters watched the stores in Tuskegee for blacks who continued to trade with whites. A black observed shopping in a downtown Tuskegee store was made the object of ridicule, though Gomillion constantly warned against such coercive action. Black maids whose duties included buying groceries for their white employers began wearing their aprons to the food stores to signal that they were not willingly breaking the boycott. Within a few days, a fish market and the town's only movie theater went out of business.[8]

Not surprisingly, the boycott elicited a harsh response from Sam Engelhardt. "Goon squads" of Tuskegee Institute students were enforcing the boycott, he charged. He said that Gomillion "completely dominates" Dr. Luther Foster, the Institute president since 1953, and threatened to oppose the state appropriation for the school if the boycott was not ended. "Downright inflammatory" was how he characterized the black demands, which called for the immediate repeal of the gerrymander bill; a functioning Board of Registrars; extension of the original city boundaries to include some black residential areas; better recreational facilities and improved sewage treatment; and more employment of blacks in Tuskegee businesses. Engelhardt said that political control was the blacks' real goal. "They had plans to annex adjacent land, insuring control." Blacks "were so confident that they refused to discuss their differences with the city fathers," he explained, and asserted that one black was already campaigning for mayor of Tuskegee.[9]

Engelhardt added insult to the Tuskegee blacks' injury in mid-July when he announced plans to abolish Macon County. He had suggested the abolition of Black Belt counties in 1951 as a means of maintaining white control. Since then he had resurrected the idea periodically, though it was never received enthusiastically, even among conservatives. But after the gerrymander passed and the boycott began, such a radical measure seemed more plausible. Engelhardt proposed simply to divide Macon County into several parts and give each of five contiguous counties one portion.[10]

State legislators from the five counties had to consider the proposal or risk being labeled integrationists, but few, if any, really liked the idea. It promised to change their counties' governmental institutions and, perhaps more important, their electorates. Each county would automatically increase its percentage of black population, and one would have to take the Institute and the VA hospital. The first meeting of legislators to divide the county revealed the difficulties. "I'll take the VA hospital if you'll take a part of Tuskegee Institute," one legislator said to another. "I'll take part of the campus, but for gosh sakes don't give me Notasulga," the legislator from Lee County, to the northeast, pleaded. "We'll take part of Tuskegee, but leave out the courthouse," a Montgomery County lawmaker said. "You are giving us more than half the county," the legislator from Bullock County, to the south, said to Engelhardt. "The Negroes already outnumber us three to one as it is; this will just make it worse." Engelhardt drew and redrew the lines dividing the county, but could never satisfy the other legislators. Finally, a bill creating a committee to study the abolition of Macon County was passed. Public hearings were to be held in early 1958.[11]

John Patterson, the Alabama attorney general, came to Tuskegee in late July to try to enforce the state's antiboycott law. Patterson questioned several blacks at the courthouse in an effort to get an admission that a boycott was indeed taking place. He searched the TCA office for the organization's membership roll and confiscated its tape recordings of the mass meetings. Four days later Patterson's chief assistant, MacDonald Gallion, again raided the TCA office, but found no current membership list; anticipating precisely this kind of harassment, the TCA had stopped keeping a roll of members several months earlier. Gallion made a radio broadcast warning blacks not to participate in the boycott and promising protection for any black who traded with whites. He summoned Institute and VA employees to the courthouse for questioning. Why are you no longer buying goods from Tuskegee merchants? Gallion asked George Busby, a VA purchasing agent. As he posed the question, Gallion had pulled back his suit jacket, revealing a holstered pistol. "What you got the gun for?" Busby asked. Gallion lectured Busby about all that whites had done for Tuskegee blacks. Busby responded by directing Gallion's attention out a window of the courthouse. "You see all that paving [equipment]?" he asked. "Do you know whose money paid for that? Negroes'." Gallion received little more cooperation from the other black witnesses.[12]

John Patterson had come to Tuskegee because he was an ambitious young politician. He had been appointed the Democratic nominee for attorney general in 1954 at age thirty-three after his father, Albert, the original nominee, was killed in Phenix City by gangsters whom he had promised to prosecute. Although his father had been a liberal on race issues, the younger Patterson quickly learned to exploit the rising racial anxieties of the mid-1950s for his own political advantage. In June 1956 he had halted all NAACP activities in Alabama when he asked for the organization's membership list during a hearing on whether the NAACP was properly registered as a "foreign corporation"—that is, an organization incorporated outside Alabama. When the NAACP refused to turn over its list, Circuit Judge Walter B. Jones of Montgomery cited the organization for contempt and fined it $100,000. The contempt citation prevented the NAACP from functioning, at least officially, and made John Patterson appear to be the savior of segregation and white supremacy.[13]

The Tuskegee boycott provided Patterson with an opportunity to enhance that image just months before the 1958 gubernatorial campaign began. "This is a serious thing that is going on at Tuskegee," Patterson announced. "The Negro citizens of this state should not be misled by the small group of Negro agitators who are urging them to violate the law." Innocent blacks were contributing money to a few "so-called leaders" who used it "to buy expensive cars, silk suits and pay for expensive trips." Patterson privately held a very high opinion of Gomillion, but publicly he repeated the common accusation that civil rights activists exploited ignorant blacks for personal gain. The person exploiting the Tuskegee situation, of course, was John Patterson.[14]

In August, Patterson asked the state courts to enjoin the TCA from conducting a boycott, because "it is calculated to destroy the economy of an entire city and destroy the means of livelihood for a large segment of Macon County." Circuit Judge Will O. Walton issued an order restraining the TCA from using violence to enforce a boycott. Gomillion responded that the order had no effect because the TCA had not forced anyone to boycott. The test for the legality of a boycott in Alabama, as he knew, was whether a group or individual was *making* a person change his buying habits. "There has been no intimidation or use of force to keep Negroes from patronizing any merchant—certainly not on instructions from the association or any of its officers," he said. In January 1958, with the gubernatorial primary only four months away, a full hearing on the injunction request took place. The TCA might not have explicitly called for a boycott, but it had "held these rallies and got people all stirred up," Patterson argued. "You can't set a fire and go off and leave it." In June 1958, after Patterson had won the Democratic nomination for governor, Walton dissolved the restraining order and rejected the motion for an injunction. Patterson, he said, had never proved that the TCA was promoting or enforcing a boycott. "Thus far in this land, every person has a right to trade with whomever he pleases, and, therefore, the right not to trade with any particular person or business," Walton declared.[15]

Engelhardt's county abolition proposal and Patterson's raids on the TCA office served only to strengthen the spirit of protest among blacks. The TCA began calling the boycott a "Crusade for Citizenship." Three thousand people—and sometimes more—attended each of the Tuesday meetings throughout July and August. They heard powerful rhetoric. Martin Luther King, Jr., the Reverend Ralph Abernathy, also from Montgomery, and the Reverend Fred Shuttlesworth of Birmingham all came to the July 2 meeting. "You are not seeking to put the stores out of business but to put justice in business," King told the Tuskegee audience. The next week a Tuskegee minister gave a concise summary of the history of Macon County blacks. "Lincoln freed us," the Reverend E. O. Braxter began. "Booker T. Washington educated us. Sam Engelhardt put us together." Gomillion saw such rhetoric as providing poor blacks with an outlet, albeit a vicarious one, for their hostility toward white Tuskegeeans. Just by being at the meetings, they were "getting back at Mr. Charlie," he said later.[16]

As for middle-class blacks in Tuskegee, the gerrymander made them see fully their common bond with poor blacks. For many years, a town-and-gown division had existed in Tuskegee, despite the Institute's traditional commitment to community improvement. Economic and educational differences reinforced that split. But the gerrymander put all blacks—rich and poor, learned and ignorant—in the same boat. Stanley Smith, a young Institute sociologist, explained that the gerrymander shocked some middle-class blacks "into the realization that we were still Negroes, with all the disabilities attached thereto in the sovereign state of Alabama." Poor blacks, Smith felt, considered that recognition long overdue. "The country people found our comeuppance rather amusing and, I think, subtly satisfying," he said. "They didn't rub it in, but there was some chortling. 'Well, now, join us' was their attitude at the first Crusade meeting. 'Welcome home.' "[17]

Anger among middle-class blacks boiled over as a result of the gerrymander. "They didn't leave us a trace of dignity," William P. Mitchell said in early August. "I think people just said that, if Tuskegee didn't want us, we didn't want Tuskegee," he explained to a reporter. A well-to-do Institute matron expressed her indignation to a northern newspaperman. "We used to go down to the square. . . . I thought of myself as having friends there. . . . Then, all together, they threw us out of their town. . . . I'd feel like a fool creeping back to those stores with my money. I can't ever go back."[18]

The gerrymander and the boycott received much attention from national magazines and northern newspapers. *Life, Time, Newsweek,* and *U.S. News & World Report* published stories in July. *Life* ran photographs of Engelhardt, Gomillion, Tuskegee's few remaining black voters, and an empty white grocery store. *Life* and *Newsweek* put the gerrymander in the context of the civil rights bill that the United States Senate was considering at the time. The Tuskegee situation "was a timely—though perhaps extreme—example of what the civil-rights argument in the Senate is all about," *Newsweek* explained. The northern black newspapers gave the boycott highly sympathetic coverage. The attention of the press showed Tuskegee blacks that their protest was being heard and strengthened their resolve to continue, while the publicity subjected whites to national ridicule for creating such a situation.[19]

Reporters elicited from Gomillion a fuller statement of his attitudes than he had ever given previously. He held deep resentments toward whites. White southerners, he told a *Time* reporter, for years had promised that when blacks obtained education, employment, and property, then they would be ready to participate in politics. But in Tuskegee, "we have all these and we seem to be worse off than if we didn't. What incentive is there for Negro youths to try to get good educations and to amount to something when they see this?" He minced no words in pointing out white hypocrisy. "If we stay away from their churches, schools and playgrounds, we are wise and understanding Negroes. But if we stay away from their stores, we are criminals."[20]

He revealed his strategy for black officeholding in Macon County: Blacks hoped first to elect a person to the Board of Education, then one to the City Council, and finally one to the Board of Revenue, the county governing body. "We thought all this would take twelve years, but finally we would be able to show the world how a city with the vote fairly balanced between Negro and white could work out its own destiny." Gomillion had reformulated the old idea of Tuskegee as a model community. "We hoped to be a pilot city in the

deep South, operating under an interracial government." The fear
that blacks wanted to take over local government was entirely unfounded. "The politicians give us credit for learning too well from
them," he said. "We have no desire to 'control.' We want only to
share."[21]

The future looked quite different to many white Tuskegeeans.
Sam Engelhardt had only done what was necessary to maintain
white control, they believed. "I had no idea," a merchant told an
Advertiser reporter, "that the Negroes were rapidly closing the gap in
the city voting strength. . . . They probably would have held the majority by 1960." But "Engelhardt realized this, and he did something about it. We should all be thankful to him." The gerrymander
was inevitable, another merchant said. "This was a matter of self-
preservation, of survival," he explained to a northern reporter. "We
couldn't have stayed around here if more and more nigger registration had taken place. Would you want to live in a nigger town?" Not
taking a chance on the reporter's reply, the merchant answered his
own question emphatically: "No, sir!" One merchant said he would
willingly sacrifice his business to stop the aggressiveness of local
blacks. "Sure, I realize it will mean that I'll go broke, but if that is
what it takes to show them we mean business then I'm prepared to
do just that. They've pushed us as far as they're going to. . . . I'm
ready to show 'em."[22]

Other merchants, however, felt these men were whistling past the
graveyard. The boycott had devastated the town's economy from
the start. It continued, with few defections, through 1957 and into
the next year. By the spring of 1958 half of Tuskegee's white-owned
retail businesses had failed. Businessmen who had managed to sur-
vive reported that their sales were off forty to sixty-five percent, figures that blacks believed underestimated the boycott's effect. "If I'd
been a nigra and told I wasn't wanted," one merchant said, "I'd
have been mighty sore, I know that." Insisting that no merchants
were informed about the boycott beforehand, another businessman
said, "I wish we could have talked this thing over first." He had an
idea that might have prevented all the trouble. "Why couldn't we
have zoned the city in some way that the nigras could have elected
one member of the city council?" A dry goods retailer scoffed at
John Patterson's effort to force blacks to shop in Tuskegee. "What
do we care about injunctions? You can't ring the cash register with
injunctions." Another merchant cited his own "pure selfishness" for
opposing what Engelhardt had done. "Tuskegee is a good town . . .
to make money in. I've made a good living here and would like to
continue to do so." But whites had to wake up to the truth. "It is

time that the white people realized that the days of slavery are over. The Negroes here are well educated and they pay taxes. They should have a voice in how things are run."[23]

Such criticism was usually given privately to a reporter who promised not to use the merchant's name. The merchants who opposed what Engelhardt had done—by one report, they numbered about twelve—felt great pressure to stay in step with the conservatives. The most blatant pressure came from Engelhardt himself, who invoked what Wilbur J. Cash called "the savage ideal"—the southern impulse toward conformity of thought—against any political opponent. When Jim Folsom let it be known that he opposed the abolition of Macon County, Engelhardt responded that "we wouldn't be having the trouble we're having in Macon [if we had a] governor who made noises like a white man." When seven Tuskegee lawyers announced their opposition to the abolition proposal, Engelhardt told the *Advertiser* that the lawyers had "every right to join hands with" the NAACP and the TCA in fighting him. "Some of us don't dare speak our piece," a Tuskegee businessman told a northern reporter. "The situation is pretty deplorable when you are against something but can't say so, yet that [is] our position." One unnamed Tuskegeean expressed his deep concern about the conformist pressure to an *Advertiser* reporter in November. "Either you agree with everything Sam says or you are a nigger-loving communist," he complained. "There is no middle ground, no reasoning at all," he continued. "The people have gone crazy."[24]

No single individual, to be sure, could create such a situation by himself. Engelhardt represented the views of a small group of wealthy men determined not to relinquish control of Macon County to the blacks. Five men from four families long involved in county politics formed the core of a conservative elite. Judge Varner was, of course, one of the five. Another was Edward Cobb Laslie, president of the City Bank of Tuskegee and chairman of the Board of Revenue. A tall, affable man in his mid-fifties, Laslie was the grandson of James Edward Cobb, who as circuit judge in the mid-1870s rid the county of black Republican officeholders and as Macon County's delegate to the 1901 constitutional convention staunchly supported disfranchisement. Laslie had apparently inherited his grandfather's opinions on race and politics and, like him, also had the power to act on his views. As chairman of the Board of Revenue, Laslie influenced virtually all county policies through the control of funds and the appointment of boards. Perhaps an even greater source of his power was his position as president and principal owner of the larger of Tuskegee's two banks. He could influence the behavior of merchants, many of whom depended on Laslie's banks for the money to stock their stores, by controlling their access to credit. While there is no evidence to suggest that he openly coerced merchants, one imagines that a small businessman in debt to the City Bank might think twice before challenging Laslie on race or politics. There were more subtle ways to enforce the savage ideal than Sam Engelhardt's.[25]

Ernest Bridges, a wealthy cotton broker who had served on the Tuskegee City Council, was a third influential conservative. His brother Forrest Bridges was the state senator who in 1948 had asked Frederick Patterson to stop Gomillion's voting rights work. Ernest Bridges enthusiastically supported the gerrymander proposal when Engelhardt first mentioned it. "I don't care what happens to Tuskegee, the niggers aren't going to take over," he had reportedly said in private conversation.

Completing the inner circle of conservative power were Greene B. "Buddy" Edwards, Jr., president of the City Council, and his brother Joe. Sons of a longtime mayor of Tuskegee, the Edwards brothers owned several large businesses and much Tuskegee real estate. Joe had successfully encouraged his friend Gordon Persons to remove Herman Bentley from the Board of Registrars in 1951. Buddy was personally close to Engelhardt and, a popular man among white Tuskegeeans, probably had more influence over city government than even the mayor, Phillip Lightfoot.[26]

These five men shared important interests and values. Each held, or had immediate access to, political power that black voting would decimate, if not completely destroy. Their families had run Macon County for many years, and they simply would not willingly hand over control—an attitude hardly uncommon among powerful men at any time or place. They all viewed blacks as racially inferior and thus by nature unfit to have power. All had supported Sam Engelhardt's political career from the start; Engelhardt's singular truculence no doubt influenced their thinking as much as they did his. All were wealthy enough to remain largely unaffected by the boycott, which they had fully expected would follow the gerrymander. (Perhaps to reduce his potential losses, Buddy Edwards had sold his Cadillac dealership in April 1957, one month before Engelhardt announced the gerrymander proposal.)[27]

As the leaders of the white community, these men strongly influenced the way whites coped with the boycott crisis. They tried first to reassure worried merchants that the boycott would not destroy them. "Everything is going to be all right," they reportedly told complaining merchants. "Just sit tight and we'll work things out. If a reporter asks how your business is doing, say, 'Just about normal.' " Ed Laslie could certainly help merchants in trouble, at least for a while. The elite's admonition to "sit tight" had history to back it up: previous boycotts had been started but had fizzled after failing to get full black participation. The conservatives portrayed the alternative to resistance as unpalatable. "Do you want to live in a nigger town?" they asked. This question was effective because most white Tuskegeeans shared the elite's racial views even if they had no power to protect or little wealth with which to insulate themselves. Perhaps more important, nearly all whites—the rank-and-file as well as the elite—feared change in general. Changes in race relations worried them most, but other political, economic, and technological developments also threatened their comfortable provincial existence. They liked their little town the way it was.[28]

Whites' racial attitudes were limned in valuable detail by a survey conducted in early 1958. Lewis W. Jones, an Institute sociologist who, like Gomillion, had studied race relations under Charles S. Johnson's tutelage at Fisk University, sought a better understanding of white thinking about the Tuskegee situation for a booklet he was writing for the Anti-Defamation League of B'nai B'rith. Jones designed a questionnaire and hired white graduate students from the University of Alabama to interview ninety-five Tuskegee whites for the Tuskegee Crisis Study.[29]

Like Engelhardt and the conservative elite, most Tuskegee whites viewed the gerrymander as necessary to prevent black political control. It provided a way to avoid the cataclysm that would inevitably follow the election of black officials, several survey respondents said. Many whites assumed that the blacks' aim was political dominance. "The Negroes want complete control and they will do anything to get it," a young housewife said. "They won't be satisfied with anything less—and we won't let them have it." The blacks' ultimate goal, she went on, was "complete integration and the destruction of our way of life."[30]

The boycott resulted from blacks' unwillingness to accept their rightful inferior status, several whites asserted. "The Negro wanted what the white [has] and wanted to be as good as the white," a life-long Tuskegee resident suggested as the cause of the current trouble. Asked whether he believed the crisis could have been avoided, another man answered that the only solution was to make blacks *"not expect to get what they can't have."* A businessman suffering from the boycott bitterly resented the blacks' pursuit of equality. "I have found out," he said, "how mean, stubborn and cruel a Negro can be. They will go to any extreme to get equal with the white. When they get equal with the white, then they will want to be better than the white man."[31]

Many whites placed the source of the trouble far away from Macon County. "Russians and Northern agitators have stirred them up," a businessman who had lived in Tuskegee his entire life explained about local blacks. "Outside agitation" by Communists and the NAACP were frequently cited as the real cause of the protest. Engelhardt had encouraged this view when he announced in July 1957 that Gomillion had been a member of the Southern Negro Youth Congress, a black civil rights organization active in the late 1930s and 1940s. The Youth Congress had made one of Senator Joseph McCarthy's lists of red-tainted organizations. Many whites therefore believed that Gomillion was a Communist and that his presence in Tuskegee explained the current problems. "Get rid of Gomillion," an insurance agent suggested as one remedy for Tuskegee's ills. "We could start [with] hanging Gomillion," a college-educated Methodist housewife answered to the question "What would you like to see done concerning the present situation?" A construction laborer suggested that "the Supreme Court and the Federal Government have caused all the trouble by meddling with the state's rights." Several respondents considered reporters to be outside agitators. A farmer who expressed anger at the Montgomery *Advertiser* and "those sorry" magazines *Life* and *Look* for covering the boycott believed that the protest would end when blacks stopped getting publicity. "They are just like children," he said. "They cry and fret but will soon stop and forget it when they are ignored."[32]

Whites ought to resist the black challenge more resolutely, several respondents said. "Remove *all* Negro agitators from jobs at [the] V.A. Hospital and Tuskegee Institute," a shop owner said, "and the rest will take care of itself." A salesman recommended that whites "withhold all the help we have given [blacks] . . . until they realize which side their bread is buttered on." A Baptist professional man advocated specific kinds of economic coercion. "White people throughout the county should organize and stop their credit—call for debts," he said. "Let them know the county can do without them. If they continue to participate as they are, every tenant worker and all who are dependent on the white will be asked to move."[33]

But others took a more conciliatory posture. Several respondents expressed the need for interracial discussion. Blacks and whites needed to get together and work out the problem "to the best of both races and forget our selfishness," a merchant suggested. "If two groups sit down and talk frankly," another businessman said, "there is no reason why they couldn't iron it out and reach agreement." Someone else suggested that the county commission and the City Council "invite Negro leaders to give their demands and see what should be done."[34]

Other opinions, however, demonstrated why no interracial effort in fact resulted. Asked to explain the absence of interracial discussion about the gerrymander and the boycott, a merchant said simply, "The white people have nothing to give." A farmer said that "the whites feel it is futile while the Negroes' demands remain unreasonable." Several respondents cited pressure from other whites as the major obstacle. "Most people are afraid and don't want to take a stand on either side," a gas station owner said. Not surprisingly, several respondents blamed the blacks for the failure. "Some whites have tried, but the Negroes will not discuss the matter with them," a retired teacher said. Gomillion was responsible for the absence of interracial discussion, the local newspaper editor said, because he insisted first on a meeting with the local governing bodies.[35]

The Negroes were pushing too fast, several persons contended. "I can't see why they're not satisfied to progress in fields in which they are best suited (music, art) until they are ready to participate in other things," a businesswoman said. A store clerk believed that, while a few blacks had made great progress in the previous fifty years, the poverty and ignorance of the majority should preempt all civil rights efforts. "If for the next 20 years they would spend their time, money, and effort uplifting the riff-raff among Negroes instead of trying to force them on us, things would be a lot better," he said. "But they are just going to cause more and more trouble if they keep trying to force them on us." That this man, a store clerk, felt besieged by poor blacks at a time when *all* blacks were boycotting white stores was a telling commentary on some whites' perception of reality.[36]

Several respondents noted with disapproval that the character of race relations in Tuskegee had changed in recent years. "There has been a gradual trend toward friction with the past two Institute presidents," one woman said, referring to Frederick Patterson and his successor, Luther Foster. Indeed, Patterson had departed from the practice of his predecessors by declining to act as arbiter between the black and white communities. The absence of a fatherly Institute president was part of the problem now, a merchant believed. "If B. T. Washington and Wright Campbell were still living," he postulated, "they could have discussed this and they would have settled it and it would never have come up." One widow, a lifelong Tuskegee resident, felt the change in race relations very personally. "My husband, children, and I have been very nice to Negroes—I want them to have good schools and get ahead—but I just don't know what's gotten into them," she said. "We've been friends for so long—We've helped them and they've helped us—but now these outsiders, agitators, and they say Communists, especially Gomillion, have come in." The boycott was "stupid and immature," she said, and it had disturbed an important relationship. "I just can't tell my maid [of twenty-five years] about anything—we can't talk to each other."[37]

A few whites looked more favorably on racial change. Asked for ideas on how to stop the boycott, a young woman with an eighth-grade education replied, "Give Negroes first class citizenship rights." A housewife who had recently moved to Tuskegee thought the boycott was justified. "I can't blame them—I would have wanted to do something too," she said. She accepted future realities that almost all white Tuskegeeans denied. "Integration is going to come sooner or later," she said. "We should spend more time preparing and planning for it instead of arguing." Several other respondents suggested fair voter registration practices, the restoration of the old city limits, and black representation on the City Council as the necessary steps to end the boycott. "The Negro is determined to have voting privileges," a lifelong resident said. "Only a liberalization [of registration policies] would bring back trade." A merchant who had lived in Tuskegee twenty-five years believed that the way to get blacks back to his store was to "give them a fair deal as citizens of Macon County and Tuskegee."[38]

The Crisis Study exposed the contours of white thinking more fully than had ever been done before. Racism pervaded the views of almost all whites; they could not conceive of dealing with blacks on the same basis as whites. Most whites did not include blacks in their conception of democratic government. They imposed a double standard for political behavior: when whites pursued and used power to their own ends, they were merely protecting their interests, but when blacks did the same thing, they were obnoxiously aggressive and selfish. It must be noted, however, that a significant minority of whites recognized this hypocrisy and believed that blacks deserved political rights.

Whites had a general fear of changes in race relations. Any change necessarily meant a loss of power for whites because they now held it all. Many believed that they would lose status if whites relinquished total control; "blacks want what we have" was a common observation, especially among lower- and middle-class whites. Nearly all whites, even the few liberals, believed that blacks were pushing for too much change too quickly. Some perceived that much had already changed, even though whites retained all positions of political power and the institution of segregation remained intact. They were, of course, correct in one sense: Tuskegee the model community—where blacks and whites coexisted harmoniously, at least on the surface of society—was gone. For some, that recognition had come only with the boycott. Forty percent of white respondents in the Crisis Study, nearly all of whom were longtime residents, said that they only recently had become aware of racial conflict in Macon County. The boycott did, indeed, represent a great change to them.

Many whites tended to ignore or misconstrue the realities of the Tuskegee situation. Most were convinced that blacks intended to get complete political control as soon as possible, despite Gomillion's disavowal of that aim. They assumed that Gomillion's goal was total power because their goal was total power. They could not conceive of sharing power; lambs and lions did not lie down together. Most whites believed that the black protest originated outside Tuskegee, though, again, little if anything substantiated that belief. Many assumed that Gomillion was a Communist, despite his constant use of democratic ideas and symbols in publicized speeches.[39]

What accounts for the failure to face reality? The "outside agitator" myth explained the current trouble without disturbing the popular belief that blacks and whites had always lived in perfect harmony in Macon County. If whites acknowledged that the challenge originated in Tuskegee, then they lost the psychic satisfaction derived from believing that their Negroes were, and always had been, happy and well treated. But the myth gained credence only because whites were largely ignorant of blacks. A vast chasm existed between the black and white communities in this town. The leaders of both communities had for many years kept the Institute insulated to avoid conflict. The Jim Crow system reinforced that separation. The voting rights challenge had further alienated blacks and whites since the early 1940s. By 1957 a great gap in understanding separated the races and allowed whites to believe patently false things about blacks. Moreover, the internal habits of the white community encouraged the avoidance of reality. Eighty percent of the Crisis Study respondents said they had not discussed the gerrymander or the boycott in any institutional or organizational setting. Many whites believed that the situation ought to be ignored, not confronted. Thus, white opinion was formed not through the rational exchange of ideas but through rumor, innuendo, and imagination.

But the overwhelming majority of the Crisis Study respondents accepted one reality: never again would Tuskegee be what it was before the gerrymander. The boycott would last forever, several whites predicted. "I'm afraid our town will never prosper again," one longtime resident said. "The relationship [between blacks and whites] will never be the same."[40]

This statement reflected the profound pessimism that white Tuskegeeans felt in early 1958. The boycott had shown no signs of ending. The mass meetings continued each Tuesday night. Many of the smaller retail businesses had failed and others were in a precarious condition. John Patterson's effort to enjoin the TCA had done nothing but antagonize the blacks further; merchants were beginning to see that he had made political hay at their expense. Many whites began to talk of moving away from Tuskegee permanently. A few did soon leave, among them City Council President Buddy Edwards.[41]

That pessimism certainly seemed justified to any conservative who attended the meeting of the Macon County Abolition Committee of the House of Representatives at the State Capitol in Montgomery on February 14, 1958. Gomillion asked to appear before this committee, which was charged with studying Sam Engelhardt's abolition plan. He and William Mitchell were the only blacks present in the crowded committee room. During the two-hour meeting the legislators never offered either man a seat. Gomillion first thanked the committee for the opportunity to speak and then recounted how Tuskegee blacks had followed Booker Washington's admonition to reduce their ignorance and increase their usefulness to society. Blacks had believed that whites were pleased with the progress they had made, only to be humiliated by the gerrymander and the abolition proposal. Blacks did not want to control Tuskegee and Macon County, he assured the committee; they merely desired to share in running them. "There is no good reason why white and Negro citizens in Macon cannot develop a community which would be a model of democratic living," he said. Ever the pedagogue, Gomillion told the legislators, Engelhardt among them, that they would not want to be remembered as the men who destroyed Macon County. "You will want history to record that you helped to build Macon County."[42]

After the statement, committee members subjected Gomillion to a series of hostile questions, most of them designed to elicit from him an admission that a boycott was taking place in Tuskegee. "It was just a transfer of trade," he maintained. Is "race-mixing in schools" a TCA objective? a legislator asked. "Our goal is to strive for democratic living," Gomillion replied. "And democratic living includes race-mixing in schools?" the legislator countered. "Yes, that is one of the ultimate objectives," Gomillion admitted.[43]

That this Negro would come to the State Capitol, stand before a hostile audience, and offer whites guidance on "democratic living" must have amazed and unnerved some conservatives. They surely recognized in Gomillion a man of courage and extraordinary determination, one who would not easily be diverted from his purpose. He was alone reason enough for Macon County's defenders of white power to be pessimistic.

But by 1958 Alabama conservatives had a much greater cause for concern than one black college professor. The previous year the United States Congress had passed a bill that established a commission to investigate violations of blacks' civil rights, especially denials of the right to vote. One of the first places to get the attention of the new federal investigators was Macon County.

8

The Invasion of Injustice

THE TUSKEGEE Civic Association had responded immediately to the introduction of civil rights legislation in Congress in early 1957. Gomillion described the restrictions put on voting in Macon County to the Senate Judiciary Committee in February. On July 30, just a month after the boycott began, William Mitchell appeared at a press conference in Washington with several pro–civil rights senators, among them Hubert Humphrey of Minnesota and Paul Douglas of Illinois, and recounted the difficulty of registering in Tuskegee. He discussed the gerrymander and the plan to abolish Macon County. Congress passed the civil rights bill in August, though by then Senate Majority Leader Lyndon Johnson had arranged a compromise with southern conservatives which removed the bill's strongest provisions, particularly the power to enforce school desegregation. The Civil Rights Act of 1957 established a Civil Rights Division of the Justice Department and gave it authority to prosecute registrars who obstructed blacks' right to vote. But the requirement of a trial by jury largely undermined this prosecutorial power: southern juries, almost always lily-white, were unlikely to convict a white voting registrar of obstructing justice.[1]

The act also established the United States Commission on Civil Rights, which proved to be the most significant feature of the law, especially to Macon Countians. The new commission sent investigators to Alabama in September 1958 to gather information for hearings on voting discrimination. The TCA, which had kept detailed records of registration practices in Macon County since 1951, assembled conclusive evidence of voting discrimination for the investigators. The commission set its first hearing in Montgomery.[2]

The television lights and cameras congested the already crowded fourth-floor courtroom of the federal courthouse on the morning of December 8. Reporters and photographers, witnesses and lawyers, state and federal officials, and a sprinkling of interested parties like Sam Engelhardt gathered for what promised to be a controversial inquiry. Six men, three northerners and three southerners, made up the commission. The northerners were John Hannah, president of Michigan State University and the chairman; Father Theodore Hesburgh, the young president of Notre Dame University; and J. Ernest Wilkins, former assistant secretary of labor and the only black commissioner. The southerners were former governor John S. Battle of Virginia, the commission's most conservative member; former governor Doyle Carlton of Florida; and Robert Storey, the dean of the Southern Methodist University law school. William Mitchell, who had testified against the Macon County registrars in this same courthouse thirteen years earlier, was the first witness. He recounted the practices of the board since 1945, emphasizing its evasions, discrimination, and failures to function. "The increasing demands on the part of Negroes to exercise their constitutional guarantees as American citizens have been met with accelerated determination to deny Negroes ... the opportunity to vote," Mitchell told the commissioners.[3]

The dean of the Tuskegee Institute School of Education followed Mitchell. The holder of a Ph.D. and a Phi Beta Kappa key, William Andrew Hunter testified that on three occasions he had waited all day at the Board of Registrars but was never allowed to make an application. On his fourth try Hunter finally did manage to apply, but the board never notified him of its decision on his application. After Hunter came the Reverend Dr. Daniel Webster Wynn, the Institute chaplain, who had voted in Massachusetts—while studying at Harvard—and in Texas but never was informed by the Macon County board about whether he qualified to vote in Alabama. Next, the Reverend Kenneth L. Buford, the Methodist minister who at the first boycott mass meeting had likened Macon County blacks to the Israelites, told the commission that the board had rejected his application because of a misunderstanding over when he became a "bona fide" resident of the state. Buford had understood his bona fide residency to date from when he completed the two-year residency requirement. The board interpreted bona fide residency, at least in Buford's case, as beginning with the date he moved into the state. When Buford asked to make that minor correction on his application, the registrars refused and told him that he would have to re-apply.[4]

Twenty-three other blacks from Macon County recounted the board's evasions. This incessant repetition of what was in essence the same story apparently affected the commissioners significantly. Father Hesburgh plainly grew more and more sympathetic to the witnesses. He asked Bettye F. Henderson, the wife of the chairman of the Institute's biology department, about the effect of her three failures to register to vote: "Mrs. Henderson, do you ever find any particular embarrassment as the wife of a rather distinguished member of the Tuskegee academic community not to be able to exercise your franchise?" Indeed she did, Mrs. Henderson replied. Hesburgh asked Eugene W. Adams, a professor of veterinary medicine, why the American Revolution had been fought. To free this country from England, Adams replied. Hesburgh wanted a particular answer.

"Do you remember the famous saying?" he asked.

" 'Taxation without representation'—"

" 'is tyranny!' " Hesburgh added.

" 'is tyranny'; yes, sir," Adams agreed.

"You have been paying taxes[?]"

"I have been paying taxes ever since I [was] old enough to," Adams replied, making the point that Hesburgh sought.[5]

The star witness proved to be not one of the learned professors but a Macon County farmer with a sixth-grade education. Hosea Guice had been born and reared near Notasulga. He farmed on shares during the 1920s and 1930s, but aspired to be more than a sharecropper. "I just thought I ought to be beyond sharecropping," he said later. "I . . . always had the desire to buy me some land, a home. I just wanted my life to accumulate that much." In 1942 the Farmers Home Administration financed Guice's purchase of a 120-acre farm near Shorter. The FHA also lent him money to make crops, a credit arrangement that Guice preferred to the crop lien system. "You know how the government is," he explained later. "They just want you to pay back what you owes." Guice thrived as a landowner. Having thus established some independence, he was free in the early 1950s to respond to encouragement from the black county farm extension agent to register to vote.[6]

"I come up to all the requirements that I was asked to come up to," Guice said of his attempt in 1954, "but I never did hear anything from it." Guice believed that he might have made a mistake by not pursuing the matter. "I didn't nurse that first one I made," he told the commissioners in a high-pitched voice that highlighted his

colorful use of language. "I didn't go back to nurse it." He tried
again in January 1956, but Herman Bentley told him he had missed
one question. Try again next month, Bentley had said encourag-
ingly. But the board became inactive with Shack Humphries's resignation at that point, and Guice had no opportunity to register for
the next eighteen months. He had since become discouraged.[7]

Commissioner Robert Storey asked him why he wanted to become a voter. Guice obviously had given the question much
thought. "I have come up to the other requirements to make myself
a citizen," he said. "I would like to be a registered voter; they ought
to give that to me. It's like I want to become a part of the government activity and so forth." Commissioner Ernest Wilkins asked
Hosea Guice why he thought he had not been registered. Again,
Guice had already considered the question carefully. "Well, I have
never been arrested and always has been a law-abiding citizen; to
the best of my opinion has no mental deficiency, and my mind
couldn't fall on nothing but only, since I come up to these other requirements, that I was just a Negro. That's all."[8]

In contrast to Guice's clear and confident testimony were the re-
sponses of Judge Varner, who was the first white Macon Countian
to testify. The judge appeared over the objection of John Patterson,
the attorney general and governor-elect, who had counseled all Alabama registrars and probate judges to ignore subpoenas from the
civil rights commission. Patterson was maintaining the posture of
defiance that had helped to elect him governor. But Varner, now
seventy years old, had apparently decided not to risk a contempt
citation, though questioning by federal officials was obviously distasteful to him. He provided almost no information. He pleaded ignorance of the Board of Registrars' policies and practices, saying
that his only dealing with the board was to keep the list of voters,
and claimed not to know the length of the registrars' term of office.
But when Governor Battle asked whether the registration requirements were applied equally to blacks and whites, Judge Varner replied in the affirmative. At that point Ernest Wilkins demanded:
"How would you know whether or not the same rules were applied
without discrimination if you never saw the records, never saw the
applications, and you were never present in the registration rooms?
How would you know?" Taking offense at the black commissioner's
aggressive questioning, Judge Varner responded, "I think that's a
ridiculous question myself."[9]

Grady Rogers, the sixty-seven-year-old retired rural mail carrier
who had served on the board for most of the past eight years, refused
to testify "on advice of counsel"; his voting records, he explained,

had been subpoenaed by the circuit solicitor. E. P. Livingston, the chairman of the Macon County board, also would not testify. A succession of registrars and judges from several other counties similarly refused to answer questions. They followed the advice of Patterson and the example of the Barbour County circuit judge, George C. Wallace, who had impounded his county's voting records as an act of defiance against the civil rights commission. Wallace believed he had lost the Democratic primary runoff for governor to Patterson the previous June because the attorney general had taken a more defiant posture against racial change. "John Patterson out-nigguhed me," Wallace reportedly said after that election. "I'm not going to be out-nigguhed again." Wallace's challenge to the commission was the first step in his effort to build a reputation as a militant conservative.[10]

The hearings received a mixed reaction from spectators and participants. The *Advertiser* reported that the Macon County blacks had "paraded to the stand like trained soldiers," and that Commissioner Wilkins had done "a superb job of leading the witnesses." The witnesses were "well-coached" by the NAACP, Sam Engelhardt said, adding that some commissioners had come to Montgomery with preconceived ideas. A more realistic assessment came from Governor Battle, who feared that voting officials "have made an error in doing that which appears to be an attempt to cover up their actions" on black registration. "The majority of the members of the next Congress will not be sympathetic to the South, and preventive legislation may be passed, and this hearing may be used in advocacy of that legislation."[11]

Battle wanted his remarks taken as friendly criticism. He explained that his grandfather had been an Alabamian, and a noted one at that. "My constant companion during my boyhood days," Battle told the Alabama officials, was Cullen A. Battle, the Confederate general who in 1870 led Macon County conservatives in their violent retrieval of political power from James Alston and the black Republicans. He was "returning to the house of my fathers," Governor Battle said, and he should be seen as a friend. "None of you white citizens and officials of Alabama believe more strongly than I do in the segregation of the races as the right and proper way of life in the South."[12]

Governor Battle's concern about the impact of the Montgomery hearings proved to be legitimate. Television reports contrasted the black witnesses, especially Hosea Guice, to the recalcitrant white registrars. Although the effect of television news reports on American public opinion was just beginning to be felt, the Army-

McCarthy hearings and the McClellan Committee sessions on racketeering had demonstrated that Americans were influenced by them. In his excellent study of the origins of voting rights legislation, Steven Lawson emphasizes the significance of the news reports on the commission's Montgomery hearings: "Television, which had brought the country an armchair view of demagogues and mobsters, now exposed a number of vicious registrars before the cameras." Although the officials "presented no tangible evidence of wrongdoing," Lawson writes, "their uncooperative behavior aroused suspicion." The analogy of Judge Varner and Grady Rogers—two grandfatherly gentlemen, by most accounts—to Joseph McCarthy and Jimmy Hoffa hardly seems fitting, but the Macon County men had left themselves open to being cast as caricatures of evil by the newsmen. Similarly, Hosea Guice conformed to another caricature: the simple, virtuous, and mistreated southern Negro. The contrast resulted in powerful, if simplistic, drama that suggested to many Americans the need for federal protection of black voting rights.[13]

Controversy over the civil rights commission's investigation continued in the weeks following the hearings. On December 11 Frank M. Johnson, Jr., a federal district judge in Montgomery, ordered six state officials, including the two Macon County registrars, to testify before the commission and to turn over all their voting records. A young but very stern judge who had gained a reputation for impartiality in civil rights cases when he helped to overturn bus segregation in Montgomery in 1956, Johnson warned the officials that failure to comply with his order would result in a jail term. No doubt having foreseen the compliance order, Grady Rogers and E. P. Livingston had resigned from the Macon County board the previous day. "We are no longer members of the Board of Registrars and we have no records to produce—that's that," Livingston said after Johnson's order. "We have nothing in the world to fear about what we have done and we didn't feel like we should be intimidated by the Civil Rights Commission."[14]

George Wallace still refused to give the commission the voting records from Barbour and Bullock counties, but in early January Judge Johnson told Wallace, his law school classmate, that any further defiance would land him in jail. Wallace thereupon secretly gave the records to his grand jury, which in turn passed them on to the commission's investigators. This indirect routing procedure was meant to save face for Wallace, but it only further angered Johnson: he called Wallace to his courtroom for a contempt hearing and announced that the Barbour County judge had pretended to defy the court's order while he actually was helping obtain the records. "This

Booker T. Washington (Courtesy Library of Congress)

*The ambiguous statue of Booker T. Washington on the campus of
Tuskegee University (Courtesy Tuskegee University)*

Charles Gomillion addressing the first mass meeting of the "Trade with Your Friends" campaign, June 1957. (Courtesy Tuskegee Civic Association)

William P. Mitchell (second from right) and Lynwood T. Dorsey (far right) at a Washington press conference in July 1957 in support of civil rights legislation. U.S. senators present are (left to right) Jacob Javits, Thomas Kuchel, and Hubert Humphrey. (Courtesy Tuskegee Civic Association)

William P. Mitchell (far right) testifying before the U.S. Civil Rights Commission in Montgomery, 1958. (Courtesy Tuskegee Civic Association)

Overflow crowd outside a Tuskegee church during the boycott, c. 1957 (Courtesy Tuskegee Civic Association)

Unidentified blacks waiting to attempt to register at a rural store in the fall of 1960. (Courtesy Tuskegee Civic Association)

Judge Frank M. Johnson (Courtesy University of Alabama)

Governor George C. Wallace (Courtesy University of Alabama)

court refuses to allow its authority and dignity to be bent or swayed by such politically generated whirlwinds," Johnson declared.

Wallace left Judge Johnson's courtroom and, ignoring the tongue-lashing he had just received, declared a victory. "These characters from the evil Civil Rights Commission and Justice Department," he told a group of admirers and reporters, "were backed to the wall—they were defied and backed down. It has been apparent they were hunting a way out. This 1959 attempt to have a second Sherman's march to the sea has been stopped in the Cradle of the Confederacy." Such florid rhetoric was evidently calculated to gain Wallace favor with the great majority of white Alabamians who did not want to accept the fact of racial change.[15]

The civil rights commission's investigators examined the Macon County voting records in early January and saw how the board had used the ambiguous registration form to reject black applicants. Fifty-seven of ninety-nine black applicants had made mistakes answering the question about the date of their "bona fide" residency. The board required black applicants to write in the day, month, and year that they began living in the county; an applicant who, for example, put down only "November 1948" was rejected. The form required the applicant to give his name several times; the board failed an applicant who missed any one space for his name, regardless of how many other times he had already provided it. Seventy percent of the black applicants had been required to write out all of Article Two of the United States Constitution, which contains slightly more than one thousand words and usually required seven pages of legal-sized paper to copy. Only twenty-seven percent of white applicants were required to copy that article, and some of these did not complete the writing. Successful white applications contained exactly the same errors marked in rejected black applications. The commission staff also learned that the board's failure to notify blacks of its decision on their applications cut off the possibility of an appeal, which had to be filed within thirty days of the denial.[16]

The Justice Department took these findings and initiated a suit against Grady Rogers and E. P. Livingston in Judge Johnson's court on February 6. Rogers and Livingston had kept down the number of black voters by "racially discriminatory acts and practices," the federal lawyers argued. MacDonald Gallion, the new Alabama attorney general, defended the Macon County registrars, maintaining that the government had no authority to sue Rogers and Livingston because they were no longer registrars. The Civil Rights Act had empowered the Justice Department to sue sitting registrars, but it had not adequately addressed the problem of boards that did not function because the registrars had resigned. A former registrar could only be held responsible for discrimination if the government could prove that he quit either to perpetuate discrimination or to avoid being held responsible for it. Judge Johnson noted that Rogers and Livingston had accepted other governmental positions soon after their resignations—Rogers as a state legislator and Livingston as a county jury commissioner—and, thus, had apparently quit the board "in good faith." They were not answerable to these charges, Johnson ruled.[17]

The judge made it clear, however, that his opinion should not be interpreted as an acceptance of voting discrimination. "Nothing stated in this opinion should be construed to mean that this Court sanctions or will sanction the proposition that registrars are free to resign at will, indiscriminately and in bad faith, and thereby cast off all their responsibilities and obligations as such officers." Johnson explicitly suggested that in civil rights matters the federal government needed the authority to sue the state, whose responsibility it was to provide a functioning board of registrars. "There is no doubt that such authority would be appropriate—and even in certain circumstances necessary—if Congress intended to give full and complete authority to the attorney general to enforce constitutional rights here involved." Johnson was adhering to the letter of the law, but he recognized that his strict constructionism in effect denied Macon County blacks the rights guaranteed by the Fifteenth Amendment.[18]

Johnson had been in a similar situation the previous October when he ruled on the legality of the Tuskegee gerrymander. In August 1958 Gomillion and eleven TCA members had sued Mayor Phillip Lightfoot and the city of Tuskegee, charging that the gerrymander had denied Tuskegee blacks their citizenship rights. In this case, styled *Gomillion v. Lightfoot,* Johnson ruled that he lacked the authority to overturn the gerrymander. "Regardless of the motive of the Legislature of the State of Alabama and regardless of the effect of its actions, insofar as these plaintiffs' right to vote in the municipal elections is concerned, this Court has no authority to declare said Act invalid after measuring it by any yardstick made known by the Constitution of the United States." Johnson was guided by Justice Felix Frankfurter's opinion in the 1946 case *Colegrove v. Green,* in which the Supreme Court declined to overturn another allegedly discriminatory gerrymander. Frankfurter had contended then that the fashioning of boundaries was "a political thicket" that courts ought not to enter. Gomillion understood that precedent dictated Johnson's decision, but he also insisted that the state's right to draw political boundaries should not override a black person's right to vote. "Perhaps the Court does not have the authority to inquire into the motives of the Legislature, but there is no doubt in my mind that it does have the right, and the duty, to inquire into the effects of the actions of the Legislature." The TCA decided to appeal Johnson's decision in order to get another hearing on the effect of the gerrymander.[19]

The federal involvement resulted in another long hiatus in the operation of the Macon County Board of Registrars. Governor Folsom passed up a final opportunity to act on his democratic values: he made no appointments after Livingston and Rogers resigned. John Patterson did not fill the positions for the first six months after he became governor in January 1959. In July, with support gathering in Washington for another civil rights bill, Patterson and the appointing board named three new registrars. But all three resigned before a single board meeting took place, citing fear of legal action against them. New appointments were made four months later, but again the appointees refused the positions. Still other appointments were declined in early 1960. Finally in May 1960, on the eve of passage of a new civil rights law, two staunch Tuskegee conservatives accepted the jobs. By then the absence of a functioning board had increased the possibility of the federal government's taking over the registration process.[20]

The idea of federal voting registrars had taken hold in the TCA during the eighteen months the board was inoperative. The civil rights commission's hearings and the resulting Justice Department suit against the registrars had suggested that the shortest route to black voting rights in Macon County might be through Washington. In June 1959 William Mitchell recommended to Clarence Mitchell, the NAACP's Washington lobbyist, that a provision for federal registrars be included in new civil rights legislation. "As long as the registration process remains in the hands of the local [and] state political hierarchy, Negroes in the South have little chance of realizing any real gains in this area of activity."[21] Charles V. Hamilton, a young Institute political scientist and a new member of the TCA, drafted a bill providing for federal registrars when local boards were inactive. The TCA sent copies of it to thirty-seven liberal senators and congressmen requesting that they introduce it. Representative Adam Clayton Powell, Jr., of New York submitted it to the Congress in August. The TCA's efforts were advanced greatly in September 1959 when the civil rights commission made its first recommendations on voting. The commissioners called the right to vote "the key to all other civil rights" and proposed that federal registrars be appointed to administer state registration laws "until local officials are prepared to register voters without discrimination."[22]

The prospect of more civil rights legislation, and especially of federal registrars, elicited anger and fear from Alabama conservatives. Governor Patterson told a Senate committee considering new civil rights legislation in February 1960 that the civil rights commission's activities had made it impossible to get "responsible people" to serve on the boards of registrars in Macon and other counties. "The responsibility for the break-down of our registration machinery in these counties rests squarely at the doorstep of the federal government," he said. Patterson insisted that unregistered blacks were not content to seek the proper redress in Alabama courts but instead wanted a procedure "whereby Negroes can be herded together and marched in battalion formation to the polling place under the watchful eyes of 'federal registrars.' " He drew the inevitable comparison to Reconstruction: "We have not had anything in the South similar to 'federal registrars' as outlined in these bills since federal troops occupied the South during reconstruction days." One must question the sincerity of Patterson, a man who had played on white Alabamians' fears through most of his brief career in politics, but he no doubt expressed the sentiments of many whites in his state.[23]

An ingenuous expression of conservative anxiety came from Grady Rogers, now representing Macon County in the state legislature. Rogers unloaded his feelings about the proposed civil rights legislation in a letter to George Andrews, the conservative congressman who represented Macon County. Rogers hoped that filibustering southern senators would be able "to stave this thing off." Then he reconsidered his original phrasing. "Stave off nothing—I hope they can beat the Hell out of it. I know it will be a Herculean task but by the living Lord if we keep losing here and there—if we lose this fight as far as the Voter Referee is concerned—we have just about lost all chance we have of keeping the Communist led N.A.A.C.P. from taking over in this section of the state." But Rogers, almost seventy years old, would not accept defeat yet. "Men like you and me," he told Andrews, "are going to fight these unholy Bastards—and I mean Yankee politicians—with all our strengths, all our hearts, and all our Souls, and with every means at our command."[24]

Despite the fear it inspired, the Civil Rights Act of 1960 did not seriously threaten white conservative power. By the time the act was signed into law in May, the Congress had cast aside the TCA's straightforward remedy of federal registrars for places with nonfunctional boards. The act empowered federal judges to appoint a voting referee where a "pattern or practice" of disfranchisement had been proved. The referee would recommend qualified applicants whom the judge could then register. Liberal critics of the bill noted that federally administered registration could come only after the Justice Department had won a voting discrimination suit. It could easily take years to win one case against one board of registrars. Senator Paul Douglas likened the new law to Abraham Lincoln's homeopathic soup—"as thin as soup made out of the shadow of a crow that has starved to death."[25]

Nonetheless, the law did sustain the voting rights struggle in Macon County. A minor provision gave the Justice Department the authority to sue states for denial of voting rights—the power that, the previous year, Judge Johnson had said was needed. The department immediately asked the United States Supreme Court to reinstate its Macon County voting suit. In June the Court ordered Johnson to reopen the case. The new law had given little relief to the mass of disfranchised southern blacks, but it provided the legal authority that would eventually secure voting rights in Macon County. That was fitting: the origins of the new law, one reporter wrote, could be traced directly to the civil rights commission's investigation of voting discrimination there. By making their predicament known to the Congress and the civil rights commission, and by pushing for federal action, Macon County blacks had helped themselves, in the finest Tuskegee tradition, to what would soon be full political rights.[26]

With the threat of federal voting referees now real, John Patterson formed a board of registrars in May 1960. Wheeler Dyson and Charles Donald Scott, the two men who accepted appointments, obstructed black registration as effectively as any previous registrars. They took only one black applicant at a time and required long writing assignments. On July 18, 1960, Dyson made Willie Turner copy Article Two of the Constitution, an exercise that took two hours and eight sheets of legal-sized paper. Dyson then asked Turner whether he had ever been convicted of a felony. Turner replied that he had not, whereupon Dyson told him that even a traffic violation counted as a felony. Again Turner stated that he had no criminal record. "You look like you would steal a loaf of bread," Dyson said.[27]

A new state law facilitated the board's obstructionist tactics. Grady Rogers had pushed through the Alabama legislature in 1959 a bill that increased the number of days the Macon County board could take applications in the county's rural precincts. Previously the board had spent one registration day every other year in each of the nine rural beats in Macon County. Rogers's new law allowed the board to spend twenty of its approximately fifty annual working days in the rural precincts. It prohibited residents of the Tuskegee beat from registering at one of the rural meetings. The law also allowed the board to use twelve days solely for office work and correspondence. The result was that the board met only eighteen times a year at the Macon County Courthouse in Tuskegee, where most blacks applied.[28]

The board meetings in the rural precincts rarely yielded a single black voter. They were held in country stores, which traditionally had served as official meeting places; the Agricultural Adjustment Administration programs had been implemented from country stores, as had public health programs. The stores also were centers of the power that controlled black sharecroppers; merchants and landlords administered the crop lien system in them. To black tenants the store itself represented white authority. Registration in the Shorter precinct in the fall of 1960 was held at Sam Engelhardt's store. Although Engelhardt was known among blacks as a fair merchant and landlord, a black sharecropper certainly would have thought long and hard before entering "Mr. Sam's" store to register to vote. Almost any country store in Macon County warranted a similar trepidation.[29]

The few blacks who did try to register in the rural precincts usually failed. Ben Williams and Herbert Fort went to the store where the board was scheduled to meet on July 5, 1960. Unable to find the registrars, Williams and Fort asked a white man named McCall for their whereabouts. Explaining that the board was at another store nearby, McCall and his wife hitched a ride with the two black men to the new location. Dyson and Scott took applications from the McCalls and then from three other whites who arrived later. Finally, at three-thirty in the afternoon, the board allowed Fort, but not Williams, to apply. A seventy-four-year-old man with a fourth-grade education, Fort copied portions of Article Two until five o'clock, when the board told him that his time had expired. "I asked them could I finish," he later reported, "and they told me it would be next year before they would be back in my precinct."[30]

Such discrimination would not continue much longer. The Justice Department reopened its suit against the Macon County board in October. "I think they're trying to scare us off," Wheeler Dyson said of the Justice Department. "Well, maybe I'm too dumb to get scared. Anyway, I don't plan to quit." He and Scott refused at first to allow the federal lawyers access to the voting records, but finally they obeyed Judge Johnson's order to turn over the files. The Justice

Department came to inspect the records on November 21, which happened to be a registration day on which the TCA had scheduled a "Stand-In for the Right to Vote." Seeing the 644 blacks who had come to "stand-in" at the board, the Justice Department attorneys quickly offered to return another day. Dyson and Scott refused the offer and enjoyed a momentary victory. They closed the board's offices and put on the door a sign for the large assembly of waiting blacks. It read: "No registration today! This office is *invaded* by agents of the '*In*Justice Dept.'"[31]

Recent events at the United States Supreme Court accounted for part of the registrars' truculence. The Court had begun hearing arguments in the case of *Gomillion v. Lightfoot* on October 18. Robert Carter, the NAACP counsel who had represented William Mitchell in the TCA's suit against the Board of Registrars in 1945, told the justices that "this is purely a case of racial discrimination." Alabama Act 140, the gerrymander law, was a deliberate, if indirect, way of denying Tuskegee blacks their voting rights. "Alabama could not openly disfranchise Negroes without violating the Constitution," Carter said. "If it had passed a law that had openly denied Negroes, as such, the right to vote in Tuskegee—there is little question but that this court would strike down that law as unconstitutional. We contend that the same principle applies when the state does things covertly, as it did in Act 140."[32]

"Well, what do you do about Colegrove?" Justice Hugo Black asked, referring to the case of *Colegrove v. Green,* the Court's 1946 decision on which Judge Johnson had based his ruling upholding the gerrymander. "Are you asking us to overrule Colegrove?" No, he was not, Carter replied. He did not think that the Court had to outlaw all gerrymandering, just this one based on racial discrimination. If, however, the justices had to throw out Colegrove to render a favorable decision on this case, then he believed that Colegrove should be overturned. Bernard Taper, who covered the pleadings for *The New Yorker,* observed that "in his endeavor to tiptoe past Colegrove, Carter was suavely assisted" by Justice Felix Frankfurter, who had written the Colegrove opinion. Frankfurter asked Carter a series of questions which elicited from the black lawyer the many ways that the gerrymander discriminated against blacks. Then for the benefit of his fellow justices, Frankfurter summarized Carter's points. Racial discrimination is clearly the real issue here, Frankfurter seemed to suggest.[33]

James J. Carter, a Montgomery lawyer arguing for Mayor Lightfoot and the city of Tuskegee, contended that the gerrymander law simply changed the boundaries of the city of Tuskegee. To decide the case on the basis of the motives of the legislation, the Court would have to ignore decisions going all the way back to Justice John Marshall's ruling in *Fletcher v. Peck,* Carter said. "Some territory has been simply detached from a municipal corporation—and that is all that the law states or that can be read into it." Chief Justice Earl Warren wanted Carter's opinion about whether the results of the law could be examined. "Suppose the results are *in*compatible with the Constitution of the United States?" Unable to contradict the obvious results of the Tuskegee gerrymander, Carter fell back on the Colegrove opinion, in which Frankfurter had warned against the Court's entering the "political thicket" of local boundaries. "This is about as highly political a thing as we can get into."[34]

The Court ruled unanimously for Gomillion on November 15. "While in form this is merely an act redefining metes and bounds," Justice Frankfurter wrote in the opinion, "the inescapable human effect of this essay in geometry and geography is to despoil colored citizens, and only colored citizens, of their theretofore enjoyed voting rights." The alternative was unthinkable. "The opposite conclusion," the justice wrote, "would sanction the achievement by a State of any impairment of voting rights whatever so long as it was cloaked in the garb of the realignment of political subdivisions." The Court sent the case back to Judge Johnson, who in February 1961 ordered the original boundaries of Tuskegee restored.[35]

Gomillion v. Lightfoot was a significant decision in American legal history. Often cited later as an instance when the Court weighed heavily the "inevitable effect" of legislation, the Gomillion decision was a departure from the Court's historic avoidance of the question of legislative motive. Perhaps more important, it set a precedent for the Court's negating a political boundary fixed by a state. In the next four years the Court would make two landmark decisions against malapportioned legislative districts, *Baker v. Carr* (1962) and *Reynolds v. Sims* (1964), which would result in legislative reapportionment that ended the rural dominance of state governments in the South and elsewhere. These "one man, one vote" decisions did not follow directly from *Gomillion,* but the Tuskegee case ushered the Court into the political thicket that the justices had previously avoided. Once there, they stayed.[36]

The climax of federal intervention in Macon County came when Frank Johnson set February 20, 1961, as the hearing date for the Justice Department's voting suit. In early February Johnson called John Doar, an assistant attorney general in the department's Civil Rights Division, to inform him of the trial date. A Republican holdover from the Eisenhower Administration, Doar later speculated that Johnson had been impatient with the lack of progress in civil rights under Eisenhower and that he "intended to find out immediately and directly" whether the new Kennedy Administration would be more aggressive. Johnson had contacted the department because, Doar believed, he "had decided that the executive and judicial branches of the federal government had to work effectively together" if blacks' civil rights were to be guaranteed. Doar had just been told by his new boss, Attorney General Robert F. Kennedy, to find a highly visible case to demonstrate to black citizens that President John Kennedy planned to enforce civil rights laws. When Johnson called, Doar immediately recognized that the Macon County voting suit was the ideal case. He told Johnson that the Justice Department would be ready on February 20.[37]

Doar and an assistant came to Tuskegee just eight days before the trial. William Mitchell immediately formed a staff of TCA members to help Doar sort through the registration records that the department had gathered at the courthouse the previous November. Mitchell gave Doar full access to the TCA's files. Doar and his assistant interviewed potential black witnesses, and he dispatched FBI agents to question successful white voter applicants who he suspected had not met the literacy requirements imposed on blacks. "There was romance in the records," Doar wrote later, referring to the perfectly consistent pattern of discrimination he found.[38]

Doar and his assistants called dozens of black witnesses who described the board's discrimination. White witnesses confirmed that they had received favored treatment. Maybelle S. Hickman testified that Grady Rogers registered her at her home in 1957. "I ain't never been to school and I can't read or write," Hickman said, explaining that she made "a little crossmark" on the application filled out by her daughter-in-law. The Justice Department's attorneys submitted thousands of documents supporting the witnesses' claims, many of which it had taken from the TCA's files. The state put up a weak defense; no registrar willingly testified in his own behalf. Determined to have some answers, Judge Johnson called several registrars as *his* witnesses. After three days he had heard enough.[39]

On March 17 he issued a short opinion and a long, sweeping decree. The Macon County registrars had "deliberately engaged in acts and practices designed to discriminate against qualified Negroes," Johnson wrote. He found six ways that the board had enforced "a double standard" in its policies: by accepting applications from whites before taking any black applications; by giving assistance to whites but not to blacks; by requiring more stringent reading and writing requirements from blacks; by failing black ap-

plicants for "technical and inconsequential" errors which it tolerated from whites; by not notifying blacks of its decision on their applications, when, on the other hand, it always informed whites
immediately that they had passed; and by not providing registration
opportunities for all blacks, which, of course, it did for whites. Johnson leveled his harshest criticism at Wheeler Dyson and Charles
Donald Scott, who had offered only "puny excuses" for their slow-
down in 1960 while a great backlog of black registrants waited for
the chance to become voters. Their belligerence no doubt accounted
in part for Johnson's strict, far-reaching decree.[40]

He ordered the board to register immediately sixty-four Macon
County blacks, including the Reverend Kenneth Buford, Hosea
Guice, and most of the others who had testified at the civil rights
commission's hearings in 1958. He directed the registrars to meet at
least two days a month in the Tuskegee precinct, to stay in session
from nine o'clock in the morning until five o'clock in the afternoon,
and to examine six applicants at a time. The board could use a writing test of no more than fifty words. He gave detailed directions for
establishing a numbered appearance schedule for applicants, an
effort to stop the endless, and until now hopeless, waiting at the
board's offices. Johnson ordered the board to inform applicants of its
decision within twenty days and to provide specific reasons for failure. He instructed the registrars to submit to him a full report of
their activities each month. He denied "for the time being" the Justice Department's request for a federal referee, but he said he would
not hesitate to name one if the board did not follow his orders.[41]

Johnson had given Macon County blacks "positive relief," rather
than simply ordering an end to voting discrimination. "I promul-
gated what they call the freezing doctrine," he told a biographer
later. "They had relaxed standards for whites, and I outlined those
relaxed standards and ordered them applied to blacks as well." The
new guidelines would not apply forever, Johnson added, but they
would be in force until Macon County had "eliminated the effects of
past discriminatory practices."[42]

Judge Johnson's order was "stronger and more specific than we
had expected," William Mitchell said. "We had not even thought of
such an all-inclusive decree." Governor Patterson called the decision
an "unwarranted and unconstitutional encroachment" on state
power. Sam Engelhardt saw dire consequences from it: whites would
either exit en masse from Macon County or "submit to Negro rule
and await a situation comparable to the Congo, with local Lu-
mumbas coming forward in ever increasing numbers."[43]

Although characteristically outrageous, Engelhardt's analogy suggested the fear that the decision aroused among most white Macon Countians. They had reason to be afraid, the editor of the Montgomery *Advertiser* pointed out two days after Johnson's decision. The Institute and the veterans hospital had brought to Macon County "a great concentration of assertive Negroes entirely qualified under the laws of Alabama to vote." Their presence had created "apprehensions" among white conservatives, which in turn led to the undemocratic practices Judge Johnson had just assailed. Macon County conservatives, the editor declared, had inadvertently brought this trouble on themselves. "The whites, some of whose forebears made possible the establishment of Tuskegee Institute, fear—and not without logic—a future Negro government." To suggest the irony of the conservatives' situation, he borrowed an image from the Old Testament prophet Hosea, who blamed the Israelites' breaking of the covenant for their crop failures. "They sowed to the wind and now reap the whirlwind," the editor concluded. He might have used the metaphor to apply the prophet's moral lesson: whites were reaping a whirlwind of conflict that four generations of exploitation and discrimination had sown.[44]

9

Hardboy Prepares

SOON AFTER John Patterson appointed him state highway director in 1959, Sam Engelhardt gave a talk to the Tuskegee Rotary Club about the new federal interstate highway that was due to pass through northern Macon County. He told the Rotarians that he planned to build an access road to the new highway through the veterans hospital compound. "There were moans and groans in the audience," Engelhardt later reported, as some Rotarians imagined the reaction of local blacks to this new effort to antagonize them. He knew, of course, that any proposal to use federal highway funds to dismember federal property would be rejected immediately in Washington; his real purpose was to intimidate the racial liberals in the group. Still, the open hostility to the suggestion surprised Engelhardt, who many times in the past decade had applied pressure to whites willing to accommodate black demands. "They were just getting where they were not afraid to speak out," Engelhardt said. With the boycott now two years old, some Tuskegee whites wanted so deeply to improve relations with the local black community that they were finally willing to resist conservative pressure.[1]

The first clear sign of change among whites came in the Tuskegee city election of 1960. Perhaps believing that the removal of blacks from the city had improved their political position, three incumbent city councilmen and Mayor Phillip Lightfoot stood for reelection. Buddy Edwards and another incumbent councilman did not run, both having moved from Tuskegee. The results were startling, marking the beginning of a new era. Three of the four incumbents were defeated. Only Foy Thompson, a councilman who had disavowed the gerrymander, was reelected. The new men were not connected with the conservative elite. Replacing Lightfoot as mayor was Howard Rutherford, a lumber mill manager. L. M. Gregg, a laundry owner who had come to Tuskegee to work at the airfield during World War II, and Johnnie L. Sides, an insurance agent who had lived in Tuskegee only fifteen years, were elected to the council. The other new councilmen, James Braswell and Roy Corbitt, were longtime residents of Tuskegee, but they did not belong to the economic and social class of Lightfoot and Edwards. "They want to get their own kind in there now," Mayor Lightfoot said of the lower- and middle-class whites who had voted for Rutherford. He might have added that, in their zeal to keep power from blacks, the conservatives had lost political control of the town.[2]

The new city government took a more conciliatory posture toward local blacks than the previous administration, which had refused to talk about problems with black leaders. Rutherford and the council met with the TCA. Gomillion was impressed in early 1961 with Rutherford's willingness to listen to the TCA's positions. The council appropriated money for building a swimming pool for black children. It oversaw the construction of Tuskegee's first public housing project. The new government wanted a return of harmony, Foy Thompson, the council president, said later. In 1961 and 1962 the effort looked successful. The boycott, which had been highly effective for nearly four years, began to lose much of its force. Although the TCA did not call off the boycott, it urged blacks to decide for themselves about shopping in Tuskegee; Gomillion and other TCA members wanted to see tangible examples of whites' willingness to share power before they actively encouraged blacks to return to Tuskegee stores. Most blacks, though not all, gradually began shopping in downtown Tuskegee once again.[3]

Several white liberals started to meet in small groups with the TCA leadership in 1961. The whites who participated regularly in these interracial meetings included Henry Neill Segrest; Sheriff Preston Hornsby; J. T. Daniel, a clothing merchant; and J. Allan Parker, president of the Alabama Exchange Bank. Other whites joined the group from time to time. Meetings were held in the offices of the various participants, in black churches, and at Tuskegee Institute. Discussions generally focused on what the black and white communitiess were thinking at the time and on what might improve race relations in Tuskegee. The rapid rise in the number of black voters after Judge Johnson's decree led to discussions about how to prepare for blacks' holding office. At a meeting in May 1963, the white liberals emphasized the fact that most whites feared the day when blacks would hold a political majority. Allan Parker urged Gomillion and Mitchell to take the initiative "to allay the white community's fears" about the impending loss of power. Sheriff Hornsby believed that better race relations now existed, but Parker cautioned that most whites had not yet accepted the idea of racial integration. William Mitchell pointed out that no blacks had been appointed to work at the polls during elections. Hornsby promised to rectify that situation. At the close of the meeting the group agreed to enlarge itself and to seek official sanction.[4]

The interracial group tried to bridge the great gulf between the black and white communities. Very little communication had existed for the past two decades and, consequently, blacks and whites were ignorant of each other in many ways. In the interracial meetings whites gained a sense of the blacks' real goals and talked with other whites who wanted Tuskegee to change. By their presence, whites demonstrated their goodwill to the black leadership—an act that they hoped would prevent a future vengeful black government. Gomillion took the whites' commitment to change as evidence of the viability of his design for a thoroughly interracial government. The meetings renewed his hope that Tuskegee would become a model of democratic living. The interracial meetings were signs to both sides that Tuskegee was achieving some harmony.[5]

A major concern of the white liberals was the posture of the Tuskegee *News* on racial matters. They saw the *News* as hindering the white community's acceptance of change. Harold Fisher, the owner and editor of the *News* since the early 1940s, ignored the black community and any events relating to Tuskegee's racial conflicts. An extreme reactionary, Fisher had grown more and more vitriolic in his defense of the status quo since World War II. He frequently lashed out at the national Democratic party, Alabama's "liberal" United States senators Lister Hill and John Sparkman, northern agitators, and the federal government. The nation's highest tribunal drove him to a singular nastiness. "There is nothing wrong with the Supreme Court that a firing squad can't cure," he wrote in 1959. After four black girls were killed in a church bombing in Birmingham in September 1963, Fisher wrote that the Supreme Court justices "have wanted violence, they have openly asked for it and they have gotten it." In an editorial the same year he responded to his question "Who is our enemy?" with an attempt at satire: "Johnitka Kennechev."[6]

Allan Parker and Robert Miller, a young Presbyterian minister, moved in early 1963 to rid Tuskegee of Fisher's pen by asking Neil

O. Davis, the editor of the *Lee County Bulletin* in nearby Auburn, to buy the *News*. Well known in Alabama for his racial liberalism, Davis was acquainted with the Tuskegee situation and Fisher's harsh views. When Parker promised to loan him the necessary money, Davis agreed to try to buy the paper. Fisher, who was ready to abandon the town that he believed was doomed, was receptive to Davis's offer. They settled on sale terms in early 1964, and Davis took over the *News* that autumn. He immediately began reporting on local racial affairs and counseling racial cooperation on his editorial page. He also became part of the interracial group.[7]

Tuskegee's white liberals were a small but diverse group, united at times only by a desire for racial change. Indeed, the defining characteristic of white liberalism in Tuskegee was simply an open acceptance of the need for changes in race relations. One might be a Goldwater Republican in national politics but, because of one's racial views, a liberal on Tuskegee issues. Several merchants favored change largely because of the damage the boycott had done to their businesses. Among them were two clothing store owners, J. T. Daniel and J. Rivers Rush; John Price, a jeweler; Charles Keever and the councilman Johnnie L. Sides, both insurance agents; and Bernard Cohn, a dry goods store owner. All depended on blacks for most of their trade, and all had suffered because of the long boycott. They may also have had other reasons, unrelated to business, for wanting change, but all had an overriding desire for a better business climate in Tuskegee. The need to boost sales was ample reason to make compromises with the black community.[8]

But the liberals in the forefront were driven by more than money. Allan Parker, who emerged as Tuskegee's leading white proponent of change in about 1960, reflected the complexity of motives among some liberals.

Parker had been born in Coffee County in the Wiregrass region of southeastern Alabama, the son of a sharecropper. After graduating from high school, he moved to Montgomery, where he worked at a local bank, attended business college, and earned a law degree at night school. He came to Tuskegee as an officer in the newly formed Alabama Exchange Bank in 1941. Although he was very successful as a banker, Parker never became a part of the social and political elite in Tuskegee. He strongly disapproved of the political atmosphere, especially after he returned from World War II to find that he could not register to vote because the Board of Registrars had resigned to prevent blacks from voting. His reserved manner and his distaste for the small-town social scene, centered on the country club, kept Parker out of Tuskegee's social elite. Even his speech, though grammatically perfect, set him apart: after many years in Tuskegee, his accent retained much of the Wiregrass farmer's twang and evidenced none of the Black Belt aristocrat's mellow, elongated vowels. Indeed, he seemed the perfect antithesis to Tuskegee's other bank president, Edward Cobb Laslie: whereas Laslie was a tall, outgoing, conservative aristocrat with a fondness for good whiskey and good bird dogs, Parker was a short, shy, bespectacled man with a serious demeanor and a strong commitment to racial change.[9]

Parker's religious affiliation further set him apart. Most whites in Tuskegee belonged to one of three churches—Baptist, Methodist, and Presbyterian—each of which occupied an attractive edifice near the town square. These three main churches had minor theological differences and good-natured rivalries among them, but all shared a social conservativism. They provided much more than spiritual comfort: each functioned as a center of social activity, to which members went at least once a week. Tuskegee whites had great loyalty to their churches. One's denominational affiliation was almost as significant as occupation in defining one's identity in Tuskegee. Although the differences among the Baptist, Methodist, and Presbyterian congregations seem insignificant to the outsider, they had great import for individual Baptists, Methodists, and Presbyterians in Tuskegee.[10]

Parker was a member of the Church of Christ, an evangelical sect that stressed the authority of Scripture in all matters. He characterized his congregation as "a minority church"; its building was located symbolically on the town's southern fringe. Besides Parker, it had few of Tuskegee's leading citizens in its flock. Moreover, it allowed black visitors to its services in the 1950s and 1960s, when they were decidedly unwelcome at Tuskegee's other white churches. The Church of Christ's liberal policy on racial matters stemmed from its strict Biblical interpretation. "If a person really has an understanding of the Scriptures," Parker explained later, "and if he tries at all to conform to them, I think that he is going to try . . . to treat other people as he would want to be treated himself."[11]

Parker had begun building bridges to the black community in the late 1940s. He went to the TCA's Brotherhood Sunday observance each February, where he was often the only white Tuskegeean present. Throughout the 1950s he discussed the Tuskegee situation with Gomillion; he was the black leader's only source of information on the white community for most of that time. He advised the TCA about whites who might serve on the Board of Registrars. When he was made president of the bank in 1960, Parker stepped forward to lead the whites who supported change. His business position allowed him the freedom to speak out. "The banking business gave me a more stable position to stand on" than most Tuskegee businessmen had, he later explained. "If a person wants to borrow money, he will put aside his personal feelings in order to get it," Parker said of those whites who disagreed with his racial views but still did business with him. His position also helped other white liberals to support change: a merchant in debt to Parker's bank did not have to worry about losing his credit if he spoke out for change.[12]

In the early 1960s Parker began trying to persuade other whites to accept changes that he believed were inevitable. In June 1963, when racial tensions in Alabama were very high as a result of the Southern Christian Leadership Conference's demonstrations against segregation in Birmingham and Governor George Wallace's threat to stop the desegregation of the University of Alabama, Parker sent two hundred Tuskegee whites the newsletter of the Alabama Council on Human Relations, which called for understanding between blacks and whites. He later sent the same people an editorial by Ralph McGill, the liberal editor of the Atlanta *Constitution*, which also counseled interracial cooperation. Parker's efforts fell on barren ground in many cases, but he set an example of a white Tuskegeean's accepting change and adjusting to it. Other whites who favored change now had a man to follow.[13]

Henry Neill Segrest and Sheriff Preston Hornsby maintained liberal positions that they had established many years earlier. Segrest, the lawyer and former legislator, was a devout Presbyterian who believed in the brotherhood of all men. Like Parker, he remained something of an outsider in Tuskegee. A native of the northern part of Macon County, Segrest had stayed apart from the social elite. He was too liberal politically to be trusted by men like Judge Varner and Edward Laslie. Segrest was joined in his law practice in the early 1960s by his son, Broward, a young man who shared his father's racial views but who, because of his more aggressive personality, was sometimes the more forceful spokesman for their viewpoint.[14]

A shrewd and popular politician, Preston Hornsby had acted on the assumption that black voters determined the outcome of county elections ever since they had provided the margin of his victory over Pat Evans in 1950. Working with blacks for better race relations was both good politics and good human relations for Hornsby. He was especially popular among poor blacks, who appreciated his friendliness and fairness. The son of a small farmer from near Notasulga, he was devoid of the aristocratic outlook common among Tuskegee whites. His mother had taught him to treat everyone kindly, "not to try to beat nobody out of nothing, or beat up nobody." He had cooperated with the TCA leadership and had regularly vouched for black voting applicants. He had strongly, if quietly, objected to the gerrymander. "You're fixing to ruin Macon County and the city of Tuskegee," Hornsby told a city councilman after the gerrymander was announced. He appointed a black deputy in 1963, an act that brought harsh criticism from many whites and led Governor Wallace to remove Hornsby's radio connection with the state highway patrol office. The sheriff applied the lessons of his religious background to the Macon County situation, saying later that he had tried to do only "what was right in the eyes of the Lord and the way everybody should be." His conscience guided him in racial matters. "I don't think I could say my prayers at night if I mistreated a person because he was a black man."[15]

Robert D. Miller came to the Tuskegee Presbyterian Church in 1961 directly from a Virginia seminary and immediately became an outspoken liberal. Miller had inherited liberal views from his parents. His father, Francis Pickens Miller, had made an unsuccessful but notable liberal challenge to the conservative Byrd machine in Virginia when he ran for governor in 1949 against John S. Battle, the later civil rights commission member and grandson of General Cullen Battle. Robert Miller's mother had supported labor organizations and international human rights causes. Miller's theological training reinforced his family's racial liberalism. The many Biblical teachings on brotherhood applied directly to race relations in Tuskegee, Miller believed. On his arrival he had been struck by the complete separation of the black and white communities. The sculpted Confederate soldier standing in the town square looked directly at Miller's church, a block to the north, and "provided a reminder of the focal point of the past" for whites. But nowhere in downtown was there any evidence that this was the home of historic Tuskegee Institute. "A person passing through downtown Tuskegee would not have known that the Institute existed," Miller said later.[16]

The one white woman recognized as a liberal in the early 1960s was Frances Rush, wife of the merchant Rivers Rush. A tall, elegantly pretty woman in her early forties, Frances Hodnett Rush passionately disliked the social elite in Tuskegee. By her own description, she had been "reared on the wrong side of the tracks." Her father operated a small farm, apparently without great success, a few miles out in the country. At school in Tuskegee, the wealthier "town" children had harassed and ostracized her. "I suffered a great deal at the hands of children who were of a higher social status than myself." She concentrated on being a good student because, she believed, "the only real way I could make a place in the sun for myself was to excel in my studies." She was determined to go to college, despite her father's strong objections, and, with encouragement from a high school English teacher, she did go to a state teacher's college in 1939. Deeply alienated from Tuskegee, and to some extent from her family, Frances Hodnett vowed not to return home. "I simply did not belong. I was a person outside and alone."[17]

In the late 1940s, however, she was compelled to come back to care for her ailing mother. However much she feared being trapped in Tuskegee, her mother's extended illness kept her there, and, while working in a temporary job, she met and married Rush, a widower and the proprietor of a local clothing store. Her marriage meant that she stayed in Tuskegee and witnessed its growing racial tensions in the 1950s. Her sympathies lay entirely with the blacks. "I knew the feeling of being considered less than somebody else," she later explained. As an active Methodist, moreover, she believed that Christian ethics mandated better treatment for blacks than they were receiving in Tuskegee. Like most of Tuskegee's white liberals, she had not acted openly on her beliefs in the 1950s, but in the 1960s she would demonstrate her commitment to change.[18]

Two strands connected these five white liberals. First, each stood outside the town's conservative establishment. Although they all lived in Tuskegee and were all relatively well-to-do, they consciously remained apart from the elite. Each had grown up elsewhere, though in the cases of Segrest, Hornsby, and Rush the distance from town was only a few miles. Nonetheless, even this distance was significant, because birth into the town elite apparently made a break with conservative orthodoxy very nearly impossible. The liberals had diverse reasons for staying out of the mainstream. Frances Rush's nonconformity stemmed from a strong psychological aversion to the upper class. To Preston Hornsby, association with the conservative establishment was politically unwise. Both Henry Neill Segrest and Allan Parker were laconic men with little desire to hobnob with Tuskegee's socially and politically prominent people. Robert Miller came from a family that was self-consciously liberal.

Second, each put race relations in Tuskegee in the context of Christian teachings on brotherhood. All five believed that white Tuskegeeans should heed the Biblical admonitions to be their brother's keeper and to treat others as they themselves would wish to be treated. This set them apart from other whites, most of whom read the same Scripture but did not apply the same lessons. Racist beliefs prevented many of those whites from extending Christian morality to blacks. Others simply lacked the independence of mind to do what they knew was right. To a very large extent, the ability to act on Christian values was based on freedom from community pressure. Because they were outsiders, Allan Parker, Henry Neill Segrest, Preston Hornsby, Robert Miller, and Frances Rush could seek Christian brotherhood in Tuskegee.

The first concern of Tuskegee's white liberals in 1961 and 1962 was to prepare Macon County for the full participation of blacks in politics. Judge Johnson's decree in March 1961 resulted in a steady growth in the number of black voters, though Wheeler Dyson, the obstructionist registrar, again had tried to slow down the process a few months after the order. He began asking black women applicants whether they had children born out of wedlock. Justice Department attorneys immediately asked Johnson to reiterate his decree to the Macon County board, noting that failure to enforce compliance would prevent many blacks from participating in the Democratic primary in May 1962. "I have leaned over backward to avoid appointing federal voting referees for Macon County," Johnson said, but vowed to do just that if Macon County and the state of Alabama did not begin immediately to cooperate with him. John Patterson quickly named two new registrars, including John Henderson, a young white farmer who greatly accelerated the registration process. At meetings in early 1962 the board accepted as many as one hundred applications in a single day. Fourteen hundred new black voters had been added to the rolls by the time of the primary, more than doubling black voting strength. Black voters rewarded Henderson for his cooperative behavior as a registrar by giving him the margin of victory in his race for county commissioner. All candidates endorsed by the Macon County Democratic Club, the TCA's political arm, were successful.[19]

The number of black voters continued to climb until it reached three thousand in the summer of 1963, almost equaling the number of white voters. William Mitchell estimated that six thousand voting-age blacks remained unregistered. Those six thousand, he believed, might be even more difficult to register than the first three thousand had been. Illiteracy, apathy, and fear of economic coercion among the thousands of poor rural people in the county promised to make further registration an arduous task. Still, the steady growth of voters since Johnson's order suggested to many whites in Macon County that a black political majority was an impending reality. They believed that within months blacks would occupy political office.[20]

But it was school desegregation, not black officeholding, that proved to be the first major transformation in race relations in

Macon County. In the fall of 1962 Detroit Lee, the VA employee who had helped to found the local NAACP chapter in 1944, asked the TCA to support a desegregation suit against the Macon County Board of Education. Lee knew that Tuskegee High was the best local high school, in part because the presence of the VA hospital qualified the school system to receive federal funds to offset the impact of federal employees on the schools. He wanted his children to benefit fully from the federal "impact" funds when they entered high school. In 1956, Lee had asked the TCA to support a desegregation suit on behalf of his oldest son but had been turned down, with Gomillion explaining that the voting issue then took precedence as the organization's top priority. Now, however, Johnson's voting decree had all but settled the voting issue and the TCA leadership decided in the fall of 1962 to pay the legal expenses for a suit on behalf of Lee's younger son Anthony and fifteen other black children.[21]

Fred D. Gray, the TCA's attorney, filed the suit styled *Lee v. Macon* in Judge Johnson's court in January 1963. In July, when Gray asked Johnson to order the Macon County Board of Education to submit a desegregation plan, Johnson made the Justice Department a party to the suit. Suspecting that Governor Wallace might try to obstruct a desegregation order, Johnson put the department squarely on the side of the plaintiffs. A few weeks earlier Wallace had made a great show of "standing in the door" at the University of Alabama to deny, momentarily, the entrance of two black students. Johnson no doubt suspected that the governor might attempt to stop other desegregation efforts, and he wanted to have the Justice Department nearby to help thwart Wallace.[22]

The stand in the door at the university may have influenced the timing of the Tuskegee desegregation order. The Kennedy Administration did not want Wallace even to appear to be the victor in any showdown over federal and state power. Johnson, who had stopped Wallace's attempt at defiance over voting records in 1959, was equally determined that Wallace not prevent or stall further the desegregation of schools. Moreover, both the Justice Department and Johnson clearly recognized the need for immediate examples of school desegregation to show Wallace and his followers where power ultimately rested. Pending school desegregation suits in Tuskegee, Birmingham, Mobile, and Huntsville offered opportunities to demonstrate immediately and unequivocally that federal authority would prevail. On August 13 Johnson ordered the Macon County board to desegregate Tuskegee High School when it opened on the first Monday in September. The board was to present him with a desegregation plan for the whole school system in December. In what seemed like lightning speed to Tuskegee blacks, the white schools had been opened to them.[23]

The sudden reality of desegregated schools in Tuskegee confounded the popular belief among many whites that integrated education would not come for many years. Indeed, in the nine years since the *Brown* decision, no black child in Alabama had attended a public school with any white child. Public officials encouraged whites to believe that desegregation would not happen. Wallace had vowed throughout his campaign for governor in 1962 to stop any attempt at school desegregation "even to the point of standing in the schoolhouse door." When he was inaugurated in January 1963, Wallace spoke his famous words of defiance: "In the name of the greatest people that have ever trod this earth, I draw the line in the dust and toss the gauntlet before the feet of tyranny, and I say, Segregation now! Segregation tomorrow! Segregation forever!" To the federal government, he said, "we give the word of a race of honor that we will tolerate [your] boot on our face no longer." To advance his own political fortunes, Wallace exploited the futile hope of many white Alabamians that federal power could be defied and racial change stopped. He had seen John Patterson successfully use this cynical strategy in the mid- and late 1950s, and now he intended to do Patterson one better.[24]

Some whites in Tuskegee had believed that Macon County's racial composition would somehow prevent a school desegregation effort. The high ratio of blacks to whites, they reasoned, would mean that white children would be engulfed by blacks, a situation that seemed to them obviously unworkable and unacceptable. Whites believed that black public schools in Macon County were better than black schools in other counties; hence, a greater incentive for desegregation would exist elsewhere. Tuskegee Institute's partial dependence on state funding would make black leaders reluctant to support school desegregation, some whites reckoned, though the history of the voting struggle belied such reasoning. Finally, there was the natural human tendency to believe that a change so fundamental—indeed, for many, so catastrophic—was something that happened elsewhere, to other people, but not to oneself.[25]

Anticipating Judge Johnson's order, the white liberals began working in the late spring of 1963 to implement peaceful desegregation. Ennis Sellers, the local Methodist minister, accepted the presidency of the Tuskegee High Parent Teachers Association in May in order to have a supporter of desegregation in that key position. Sellers and other liberals were hardly happy about the prospect of school desegregation, but they were convinced of its inevitability.

"It's a dose we don't like," the liberals explained to white Tuskegeeans, "but let's go ahead and make the best of it." The liberals elicited a promise of cooperation from the Tuskegee City Council. Riley Lumpkin, a young physician who had recently been appointed to the council, encouraged the city fathers to support the desegregation effort. After Johnson made his order, the school board agreed not to appeal. They too would cooperate.[26]

C. A. "Hardboy" Pruitt, the superintendent of schools, worked hardest for compliance, despite his previous objections to desegregation. "Personally, I feel the majority of Negroes in Macon County do not want integration any more than white people," Pruitt had said in response to a desegregation petition in 1955. "I hope the fine relations which have existed between the races in Macon County will not be destroyed by a few hotheads of both races." But now Pruitt, a former football player at Alabama Polytechnic Institute and coach at Notasulga High School, began a personal campaign for acceptance of desegregation. He lobbied with local merchants and ministers, encouraging them to use their influence for peaceful acceptance of the order. He spoke before the Civitan and Rotary clubs, making a similar plea. He prevailed on the Tuskegee High football coach to encourage his athletes, the school's most influential students, to cooperate with the desegregation process. A stocky, white-haired man in his mid-sixties, Pruitt personally went to the Tuskegee High Student Council and asked for its support. The purpose of his efforts, he would later explain, was "to do all that I could to bring about mature thinking in the community, and to . . . carry out this Court order without any trouble."[27]

Judge Johnson had ordered the Macon board to desegregate Tuskegee High through the use of the Alabama Pupil Placement Law, a 1955 antidesegregation statute which gave local boards of education the power to decide where each student in their jurisdiction should be assigned. The board asked for applications for transfer from local black students. Forty-eight applied. Each applicant was given a battery of achievement and personality tests. A Justice Department official was consulted on the applicants' personal qualities and scholastic ability and on the number of applicants to be accepted. On August 29 the board voted unanimously to transfer thirteen black students, Detroit Lee's son Anthony among them, to Tuskegee High. That same day the board met with Mayor Rutherford and four city councilmen and discussed the potential for danger when the black children entered the school the following Monday, September 2. "Our local police and sheriff's department will be adequate," Pruitt said after the meeting. "I think this will be done without any trouble." Sheriff Hornsby had already stated publicly that he expected no trouble when the school opened. City Council President Foy Thompson was, however, more tentative. "We are hopeful [that there will be no trouble], but we don't know."[28]

A meeting of the PTA at Tuskegee High on the evening of August 29 did foreshadow trouble, however. "An unfortunate affair," Erwing W. Wadsworth, the Tuskegee High principal, would later say of this meeting, which was called to inform parents about the desegregation effort. The liberals also hoped that it would defuse any opposition to their plans. Four hundred whites crowded into the high school auditorium. The unusually high attendance revealed the degree of concern over what was about to happen. Ennis Sellers began the meeting by asking the school board president to explain how the desegregation order had evolved. Harry Raymon, a local lawyer, recounted the development of the suit and gave the details of Judge Johnson's order. Superintendent Pruitt then explained how the thirteen black students had been chosen, noting that a representative of the Justice Department had conferred with the board on each selection. Wadsworth told the group that all white students would receive instructions about proper behavior before the black students were brought to Tuskegee High the following Monday morning.[29]

Sellers then opened the meeting for discussion, but announced that he would allow only teachers and parents of students at Tuskegee High to speak. Each speaker was to give his name and the names of his children. Tension surfaced immediately. Woodrow Ruff, a cashier at the local state-run liquor store, suggested that Governor Wallace be asked to intervene to stop this integration. Why don't we postpone the opening of school for a week to see whether the integration can be stopped? he asked. David Jenkins, a Tuskegee accountant, rose to say that he and his wife had already been to see Wallace to discuss the Tuskegee school situation. The governor had told them that they were the only parents of Tuskegee schoolchildren who had come to see him, Jenkins said. Wallace offered to provide transportation for white students to other schools or to call a special session of the legislature to have Macon County's public schools closed. Mrs. Jenkins seconded Ruff's suggestion that the opening of school be postponed a week to give Wallace time to act.[30]

Several persons, including John Henderson, the county commissioner, objected angrily to the idea of postponing the opening of school and called for support of the board's position. John T. Morgan, a young salesman, then accused the board of cowering before the federal government. Why have you ignored Governor Wallace?

he demanded. Superintendent Pruitt replied that he had met with the governor and listened to his objections to the board's position. The fact remained, however, that Wallace did not have the authority to block a federal judge's order. Mrs. Willie Jo Flurry said that the school integration was "cut and dried," that the Negroes were going to attend the school. She pleaded: can't something be done?[31]

Real damage to the cause of compliance was done when a man named Hugh Adams took the floor in defiance of Sellers's ground rules. Adams explained that he lived in Montgomery and was assistant director of the State Building Commission. He announced that "Montgomery," meaning the state government, had a plan for resolving the Macon County situation. If the schools are integrated, Adams suggested, the state plans to close them and organize a private school system. Adams had said that he was a member of the Montgomery County Private School Commission, which had sent investigators to Prince Edward County, Virginia, where a private, segregated school system had been flourishing for several years. He advised the Tuskegee audience to postpone the opening of the school for a week, until the groundwork for a private system could be laid. If anyone in Tuskegee wanted an audience with the governor to discuss such a plan, Adams said, he could arrange it.[32]

Adams's plan drew immediate fire. State Representative Andrew Cooper told the group that if anyone wanted to talk to Governor Wallace, he would be the one to arrange it. City Councilman Riley Lumpkin said that Wallace "had never done anything for Macon County and [there] was no cause to believe that he would [now]." There was actually very little Wallace could do, Allan Parker added. To support his contention, Parker recited some recent history. Governor Orval Faubus of Arkansas had defied the United States Supreme Court in 1957, but the black children in Little Rock had ended up in that school. Governor Ross Barnett of Mississippi had challenged the federal government in the fall of 1962, less than a year before. Two people had been killed, a university campus was severely damaged, a former U.S. Army general was sent to an insane asylum, but James Meredith still went to school at Ole Miss. Meredith had gotten his diploma the previous week, Parker noted. Governor Wallace had stood in the door in Tuscaloosa in June, in open defiance of the federal government, and had delayed the desegregation of the University of Alabama for all of three hours. Wallace could, Parker suggested, stand in the door at Tuskegee High long enough for federal troops to get there from Fort Benning in Columbus, Georgia, fifty miles away. The troops would be there in about two hours, Parker reckoned. He closed his remarks by praising the school board and calling for compliance with the order.[33]

Frank Bufford, a postal worker, expressed what apparently was a deep-seated sentiment among many whites in Macon County. White people, Bufford said, had to take a stand against integration. The situation in the country was growing steadily worse. Communists, the NAACP, and the federal government were on the verge of running over white people. They had to be stopped, he said, though white resistance would probably mean bloodshed. Whites simply could not accept integration, and certainly not what was happening in Tuskegee. Bufford's remarks reflected the feeling among many whites that their institutions, their way of life, and even their families were under siege. Outside powers were trying to force change—indeed, destruction—on them. They felt a defensiveness remarkably similar to what white Alabamians of the 1850s had felt when abolitionists and the Republican Party had attacked the South and the institution of slavery. Like their ancestors, these white Tuskegeeans believed that they had to fight back to try to hold on to control of their society.[34]

Emotions stayed at a high level throughout the two-and-one-half-hour meeting. Some speakers were so upset that they had difficulty talking. In a town that had long suppressed conflict, a deep rift had come into the open. Anxieties about change and a fear of the future were fully exposed, perhaps for the first time. For Tuskegee, where decision-making was traditionally the province of an oligarchy of conservative men, this all-white meeting was perhaps the most democratic exercise in its history. But the new experience was hardly a happy one. The open confrontation of emotions and ideas was a divisive and troubling affair, which, the liberals believed, had been fruitless, if not destructive.[35]

Despite the unsettling meeting, local officials still expected the opening of school on Monday to go smoothly. Judge Johnson had ruled, the school board had complied, and that was that. The persons who had expressed the greatest opposition to desegregation were not local officials. Superintendent Pruitt was confident that the thirteen black students were intelligent and psychologically capable of coping with the difficult situations they were expected to face. The board had secured the full cooperation of the Tuskegee police department and Sheriff Hornsby's office, both of which had made arrangements with law enforcement officials in neighboring towns and counties to be on alert to help if needed. The teachers at Tuskegee High had been consulted on how to handle the situation and all had agreed to cooperate fully. A man whose nickname belied his gentle manner, Hardboy Pruitt went to bed on the Sunday night before the opening of Tuskegee's school year believing that "everything had been done that was possible to . . . open the schools without any disturbance at all. I felt that we would be successful in carrying out the orders of the Court." But very early the next morning Pruitt would experience the futility of all his efforts.[36]

10

The End and
the Beginning

AT DAWN that Monday, an Alabama state trooper knocked on Superintendent Pruitt's door and handed him the governor's Executive Order Number Nine. "There now exist in the State of Alabama," George Wallace had written, "conditions calculated to result in a disruption of the peace and tranquility of this State and to occasion peril to the lives and property of the citizens thereof, this situation resulting from the threat of forced and unwarranted integration of the public schools of this State." Wallace directed the Macon County school board to postpone the opening of Tuskegee High School for one week for "the sole and express purpose of allowing the Governor of the State of Alabama to preserve the peace, maintain domestic tranquility and to protect the lives and property of all citizens of the State of Alabama." The governor has ordered us to keep everyone out of the high school, the trooper told Pruitt.[1]

Ennis Sellers looked out a front window of the Methodist parsonage at 5:30 and saw state troopers arriving at the high school across South Main Street. By 6:30 two hundred state troopers dressed in handsome Confederate-gray uniforms and riot helmets encircled Tuskegee High, a two-story brick building standing on several acres of flat, shaded lawn one block south of the town square. The troopers barricaded the streets running alongside and behind the school. The summer sun heated the campus even in the early morning of September 2, which was Labor Day. The remainder of Tuskegee's white citizens learned of Wallace's action only when they delivered their children to Tuskegee High, though by then reporters, photog-

raphers, and hundreds of spectators had arrived. Ed Bearden, a retired insurance agent, faced the troopers and loudly demanded to
see their boss. "Where's Al Lingo?" he shouted, referring to the state
public safety director who had gained notoriety earlier in the year
for arming troopers with electric cattle prods to use against civil
rights workers in Birmingham. "Tell Al Lingo to get 'em out! Get
your durn troopers out of this place. We want our children to go to
school." The troopers turned away the bus bringing the thirteen
black children to Tuskegee High. "I've heard a lot about state's
rights," Mayor Howard Rutherford exclaimed, "but what about
city's rights?"[2]

Sellers and his wife attempted to take their two children, a third-
grader and a first-grader, through the troopers into the grammar
school, located behind Tuskegee High. The troopers turned Sellers
back and referred him to Lingo. When Sellers, a tall, powerfully
built former football tackle, approached Lingo, ten troopers sur-
rounded the two men. The order said nothing about closing the
grammar school, Sellers told Lingo, but Lingo replied that the
whole system was closed. As Sellers turned away, a trooper trained a
movie camera on him and photographed the young minister for several moments. This blatant effort to intimidate him further angered
Sellers, who then left the trooper barricade. Alice Lee Wadsworth,
the mother of three school-aged children, was outraged at the idea of
the state closing Tuskegee High. She tried to break through the
troopers, pulling her children with her. The troopers repulsed her,
and, trembling, she left the school grounds.[3]

Several white liberals stood outside the trooper barricade and denounced Wallace's action. Broward Segrest, the county solicitor,
told reporters that the county would ask Judge Johnson to order the
troops removed. "This is an invasion of Macon County by the governor, who talks about letting local people solve their problems
but then violates these principles," he said. Robert Miller said he
had hoped that Wallace had meant what he said "when he asked
us to take charge of affairs." Wallace had made a serious mistake,
Allan Parker said. "He has alienated his own supporters. We have
an elected school board. They are reputable people." Parker estimated that ninety percent of the people supported the school board's
compliance. Events would demonstrate, however, that he had
greatly overestimated the number of whites willing to accept desegregation.[4]

Superintendent Pruitt called Richmond Flowers, the Alabama
attorney general, to ask whether Wallace had the authority to block
the desegregation order. Flowers, a political foe of Wallace, drove

immediately to Tuskegee and counseled Pruitt and the school board
to continue their compliance effort. "If federal troops are called into
Alabama," Flowers told reporters, "it is George Wallace's fault, not
mine or the school board's. He knows as well as I do that if they
come, he will back down again as he did at the University of Alabama." The governor dispatched three aides to Tuskegee to try to
persuade the local board to affirm his delaying order, but the board
refused. Ignoring the Tuskegeeans' harsh criticism of him, Wallace
maintained that the school board had been subjected "to the most
intense pressure and intimidation from federal authorities." The
governor accused Flowers of abandoning the local board and of
being the pawn of the Justice Department. Wallace himself was far
away from the Tuskegee turmoil, in Tuscumbia in northern Alabama, where he told a Labor Day audience that "we're going to
preserve our school system just as it is, and not allow a jungle system in Alabama."[5]

Why had Wallace closed Tuskegee High? He understood that
most white Alabamians feared the changes taking place in their society and that they desperately hoped for some means to maintain
the status quo. Wallace nurtured those false hopes—and endeared
himself to many white Alabamians—by posing as the defender of
segregation against an aggressive federal government. For the strategy to succeed fully, he needed to make the federal government use
force to desegregate Alabama's public schools. "I'm gonna make 'em
bring troops into this state," he reportedly told Richmond Flowers.
The image of armed federal troops taking Negroes into white schools
would make powerful propaganda for his political campaigns, Wallace clearly believed. He closed Tuskegee High School, then, to try
to provoke the Kennedy Administration into using federal power to
enforce the desegregation orders. If Tuskegee High had desegregated peacefully, as it apparently was going to, Wallace's strategy
might have foundered: He not only would have failed to elicit a
show of federal power, but would have had to confront an example
of whites' accepting desegregation willingly. The whole posture of
defiance would have been undermined.[6]

Wallace had had prior indications of support for his intervention
in Tuskegee. At least one Tuskegee couple, the David Jenkinses, had
met with him the week before school was to open and asked him to
stop the desegregation. Two ranking officers in the Alabama state
troopers had attended the PTA meeting on August 29 and filed a
long report which clearly encouraged Wallace's intervention. The
troopers emphasized the strength of the opposition to compliance
and noted that two other troopers who worked in the Tuskegee area

"were certain that there would probably be trouble when the school integrated on Monday." Some persons at the meeting were known to the two troopers "to be staunch segregationists . . . [who] would not take it setting [*sic*] down." The suggestion of the possibility of violence gave Wallace, who had defended his schoolhouse-door stand in Tuscaloosa as a strategy to prevent Ku Klux Klan violence, an added rationale to intercede. Although race relations in Tuskegee had never been as happy as some residents wanted to believe, the town had experienced almost none of the ugly racial violence that had surfaced in Birmingham and Montgomery. In all likelihood, the troopers were deliberately telling the governor what he wanted to hear.[7]

Opposition to compliance had grown after Thursday night's PTA meeting, which had given local segregationists an opportunity to identify like-minded persons. A petition asking Wallace to intervene was circulated in Tuskegee over the weekend. The petition would provide Wallace with evidence that Tuskegeeans wanted his intervention. Several other persons apparently contacted the governor and asked him to act. One who did was Perry Motley Wadsworth, a forty-eight-year-old mailman. Mott Wadsworth left an informal discussion of the school situation among several men at the local hotel on Sunday night to call Wallace's office in Montgomery. Worried about the prospect of his children, and especially his daughter Rebecca, going to school with blacks, Wadsworth told a Wallace aide that something had to be done to stop the integration of Tuskegee High School. He was tormented by the disruption taking place in his community and said later that he had sought the solace of liquor more during the days of the school desegregation crisis than at any other time in his life. His concern turned to horror the next morning when he learned that, after Wallace closed the school, his own wife had tried to break through the trooper barricade.[8]

The two hundred troopers remained in Tuskegee on Tuesday to enforce Wallace's order. Also on hand to help keep the students out of Tuskegee High were Sheriff Jim Clark of Selma, ninety miles to the west, and his mounted posse. Clark and the posse would shock millions of Americans in March 1965 with their bloody attack on civil rights marchers on the Edmund Pettus Bridge in Selma. With no teenagers to clutter the school grounds, Clark's men tethered their horses to trees on the campus. Late on Tuesday the trooper contingent was cut to twenty-five, and Clark and his posse went home.[9]

Wallace persuaded school officials in Huntsville and Mobile to delay planned desegregation for that week. Two schools in Birmingham admitted black children without incident on Wednesday, but later that day the home of Arthur Shores, the NAACP attorney, was bombed. A riot of angry blacks then erupted. Fearing more violence, the Birmingham school board closed three schools scheduled to desegregate. Officials in Huntsville decided to go ahead with their desegregation plans, only to have Wallace send troopers to stop them. A "tyrannical use of power," the Huntsville police chief said of Wallace's action. Grover Hall, Jr., the editor of the *Advertiser* and a Wallace supporter, also condemned the governor. "The Advertiser must sorrowfully conclude that, in this instance, its friend has gone wild," he wrote. "Alabama is not a banana republic. It is in no need of an adventurer to ride down upon local authority."[10]

Wallace began to backpedal a bit. He allowed four black children to enter public schools in Huntsville on Monday, September 9. But he intervened again in Tuskegee, Birmingham, and Mobile. A trooper boarded a school bus bearing the thirteen black students to Tuskegee High that morning and passed out a Wallace order denying them entry to the school. The Justice Department quickly asked for and received a restraining order against Wallace. The governor then called out the National Guard to stop the desegregation efforts. President Kennedy immediately federalized the guard and sent it back to the barracks, leaving only local authorities to keep the peace. The president was determined that Wallace not get the show of federal military force he wanted. The next day Tuskegee High and schools in Mobile and Birmingham were desegregated.[11]

The triumph of federal power would be a pyrrhic victory in Tuskegee. During the week that Tuskegee High was closed, a group had begun to organize a private, segregated school. The initial meeting was held at the Veterans of Foreign Wars post the day after Tuskegee High was closed. Frances Wadsworth, sister-in-law of Mott Wadsworth and the group's temporary chairman, tried to correct what she thought was a false impression about the racial views of white Macon Countians. "The picture has been printed all over the country that Macon County is ready to accept integration in their schools," she said, no doubt referring to the recent public statements of Allan Parker, Broward Segrest, and Robert Miller, who was her minister. "There are a lot of people here who do not agree with the statements that have been made." Wadsworth and several other citizens had informed Governor Wallace that, because of "the friction, danger, and ill will generated by the threat of forced public school integration," they were forming a private school. They asked for Wallace's help in invoking a 1957 antisegregation law which allowed school boards to close public schools and use school funds for grants-in-aid to parents who sent their children to private schools. Wallace immediately had promised his support for grant-in-aid requests. A petition asking the Macon County school board to close Tuskegee High was circulated at the meeting.[12]

The plans for a private school influenced what happened when the school finally opened. On Monday, September 9, only 125 of an expected 565 white students appeared. On Tuesday, the day the 13 black students first entered Tuskegee High, 150 whites attended, though most of them arrived late, having waited to see whether any trouble would develop. School officials announced that they expected the number of whites in attendance to rise now that the crisis was over. Their hopes received a blow later that day when the Tuskegee High football team voted to disband. "An overwhelming majority of the Tuskegee football team has voted not to play another game as representative of Tuskegee High School," Wayne McLendon, the team captain, announced. "We take this action because we object to the forced integration of our school." In a state fanatically devoted to football, in a small town where high school games were major community events, the dissolution of the football team was a highly significant development. Governor Wallace quickly wired McLendon his congratulations and offered to provide the necessary equipment should the team decide to reactivate "in conjunction" with the new private school. On Wednesday the number of white students dropped drastically, and by the end of that day all white students had withdrawn from the high school, though most white children stayed in the still-segregated grammar school. Tuskegee High was once again a segregated school.[13]

What accounted for the complete white exodus from the high school? Even liberals like Allan Parker, Henry Neill Segrest, and Preston Hornsby withdrew their children. The great tension surrounding the school opening frightened most parents and raised legitimate questions about whether their children could study and learn at Tuskegee High. Regardless of their political feelings about what had happened, most parents put their children's welfare first. If there was an alternative to exposure to such tension, then most parents opted for it. The pressure among whites to abandon Tuskegee High had mounted each day after the school was closed. Fearing that their friends would be elsewhere, the students themselves began to agitate for withdrawal.[14]

Alternatives to Tuskegee High emerged. Many white students were allowed to transfer to two other, still-segregated high schools in the county. One hundred thirty students went to Shorter High in the western part of Macon County, and thirty-four went to Notasulga's high school. Others went to schools in adjoining counties, and some lived with relatives in distant places. Several students transferred to desegregated high schools in other states. But many simply waited in Tuskegee for the opening of the private school, which, to a growing number of parents, was the best alternative.[15]

On September 12, the day after the last white student withdrew from Tuskegee High, eight hundred persons attended another organizational meeting for the private school at the VFW post. John Fletcher Segrest, the Tuskegee postmaster and a cousin to Henry Neill Segrest, was chosen president of the foundation that would direct the school. An urbane, intelligent man and one of Macon County's few Republicans, John Fletcher Segrest suspected that his fellow Republican Frank Johnson had conspired with the Justice Department to pick Macon County as the site for the first desegregation effort. "If massive integration was going to work," Segrest thought the Justice Department had reasoned, then "Macon County would be the county where it would work." The father of three teenagers, Segrest viewed the number of blacks transferred to the Tuskegee school as dangerously high; no white school in the South had been forced to take *thirteen* blacks. A place like Tuskegee, where whites were in an extreme minority, should be the last place to have so many blacks put in its white school, he felt. Segrest had resolved to resist the government's strategy. He had spent much of World War II in a German prisoner-of-war camp, and that experience helped to prepare him for this challenge. "I didn't have any problem standing up to the Justice Department," Segrest later said. "They didn't scare me. I had stood up to the Germans."[16]

"It will be a tough fight but we have the power and the forces to win this battle," Segrest told the large crowd. Hugh Locke, a Birmingham lawyer who had been active in state prosegregation organizations for many years, was on hand to warn anyone who had any doubts about the evils of school integration. Locke had just returned from Washington, D.C., where he had "studied the school and race issue for several days." He had learned in Washington that "the way to ruin education for both races is to integrate." The negative impact of desegregation could not be exaggerated. "It not only ruins the school but ruins the community," Locke said, and it "is usually followed by migration of the white people from the area."[17]

The organization of the private school, to be called Macon Academy, was swift and successful. An unoccupied mansion directly across the street from Tuskegee High was renovated to serve as Macon Academy's temporary quarters. John Fletcher Segrest, Mac-

Donald Gallion, Mayor Howard Rutherford, and state representative Andrew Cooper—the last two only lately converted to the private school cause—were dispatched to Prince Edward County, Virginia, to investigate the segregationist academies there. On his return, Segrest lauded the dedication and "the pioneer spirit" of the Virginia segregationists and quoted one about the significance of his cause: "He told us he knew how Noah must have felt as he prepared the Ark while the sun was shining."[18]

More than six thousand dollars in donations poured in the first week, and almost twenty-five thousand had been gathered by the end of September. Governor Wallace solicited contributions from state employees for Macon Academy; in October they donated more than two thousand dollars. An advertisement in the Montgomery *Advertiser* appealed for aid: "TUSKEGEE CITIZENS ASK FOR HELP. Our cause is right, our cause is just. . . . We will never surrender our heritage. Join us in the establishment of a private new school. Our high school has been killed by federal fiat." Students washed cars and sold box lunches for the benefit of Macon Academy. The American Legion held a bake sale and a local business organized a barbecue. "Necessity is the mother of invention," one conservative proudly observed.[19]

To many supporters the establishment of the private school was a moral crusade. One woman proclaimed that she would "clean toilets to help keep my blood kin out of an integrated school." Another was equally devoted to the cause but more delicate in her choice of images. "On September 2, it was as though a great trumpet had sounded to awaken us from a long sleep," Frances Woodall wrote to the *Advertiser*. "The majority arose as one and went to work, not just for ourselves but for our neighbors. . . . We are undertaking a big task here in Tuskegee but with everyone putting their shoulder to the wheel and with God's help, we cannot fail."[20]

Sylvia Scott expressed the basic premise of many supporters of the private school: "If God had meant for our children to mix and mingle and go to school together, he would have made us the same color." She believed that Communists were behind the dissatisfaction among Negroes, and that John Kennedy, "our dictator," was trying to change her belief in racial differences. If one examined the motives of those white Tuskegeeans favoring desegregation, she wrote to the *Advertiser*, "you would find not the will to do what they think right, but fear and, in some cases, greed. They fear that their town will be boycotted again. . . . There are those in any situation who can be bought if the price is right." But Sylvia Scott had reason for optimism. "For this I will thank God—we have one of the greatest leaders in the world fighting for us and our beliefs—Gov. George Wallace."[21]

Macon Academy was from its beginning a very important institution to many whites. They saw it as an exercise in preserving cherished values: racial purity, segregation, and white political control. It demonstrated that they would not willingly accept integration without a fight. The building of the school provided nourishment to the egos of people who felt that outside forces—the federal government, the NAACP, and northern politicians—were trying to control their community. Macon Academy showed Gomillion, Frank Johnson, and the Kennedys that whites intended to maintain some authority over their fate. Thus the school provided psychic satisfaction to those who knew that they had lost power and status. We may not control government in Tuskegee much longer, some whites believed, but at least our children do not have to go to school with blacks. It gave whites a means to save face if they stayed in the community: there was a growing feeling among them that Tuskegee was becoming an unfit place for whites to live, but the private school gave them reason to hope that the community would not be altogether hostile to white values and concerns. In future years Macon Academy would be the only thing that held some whites in the county.

By the end of September the school crisis had bitterly divided the Tuskegee white community. Although no whites attended Tuskegee High, a contingent of public-school supporters hoped to reenroll most white children as soon as tensions subsided. They condemned the new private school as another hopeless gesture, like the gerrymander, to try to deny the reality of change in race relations in Macon County. Allan Parker, Preston Hornsby, Henry Neill Segrest, Frances Rush, and several merchants formed the core of the public-school group. But a majority of white Macon Countians supported the private school. This group included some older, wealthy conservatives, who tended not to take leadership roles in the new undertaking, and many younger, middle-class persons who generally managed the private school's affairs. They appeared to view public-school proponents as unprincipled opportunists willing to give up anything to placate the blacks. At bottom, the rift was over whether to accept fundamental changes taking place in their society.[22]

The bitterness was manifested in some overt harassment and much social ostracism. Harry Raymon, the school board chairman, found a cross burned in his yard. Vandals persistently flattened the automobile tires of a Tuskegee High teacher conducting classes for the thirteen black students. Another Tuskegee High teacher, Mrs. William Varner, Jr., received threatening phone calls. After Robert Miller condemned Governor Wallace before television news cameras, he detected some friends and parishioners avoiding him on the street. Allan Parker also noticed that acquaintances sometimes quickly ducked into stores when they saw him approaching on the town square. Some opponents were more straightforward: they yelled "nigger lover!" at Parker, his wife, and his children. Hardboy Pruitt had taught a men's Sunday school class at the Methodist church for nine years but, because of "the things that have been said to me, the things that have been done," he decided to end his affiliation with the church. Erwing Wadsworth, the Tuskegee High principal, also left the Methodist church, and resigned as well from his position as president of the Tuskegee Rotary Club.

The ill will, it should be noted, flowed both ways. Public-school supporters exaggerated the cost of the private school and disparaged its educational quality. The epithet "redneck" was used in the same mean spirit as "nigger lover." Some things done against private-school supporters were "reprehensible," John Fletcher Segrest would say years later.[23]

The division devastated white Tuskegee's social institutions. Both the American Legion and Veterans of Foreign Wars posts became bastions of private-school supporters; Parker, who had been active in both organizations since the war, stopped going to the posts. The women's garden clubs and book clubs experienced the same splits. The social activities of children and teenagers also conformed to the division: the offspring of public-school supporters did not attend the same Coke and slumber parties or participate in the same touch football games as the progeny of private-school supporters. For the many children who did not understand the reasons for the bitterness and division, the split was bewildering and painful. "I think it was worst for the children," Frances Rush, the mother of two, said later.[24]

The school controversy racked many white families. Alice Lee and Mott Wadsworth were a couple in their mid-forties when the school crisis developed. Mott was a rural mailman and Alice Lee a clerk for the city of Tuskegee. They had four children, including a sixteen-year-old daughter in high school and two sons in grammar school. Both Alice Lee and Mott descended from old Macon County families and were firmly attached by birth and experience to their home. Although he had lived virtually his entire life in a county that was four-fifths black, Mott had never known any blacks very well personally. He later cited this fact as part of the basis for his segregationist views. "I just never was thrown with the nigras," he explained.[25]

Mott adamantly opposed school desegregation. He worried primarily about the danger that he believed desegregation presented to Rebecca, his teenaged daughter; the prospect of school integration heightened in Mott deep-seated fears of rape and miscegenation. His family held the same views, though probably even more strongly; his mother was an ardent segregationist, and so were his older brother Tamp and sister-in-law Frances, who became leaders in the private-school movement. Alice Lee's attempt to force her way through the state troopers was not only a violation of his segregationist principles but an embarrassment to him, for she was immediately the talk of Tuskegee. She had been photographed trying to push past the troopers, and, to Mott's horror, that image appeared in newspapers all the way to Japan.[26]

Alice Lee had also spent her whole life in Macon County, but, unlike Mott, she had known many blacks well. She grew up on a plantation four miles from Tuskegee, where her only playmates outside the family were black children; she had cried when she learned that they would not be going to school with her. Her parents and grandmother had taught her always to treat blacks kindly and never "to talk down to them." She would later recall an incident in her childhood which influenced her attitude about race relations. On the way to Sunday school one day her family narrowly averted an automobile collision with a car being driven recklessly by a black man. When Alice Lee's father angrily confronted the man about his dangerous driving, the Negro responded quickly, "My Mama always told me to be kind to other people." Alice later wrote that the man had taught her an important lesson about the virtue of forgiveness and had made her keenly aware of how blacks' existence often depended only on the mercy of whites.[27]

As an adult, Alice Lee became very active in the Tuskegee Presbyterian Church. She helped the Reverend Pat White—a young liberal-minded minister who served the church in the mid-1950s and married her sister—to build a church for the black Presbyterian congregation in Tuskegee. Despite the separate congregations in Tuskegee, Alice Lee believed strongly in the idea of one universal church. In an autobiographical essay written in the mid-1960s she cited St. Paul's letter to the Ephesians, in which he wrote that all nationalities and peoples belonged to the universal church of Christ. "There is one body and one Spirit," Alice Lee quoted the Apostle, "one Lord, one faith, one baptism, one God and Father of us all, who is above all and through all and in all." Alice Lee's religious faith reinforced feelings acquired during childhood about the unity of human experience and helped her to understand why blacks wanted change. She accepted the fact of change with little fear. She had not, however, taken a public position on the coming changes until the morning in 1963 when the school was scheduled to open.[28]

After she was repulsed by the state troopers that morning, Alice Lee went to her office at Tuskegee City Hall. Overwrought by what had happened, she was unable to work. She finally left her desk, went next door to the Presbyterian church, knelt at the altar, and cried and prayed. Robert Miller eventually came in and comforted her. As word of her feelings spread through Tuskegee, Alice Lee began to be harassed. She received abusive telephone calls late at night. Ku Klux Klan leaflets were hung on her front door. She was refused service in a local restaurant. But to her mind, the worst abuse was that aimed at her two young sons. Grown men sitting on the town square shouted "Nigger lover!" at Frank and Howard Wadsworth as they walked home from grammar school.[29]

Alice Lee remained adamant in her commitment to the public school through the weeks of harassment. Mott was equally determined that their daughter not attend Tuskegee High. Both Pat White, her brother-in-law, and Robert Miller tried to mediate the conflict. As a compromise, the Wadsworths sent their daughter to live with White and Alice Lee's sister in Alexander City, Alabama, forty miles away. In another, more permanent compromise, Mott and Alice Lee decided in the next few months to move from Tuskegee to Auburn, twenty miles to the northeast, where their sons could attend a public school that was still all-white. Mott's brother Tamp criticized his decision to leave Tuskegee, and Mott himself had strong misgivings about abandoning his home. But, with his family divided and abused and the high school invaded by blacks, Mott Wadsworth felt that he had to leave Tuskegee to regain some peace and to save his family. For Alice Lee, Tuskegee had become a morally bankrupt town where people allowed fear and hatred to destroy an institution as fundamental as the public school. Her disaffection had been reinforced on November 22 when the news of President Kennedy's assassination elicited cheers from whites in Tuskegee City Hall. In Auburn the next year, the crisis for Mott and Alice Lee simmered down and finally passed. "They loved each other or they would never have made it through that," a longtime Tuskegee resident later observed.[30]

The school conflict created serious problems in the Methodist and Presbyterian churches. At the Methodist church, Ennis Sellers had inherited in 1960 a congregation dispirited by the social and economic turmoil resulting from the boycott. To make matters worse, he found himself at odds with members of his congregation soon after he arrived. The church's finance chairman informed Sellers that he intended to withdraw the church's contribution to World Service, a denominational fund that, he suspected, had supported efforts to end segregation. Sellers vowed to fight to maintain the contribution, which he saw as the church's primary connection to Christians outside Tuskegee. Seeing Sellers's determination, the finance chairman relented.[31]

Sellers opposed the church's three most powerful members—the banker Edward Laslie, the millionaire cotton broker Ernest Bridges, and Howard Lamar, a wealthy farmer and building contractor— over the use of land that the church had inherited. When Sellers refused to accede to the wishes of Bridges, who had a clear conflict of interest with the church over the disposition of the property, the three men withheld their financial support from the church. But Sellers got along well with most of the congregation and enjoyed a successful ministry through his first three years. He added many new members, performed dozens of weddings and funerals, and kept the church on a sound financial basis despite the withdrawal of support.[32]

The school crisis undid much of Sellers's success. His highly visible pro-public-school stand alienated a significant number of his parishioners. His uncompromising stance put him into direct conflict with the segregationists. He had to threaten a church usher with physical violence to prevent the man from locking the church doors—out of fear that a black might try to enter—one Sunday in the midst of the school crisis. When John Fletcher Segrest, a member, asked the church board for permission to use church facilities for the new private school, Sellers, whose consent was necessary according to church rules, flatly refused. Would you agree to its use if the congregation approved? the chairman of the church board asked. "If we had a congregational meeting and everybody there voted to do it," Sellers replied, "I still wouldn't give my permission." He noted the number of public-school teachers in the congregation. "It would split the church right down the middle."[33]

It did lose many of its members, including most of those connected with the public-school system. Attendance at services fell as the division in the community widened. Some private-school backers stopped giving their tithe to the church and started contributing it to Macon Academy. Sellers began to believe in the winter of 1963–64 that the church would lose more members and financial support if he stayed. At last, in June 1964, he asked his superiors in the church hierarchy to transfer him out of Tuskegee. But he left with some misgivings. It was easy, he wrote later that year, " 'to deliver one's conscious' [*sic*] in some spectacular fashion and then 'wipe the dust of that community from your feet.' It is much more difficult to live in a community day in, day out, and year in, year out ... bearing your Christian witness in a less spectacular but more constructive fashion. There are many ordinary persons in Tuskegee doing just this—bearing their witness day by day." The Sunday after Sellers left, the ushers of the Methodist church began locking the front door.[34]

The liberal stance of Robert Miller resulted in similar difficulties at the Presbyterian church. When Miller interviewed for the Presbyterian pastorate in 1961, he asked members of the session, the church's governing body, whether the church had an open-pulpit policy. "What do you mean?" asked Richard Lightfoot, a cotton-gin owner and brother of the former mayor. "Am I free to preach from the Bible?" Miller asked. "If you preach from the Bible, it will be all right," Lightfoot replied. "What if we turn different pages?" Miller inquired further. "As long as you preach from the Bible, it will be okay," Lightfoot answered again. This response persuaded Miller to accept the pulpit of the Tuskegee church.[35]

It became apparent immediately that Miller and his congregation were indeed turning different pages. His work in the interracial group and his outspoken stand for school desegregation alienated many parishioners. Whereas previous ministers had avoided or at best dealt obliquely with racial problems in their sermons, Miller addressed the Tuskegee racial situation directly. He tried to make it impossible for his congregation to separate Christian morality from the town's racial problems. But he encountered great resistance. When Miller cited Scripture in support of a liberal racial position during a session meeting in 1964, Richard Lightfoot slammed his fist onto a table and shouted to Miller, "Leave the *Bible* out of this. Read *The Rise and Fall of the Roman Empire,* and you'll see what's happening around here."[36]

Most members of the Presbyterian church shared Lightfoot's view about mixing race and religion. No more than two dozen church members agreed with Miller, though others liked him personally. Henry Neill and Broward Segrest were his staunchest supporters, and Alice Lee Wadsworth drew similar lessons from the Bible. The Lightfoots, most of the Wadsworths, and some of the large Segrest family disapproved of Miller's stand. When the church session voted in 1963 on whether to allow blacks to attend their services, Miller and Henry Neill Segrest were the only two of eight session members to approve the change. During Miller's tenure, church attendance fell precipitously.[37]

Miller's relationship with his congregation reached a breaking point on Sunday, July 17, 1964. That day two Tuskegee Institute professors, one white and one black, entered the church sanctuary for the morning's service. When Miller and the members of the session were told of the black man's presence, Richard Lightfoot announced that he would "take care of" the situation. Miller responded quickly, "No, there's nothing to take care of." He reminded Lightfoot and the others that, when the vote had been taken the previous year to exclude blacks, Miller had insisted that no one, not even a black, should be ejected from the sanctuary. If you are going to keep blacks out, Miller had said, "you're going to have to stand out on the front steps and keep them out."[38]

The service began quietly, perhaps because some of the congregation had left when they saw the black man enter, and it proceeded uneventfully through the liturgy until all that remained was the sermon and the sacrament of Holy Communion. Miller's sermon recounted the most familiar Old Testament stories of man's failure and sinfulness—Adam's Fall, Cain's murder of Abel, and Jacob's betrayal of Esau. "The story of the Old Testament is the story of man's bringing to an end his possibility and potential," Miller said. But God never ceased offering new beginnings. The young minister made his point lyrically:

> The end and the beginning, the end and the beginning
> In ceaseless cycle they seem to go
> The touch of God and the spoil of man
> The height of creation and the earth laid low.

He began to relate the Biblical history to that moment in Tuskegee. "We have forgotten, like the old Adam, that we are here to serve the God who created us," Miller said. He noted the tendency to judge one's neighbors harshly. Like Cain, "we cannot stand our brother." Holy Communion, which symbolized the rebirth that Christ made possible, offered one more opportunity for a new beginning. "If you intend to lead a new life," Miller said to his congregation, "and are in love and charity with your neighbor, full of sorrow for what you have been, and eagerly seek this new beginning, I invite you to this table." Miller knew that some who were present did not love their neighbors. "But if you do not intend to change your ways, if the old Adam yet will rule you, I forbid you to come at all."[39]

The two elders assigned to pass the communion plates were Henry Neill Segrest and Richard Lightfoot. Miller gave the two men plates of bread and bowed his head to pray. But, remembering the situation, he looked up just as Lightfoot passed by the black man and his white friend without serving them. Miller became very angry. At that moment he happened to look at the communion table nearby. "A piece of bread had fallen out on it, which never had happened," Miller explained later. When Lightfoot and Segrest returned with the bread plates, Miller took Lightfoot's plate and put the spilled piece of bread on it. Then, leaving the elders standing before the altar, he walked from behind it and down the aisle to the pew where the two visitors sat. He served them the single piece of bread, then walked back to his place behind the altar and issued the sacramental wine to Segrest and Lightfoot. Segrest served the two visitors the wine.[40]

Immediately after the service, members of the congregation called for Miller's resignation. He refused to quit; he believed that his message of interracial brotherhood was reaching some of the congregation. Later, however, he began to see that he had lost his effectiveness. He resigned in early 1965 and accepted the pulpit of an interracial church in Florida. His leaving troubled many in the congregation, even some who disliked his racial views. After church on his final Sunday in Tuskegee, Martha Lightfoot, Richard's wife, came to Miller and stood before him in tears. "She knew that the social pressures had taken their toll," he said later.[41]

Almost overlooked by the whites were the thirteen black students attending Tuskegee High in the fall of 1963. Theirs was a strange and lonely existence, but they tried to make the best of it. They had relatively few problems at school, though one of the boys was expelled for allegedly whistling at a white girl. The most difficult part of the experience came after the students returned home each day: they received a constant stream of abusive telephone calls throughout the school year. The white teachers at Tuskegee High found them to be courteous, well behaved, and eager to learn. "I never taught a more co-operative or interested group of students," Mrs. J. C. Akin, a social studies teacher, said. "Lesson assignments and extra reading materials were always completed and handed in on time. . . . They showed a deep appreciation for any and all consideration given them by the teachers." Akin clearly admired the character exhibited by these teenagers. "They did everything to try to prove that they had come to get a better education." Getting an education, however, was no longer the real issue at Tuskegee High.[42]

Governor Wallace again intervened in Macon County in January 1964, acting through the state board of education, a body of nine persons which he appointed. On orders from the state board, the

Macon County system had provided bus transportation for about 150 white students to the still-segregated high schools in Shorter and Notasulga during the fall of 1963. Judge Johnson ordered the local board to cease the practice in December, whereupon Wallace had the students driven to school by state troopers. Apparently seeing the impracticability of this arrangement, Wallace asked the local board to resume bus transportation. The board refused. Then, at Wallace's behest, the state board in late January ordered Tuskegee High closed in accordance with the state's policy of closing schools "where the teacher load is not sufficient to justify paying teachers." It ordered the students at Tuskegee High transferred to other schools "in the Tuskegee area," which meant to the town's other high school, all-black Tuskegee Institute High. It also ordered the Macon board to supply bus transportation for the children attending the Shorter and Notasulga schools.[43]

On February 1 the Macon County board, wearying of its effort to comply, voted to do as the state board had ordered, only to learn that the state was frantically trying to rescind its directive. State attorneys had realized that Wallace had blundered badly. The order to close the school provided incontrovertible evidence that the state board actually controlled education in Alabama. With this evidence, a civil rights lawyer or the Justice Department could ask a federal court to order the state to desegregate every school system in Alabama. Fred Gray, the TCA's attorney, immediately filed an amended complaint asking for a statewide desegregation order. Gray also asked Judge Johnson to prevent the state from resegregating the Macon County schools. On February 3 Johnson postponed a decision on the statewide order but delivered a restraining order directing Wallace, the state board, and the local board not to interfere with the desegregation of the Notasulga and Shorter schools, and then ordered the Macon County board to transfer six of the twelve black students to Shorter High and the other six to Notasulga. According to Wallace, Judge Johnson had thrown a "judicial tantrum" and was "attempting to run this state by usurpation of authority and the threat of bayonets."[44]

On February 5, the day of the scheduled desegregation of the Shorter and Notasulga high schools, tension in Macon County was high. Two nights earlier, crosses had been burned at the homes of three school board members. The previous night a fourth board member's hay barn burned to the ground, destroyed by arson. The six black students who went to Shorter on the morning of February 5 had few problems, but trouble developed at Notasulga. A crowd cursed the students when their bus pulled onto the school grounds. On the scene once again was Jim Clark and his mounted posse from Selma. When the bus stopped, Clark climbed inside and dragged off Vernon Merritt, a professional photographer for the Black Star syndicate who had, unbeknownst to school officials, slipped onto the bus in Tuskegee. Clark threw Merritt to the ground and struck him in the neck and the back with his electric cattle prod, all the while shouting to Merritt, "Don't you strike me! Don't you strike me!" He destroyed Merritt's camera. Merritt later explained that striking Clark "was the last thing I planned to do." Perhaps to their own relief, the six black students were refused entry to the school. James N. "Kayo" Rea, the mayor of Notasulga, was poised defiantly in the school door to prevent their entry. Rea announced that the entry of the six blacks would violate a recently passed city fire ordinance, which limited the school building's occupancy to the number of whites then enrolled.[45]

Judge Johnson quickly labeled Rea's new fire ordinance a ruse and ordered him and other Notasulga officials not to interfere with the desegregation process. The black students entered Notasulga High, and, once again, the white students withdrew. The whites also left Shorter High. Most of the white students from Notasulga and Shorter soon enrolled at Macon Academy, a development that greatly strengthened the private school. John Fletcher Segrest later said that, when Johnson ordered the desegregation of the Shorter and Notasulga schools, "he gave us Macon County." Now all whites in the county were involved in the school crisis.[46]

More lawlessness followed. On the night of April 16 someone defaced the Notasulga school. Painted on its sides was the inscription, "Judge Johnson's and Bobby Kennedy's school." The judge and the attorney general were identified as "Godfathers of all Niggers." The next night the school burned to the ground; state investigators suspected arson and set the loss at $250,000. A few days later, police in Tuskegee arrested two teenaged boys for stealing five thousand dollars' worth of science, music, and athletic equipment from Tuskegee High. The local grand jury failed to indict the two boys, and the police were criticized for making the arrests. Some Tuskegee whites felt that the stolen equipment had been rightfully reclaimed, since their contributions had paid for it. A few persons blamed defiant adults for encouraging such actions, though a reporter found that most whites simply had nothing to say about the disregard of the law.[47]

The events in Macon County did elicit expressions of outrage from observers outside its boundaries. Macon County "has been destroyed on the altar of political demagoguery," said Winton "Red"

Blount, a wealthy Montgomery contractor and former Tuskegee resident who would later serve as postmaster general under President Richard Nixon. "We must not ever let this happen again in the State of Alabama." The editor of the Montgomery *Alabama Journal* blamed the state's intervention for the violence in Macon County. "At least it encouraged defiance, which translated in the feeble minds of violent men does not mean constitutional issues or legal resistance but bombing, barn-burning, and school-burning." The editor pointed out that Wallace's defiance, and particularly the state school board's order to close Tuskegee High, had precisely the opposite effect from what he intended. "If all the attorneys of the NAACP, joined by the entire U.S. Attorney General's staff, had devoted their full time to entrapping Alabama on school desegregation, they could not have been more effective than the State Board of Education and Gov. Wallace. They devised a virtually escape-proof trap for themselves, walked in and waited for Judge Johnson to spring it."[48]

The spring of 1964 was a time of despair for Tuskegee's white liberals. Just months earlier they had had great hopes of bringing peaceful change and communal harmony to Tuskegee. Now all that seemed lost. The desegregation of the schools had failed completely. A year earlier they could hardly have imagined a worse outcome than the total withdrawal of whites from the public schools. The school crisis had resulted in neighbors turning on one another, families dividing bitterly, social institutions becoming battlegrounds over race. Perhaps most disturbing, the school crisis accelerated a tendency among whites, begun during the boycott, to abandon Tuskegee altogether. Families began to pack quickly and move away. Perhaps as many as twenty families joined Alice Lee and Mott Wadsworth in Auburn in 1964. Others moved to Montgomery. Those who stayed viewed the exodus as a sign of their town's decline. For the moment, the liberals focused their anger and frustration on the man they believed had foiled their plans. Removed from the turmoil but still bitter about what happened, Alice Lee Wadsworth wrote privately that George Wallace "has taken away my home, my job, my school, and is well on the way to destroying my church. . . . Someone has to stop the Little Dictator."[49]

Other white Macon Countians—indeed, many of Alice Lee's relatives—took a completely different view of Governor Wallace and recent events: Wallace had helped to save whites from domination by blacks and the federal government. He had assisted greatly in the establishment of Macon Academy, the institution into which whites could put their energy and hopes. Through it, they could resist the forces that were trying to destroy their society, and they could retain some control over their future. But the private school did not solve all the problems they confronted. There would be city, county, and national elections in 1964, and no realistic white conservative in Macon County could look to them with anything but foreboding.

11

Let the Children Lead

THE MACON COUNTY Democratic Club approached the Democratic primary in May 1964 with great anticipation. The TCA leadership had formed the Democratic Club in 1954 to support the unsuccessful candidacy of Jessie P. Guzman for the Board of Education. Ten years of conflict had made club members more realistic about politics than they had been in 1954, but they now had good reason for optimism: blacks composed a majority of voters in the county. Under Gomillion's direction, the Democratic Club had made preparations to see that black voting strength was felt fully in the coming election. It organized the county by precincts and chose men like Hosea Guice of Shorter to lead the voters of the rural beats. It arranged the appointment of blacks to work at the polls, an effort to counter possible intimidation of new voters. It held a series of candidates' forums throughout the county where, for the first time since Reconstruction, white candidates appeared in public to ask for black votes.[1]

The Democratic Club endorsed candidates in seven local races. It recommended three whites, including Sheriff Hornsby, who was running for the probate judgeship (because of poor health, Judge Varner had resigned that office in 1963), and candidates for positions on the county commission and the county school board. The club supported four blacks: William C. Allen, the proprietor of a general store, and William J. Childs, the owner of a service station, received endorsements for justice of the peace, the lowest level of county magistrate; V. A. Edwards, a retired religion professor at the

Institute, for a second seat open on the county commission; and Gomillion for a second position on the Board of Education. These endorsements bore the distinct markings of Gomillion's gradualist,
interracial approach: he wanted blacks to move into officeholding
slowly.[2]

Gomillion chose a gradualist course because he believed that the
Tuskegee example would influence the way other Alabamians and
southerners viewed black political participation. He was determined
not to fulfill conservatives' prediction that Tuskegee would reenact
the worst horror of the Reconstruction myth—a political takeover
by ignorant and unscrupulous blacks. Tuskegee would demonstrate
that blacks and whites could govern a southern community as equal
partners. The Tuskegee model would "encourage whites elsewhere
to be willing to appoint or elect qualified Negroes, even in places
where Negroes were less numerous than in Macon County." Gomillion hoped to show that blacks would not do to whites what had
been done to them. Blacks in Tuskegee would abide by "principles
that we had accused the white power structure of failing to honor in
the past. . . . We were not interested in replacing white demagoguery
with black demagoguery." A black takeover, Gomillion feared,
might inspire spiteful whites, especially outgoing officeholders, to try
to make new black politicians look inept or dishonest. "And then we
would have been saddled with the blame," Gomillion said. Blacks'
lack of experience in government made patience the practical
course. "The truth is we *are* just beginners at this, by virtue of having
been kept on the sidelines so long, and we *do* have much to learn."
Gomillion's strategy prevailed in the primary: all seven local candidates endorsed by the Democratic Club won their races.[3]

The city election on August 11 promised to be even more interesting than the county races had been. Blacks made up only about 900
of the 1,900 city voters—on a strictly racial vote, whites could still
prevail. The Macon County Democratic Club again endorsed an
interracial slate. It picked the incumbent white councilmen L. M.
Gregg and John Sides, who had proved to be friendly and cooperative with black Tuskegee. It endorsed Allan Parker for another
council position and Alton B. Taylor, a white retired army sergeant,
for mayor. The club gave its strongest support to two black council
candidates: Kenneth L. Buford and Stanley Smith. Smith was a
young sociologist who had also been active in the TCA.[4]

The three white council candidates endorsed by the club won in
the first election. Buford and Smith each faced white incumbent
councilmen in the runoff. Black voters defected in large numbers
from Taylor, the club's white mayoral candidate; most of them in-

stead supported Charles Keever, a local white businessman and political liberal who had campaigned vigorously among blacks. Keever
and incumbent mayor Howard Rutherford, whose support for the
private school had damaged his initially good reputation among the
black leadership, were forced into a runoff.[5]

Buford and Smith would probably have won in the first election
except for the presence of other black candidates in their races.
Council candidates supported by the Non-Partisan Voters League
of Macon County, an independent political group formed in early
1964, drew about twenty percent of the black vote. Led by Paul
Puryear, a young Institute political scientist, the Non-Partisan
League supported five black candidates. Unlike the Democratic
Club, which attempted only "to educate" its members about school
candidates and issues, the league put forth a specific platform calling for better city services, more low-income housing, vocational
education for the unemployed, and more federal assistance to city
government. The league geared its concerns to the interests of
lower-income blacks, though its candidates, including Puryear, were
solidly middle class. None, however, had been part of the TCA
leadership.[6]

The Non-Partisan League directly challenged Gomillion's gradualist strategy. Puryear assailed the assumption that blacks' lack of
experience in government necessitated a deliberate entry into politics. That thinking, Puryear wrote to the *Advertiser* a few days after
the election, assumed that blacks were a " 'child-race' unable to
cope with the complexities of modern life." Puryear and a significant minority of Macon County blacks believed that the newly acquired political power should be used to put as many blacks as
possible into positions of authority. Several black citizens had begun
to see themselves as political candidates. Detroit Lee had told the
Democratic Club in early 1964 that he wanted to run for probate
judge that year. "Don't rock the boat, Mr. Lee," Beulah Johnson, a
longtime TCA activist and staunch Gomillion loyalist, had responded, knowing that Gomillion did not believe a black ought to
run for probate judge at this time. "I may turn the damn boat over,"
Lee replied. He soon approached Puryear about forming a new political organization. Thus, the Non-Partisan League was born.[7]

Gomillion and the Democratic Club leadership viewed the runoff
election on September 15 as a critical moment for Macon County.
In August Gomillion wrote to Neil Davis, the new editor of the Tuskegee *News,* expressing his fear that "even among the most 'liberal'
white citizens there is not now the readiness to act courageously in
moving toward more responsible civic behavior." The consequences

of a failure to act "responsibly" could be serious, Gomillion suggested. "If white citizens do not cooperate with Negro citizens on September 15 in the election of Reverend Buford and Dr. Smith, in view of what Negro voters did on August 11, white officials and white citizens might as well expect on September 16 the beginning of an all-out effort to take over the government of the city and the county, in which Negroes are now willing to share." Gomillion called for whites to make "a noticeable demonstration of democratic behavior," which he defined as one hundred white votes for Buford and Smith.[8]

The white liberals had already surmised what Gomillion made explicit. The Non-Partisan League's presence showed them what the future might hold if Gomillion's leadership were undermined. The liberals mustered, if only barely, the requisite white support for the two black candidates. According to the Democratic Club's calculations, Smith received at least 120 white votes and Buford 89 in winning their races. With solid black support, Charles Keever defeated Howard Rutherford for the mayoralty.[9]

The results of the city election sparked new optimism among blacks and liberal whites. The idea of Tuskegee as a model community reemerged, and liberal whites grasped the notion with enthusiasm. Indeed, Charles Keever had used the idea in his campaign literature: "This is our opportunity to establish with certainty that Southern civic government can function with the good of *all of its people* in mind." The new City Council announced at its first meeting that it was consciously breaking with the past and would henceforth base its policies on justice and fairness to all Tuskegeeans. "We shall work for a community composed of citizens whose hearts are united in brotherly love," the councilmen said. "I believe that this little community can become the showplace of the world," Neil Davis said a few months later. The white liberals now publicly espoused the goal toward which Gomillion had been working for twenty-five years: a community in which blacks and whites shared political power and worked together for common ends.[10]

The new city government succeeded in becoming thoroughly interracial. Blacks were appointed to municipal boards and committees. Allan Parker, now a leader of the city council, formed a Community Action Committee to seek and administer federal poverty program funds. The council named twelve blacks and nine whites to an official interracial committee to advise the city on racial matters. Formed at about the same time was an unofficial interracial group, the Committee for a Greater Tuskegee, to which all elected officials, most leading blacks, and the white liberals belonged. This commitee worked for economic development in Tuskegee and supported the public-school system.[11]

White liberals reasserted their support for the public schools in the summer of 1964. They resolved to reenroll their children in Tuskegee High and expressed the hope that other whites, perhaps overburdened by the private-school tuition, would do the same. They were reasonably certain that the state would not interfere again. In July a three-judge panel ordered Governor Wallace and the state Board of Education to stay out of local desegregation efforts, and particularly to let Macon County alone. Only "through the exercise of considerable judicial restraint" were they not issuing a statewide school desegregation order, the judges warned Wallace. The local school board, which had given in to Wallace's demands for more defiance the previous February, once again supported compliance. The appointment of Frances Rush, a staunch public-school supporter, to the board in June had strengthened its resolve. Superintendent Pruitt, however, wanted no part of another desegregation try; he retired on July 1, 1964, to be replaced by Joe Wilson, a younger man who also favored compliance. Tuskegee High had fifty-nine white students and fourteen blacks when it opened in September 1964. The number of whites would grow to 133 by the end of the school year.[12]

Nonetheless, white support for Tuskegee High did not inhibit the growth of Macon Academy. The private institution added a grammar school, new classrooms, more books to its library, Latin and Spanish to its curriculum, and basketball and football teams to its athletic program in 1964 and 1965. The school continued to be the focus of conservative energy and hopes. With the liberals now rallied around Tuskegee High, the division among whites over the schools looked to be a long-term reality.[13]

But by the fall of 1964 a schism in the black community began to overshadow the white division. The Non-Partisan League nominated Detroit Lee to run against Preston Hornsby for probate judge in the November general election. Lee believed that he was as well qualified as Hornsby for the office and that his years of activism had earned him a political reward. The probate office had a special attraction for him: as a boy growing up in Mt. Pleasant, Texas, Lee had been friendly with the local probate judge and his family. He had spent many hours in the Mt. Pleasant probate office, and he believed that he knew well the functions of the probate court.[14]

Gomillion respected Detroit Lee's integrity and commitment to the civil rights cause, but he doubted that Lee would make a good judge. The probate judgeship should go only to an eminently qualified black, Gomillion felt. He also thought it was too early to run a black for that office. Although Gomillion was not personally close to Preston Hornsby, the sheriff had been a friend to the black community when it had had few white friends. Gomillion also believed that support for the Democratic party would best serve black interests in the long run. In a letter to the Democratic Club precinct leaders encouraging their backing of the entire Democratic ticket, Gomillion used only the last reason to explain the club's endorsement of Hornsby. "The important issue here is whether or not we want to continue to act and be treated as Negroes, or move into the larger area of politics and act as Democrats who *happen* to be Negroes."[15]

In case the appeal to assimilationist values was not fully persuasive, Gomillion enclosed a copy of a White Citizens Council leaflet promoting a write-in strategy to elect to the probate judgeship James N. "Kayo" Rea, the Notasulga mayor who had blocked the door at the high school the previous February. "If the negro block [*sic*] splits between the negro candidate and Sheriff Hornsby," the Citizens Council strategist explained, "its [*sic*] possible for the white people of Macon County to elect a real white man to this office." Most black voters again followed Gomillion's advice, and Hornsby won easily.[16]

After the election Paul Puryear denounced the Democratic Club's support of Hornsby. "While many of the nation were exercising discriminating judgment by voting for the candidates deemed most fit," he wrote to the *Advertiser*, "the Negro leaders of Macon County continued to adhere slavishly to the notion that the viability of the Alabama Democratic Party must be maintained at all cost." Puryear hoped that as Macon County blacks became "more sophisticated in the use of the ballot" they would vote independently "without regard to race, party, or organizational affiliation." The Democratic Club's political strategy retarded progress for Tuskegee blacks, Puryear believed. "The pace of social change in Tuskegee is unconscionably slow."[17]

Puryear accused Gomillion and the TCA leadership of exercising an oligarchical control over Macon County blacks. The Non-Partisan League, he explained to a reporter, was concerned "with what is going to emerge as one of the key political issues of the time . . . that of democratizing the Negro leadership." In Tuskegee and other places in the South "everybody has been so busy obtaining the right to vote that we've all neglected to notice that time and again the drive for freedom has resulted in the establishment of a black oligarchy—a narrow leadership that presumes to speak for the mass of Negroes and to treat with the white power structure in the manner of an ambassador." While acknowledging "the heroic way" Gomillion had worked for so many years, Puryear said that the TCA leadership "has become sterile and limited in its approach, and perhaps satisfied that it knows all the answers."[18]

Puryear and Gomillion viewed the Tuskegee situation from widely different perspectives. Age accounted for many of their differences. Gomillion, now approaching sixty-five, had matured during the 1920s and 1930s, a time of relatively little progress for blacks. For most of his adult life he had worked to make small gains for black rights; only in the previous five years had the pace of change accelerated significantly. Puryear was twenty-eight. He had matured during the 1950s, when blacks had much higher expectations, and realizations, of change. So much change in race relations had taken place since 1960—national civil rights legislation, the virtual end of segregation in public accommodations, real progress in getting blacks the right to vote—that men and women of Puryear's generation began to look on rapid change as the norm. They tended to assume that change had come easily. Gomillion knew it had not.

Gomillion had power and influence that Puryear and other blacks wanted. He had charted the course of black activism in Tuskegee for almost twenty-five years. The TCA had always followed his lead on policy decisions, although he was not a domineering personality. The TCA cabinet generally was composed of about twelve persons with great loyalty to Gomillion. William Mitchell, the influential and hard-working executive secretary, did not apologize for following Gomillion's directions "as closely as possible." But the TCA leadership had not been a closed circle. Young men like Stanley Smith and Kenneth Buford had quickly been accepted into the TCA cabinet and were given opportunities for leadership. But they had accepted, apparently with no misgivings, Gomillion's leadership on policy matters. Because he was not willing to adopt the Gomillion style or to defer to his thinking, Puryear could not be a part of the TCA leadership, and thus he challenged the legitimacy of the leadership itself.[19]

Puryear represented only the second significant challenge to Gomillion's leadership since the late 1930s. The first had come in 1960 from Charles V. Hamilton, also a political scientist. Hamilton had arrived at Tuskegee Institute in 1958, a man in his late twenties who was happy about the opportunity to work with Gomillion on the Tuskegee voting struggle. He became Mitchell's assistant in running the daily affairs of the TCA and wrote the voting rights bill that the TCA submitted to Congress in 1959, a feat that impressed the organization's officers. But he soon came into conflict with his older colleagues regarding the proper strategy for civil rights activism. In Hamilton's view, the organization's approach was far too cautious. He gave talks at TCA meetings on the limitations of the gradualist style. He and Charlotte Lewis, a young lawyer who had also recently joined the TCA, advocated protest marches and other direct action to accelerate the pace of change. Lewis charged that the TCA leadership was "bourgeois" and out of touch with the "grass roots."[20]

The TCA leadership received such criticism unsympathetically. Gomillion, Mitchell, and the older TCA members believed that their tactics were proper for the Tuskegee situation. Gomillion wanted no part of direct confrontation with whites, and most TCA members shared that feeling, though many had engaged in a kind of direct-action protest at the Board of Registrars over the years. In early 1960, Hamilton was summarily removed from the executive committee and ostracized by the organization. Gomillion later explained that Hamilton had disobeyed an organizational directive on how to vote on a policy matter before a regional meeting of voting rights activists; but Hamilton believed it was his advocacy of a more aggressive approach that had been his undoing at the TCA.[21]

Hamilton's alienation from Tuskegee became complete in February 1960, when he led a march of several hundred students from the campus to downtown Tuskegee in a response to the sit-in movement just then beginning to sweep the South. The demonstration was silent and peaceful except for an altercation between one student and a local white man, who apparently provoked the incident. Luther Foster, the Institute president, had discouraged the march, but afterward described the students' action as an effort "to express their earnest support of efforts by many other youth groups throughout the nation to help advance the cause of full democracy in America." The Institute's attitude toward Hamilton's involvement may well not have been so tolerant, though Foster contended that the march had nothing to do with Hamilton's firing in April 1960. Hamilton later reported that Gomillion, who was chairman of the Institute's social science division, said his participation in the march had "figured in" the decision not to renew his contact. A brief student protest resulted. Placards asking "Are There Uncle Toms Among Us?" were planted on Gomillion's and Foster's lawns. The American Association of University Professors appealed Hamilton's dismissal, but managed to get only an additional three months' salary for him.[22]

Hamilton believed that his firing resulted from his encouragement of student participation in the march. To protect the school from conservative harassment, Gomillion and other Institute employees had formally separated their civil rights activities from their roles at the Institute. Frederick Patterson had established that policy to protect Gomillion, and Foster had continued it since 1953. By encouraging the protest and marching with the students, Hamilton had breached the separation, thus possibly creating political problems for the Institute.[23]

Hamilton also had publicly forsaken the gradualist style. Since the time of Booker Washington, Tuskegee blacks had sought a slow spiral of progress. The pace had picked up in the late 1950s, and that pleased the TCA leadership, which had long felt that change had not come quickly enough. But they did not want the disorder that might result from radical or rapid change; enough disorder had come from the recent acceleration. Nevertheless, the pressure for faster change would mount steadily after 1960. Both the Hamilton challenge and the Puryear challenge in 1964 demonstrated that some segments of the black community were no longer content with the gradual approach. Among those likely to rebel against gradualism were persons who were younger than the TCA leadership; who considered themselves capable of leadership; and who were in touch with the shift to a more aggressive, militant approach among civil rights activists outside Tuskegee. Many such people lived within the boundaries of Macon County by 1965.

After five years of quietude, the Institute students suddenly awakened in early 1965. The Student Nonviolent Coordinating Committee had sent organizers to the campus in the winter of 1964–65 to recruit participants for voting rights campaigns in the Alabama Black Belt. The Tuskegee students were a large pool of potential activists to help with SNCC's Selma campaign in Dallas County. SNCC workers visited the Institute dormitories and taught students "freedom songs," the protest music of the civil rights movement. James Forman, SNCC executive director, persuaded several talented students to join the SNCC cause. George Ware, a graduate student in chemistry from Birmingham, became a leader in the Tuskegee SNCC contingent. Forman, who had become highly disaffected from the leadership of Dr. Martin Luther King, Jr., and the Southern Christian Leadership Conference, brought to Tuskegee a militant strategy for the civil rights cause. "If we can't sit at the table of democracy," Forman said in March 1965, "then we'll knock the fucking legs off."[24]

The students formed the Tuskegee Institute Advancement League in February 1965 to support the Selma movement, which SNCC and SCLC had escalated into a major protest against voting discrimination. King and other protesters had marched on the Dallas

County Courthouse many days during January and February. TIAL planned a march of Tuskegee students on the state capitol for March 10 to show their sympathy with the Selma protest. After state troopers and Jim Clark's posse bludgeoned the Selma protesters on the Edmund Pettus Bridge on Sunday, March 7, Judge Johnson issued a temporary restraining order against more marches. Confident that Johnson would allow the march to proceed once protection for participants was secured, King sent a telegram to the Tuskegee Institute campus asking the students to postpone their Montgomery protest. Institute administrators put a copy of King's telegram at each student's place in the dining hall the night before the march was to take place. But the students' loyalty was to SNCC. They began a rhythmic tapping on the dining hall tables as they read the telegram. "March, march, march," they chanted in response.[25]

March 10 proved to be a chaotic day for the seven hundred students and faculty members who rode chartered buses to Montgomery. Upon their arrival, a debate developed between student leaders and several local clergymen about who would lead the protest. This is a *student* protest, George Ware insisted, and students will lead it. At the state capitol, the protesters encountered a state trooper contingent and more than a hundred Montgomery city policemen. Ware and another student leader attempted to read a petition demanding voting rights for black people, but a city detective arrested them. The local ministers and Dr. P. B. Phillips, the Institute dean of students, then attempted to persuade the students to give up the protest and return to Tuskegee. Frustrated by the result of their efforts, the students refused to leave. They sat down on the sidewalk in front of the state capitol. City policemen encircled the students and did not allow any protester to reenter the circle once he had left. The number began to dwindle, but most students were adamant. After several hours of confinement, some urinated within the circle, albeit as modestly as possible. Finally at nightfall half the students gave up. The others remained for several hours and then retired to a local black church, where they spent the night. The next morning they returned to Tuskegee.[26]

The Montgomery protest profoundly affected many Tuskegee students. "After the march, a lot of people couldn't take Tuskegee any more," said Gwen Patton, a junior from Montgomery who joined SNCC after the protest. Students began to object to compulsory class attendance and to accuse the administration of treating them like "babies." In April Patton ran successfully for president of the Institute Student Council on a student rights platform. Several TIAL members left school to work on SNCC projects away from

Tuskegee. Among the students most affected by the Montgomery protest were several descendants of prominent black families in Tuskegee. Wendell Paris, Simuel Schutz, Eldridge Burns, and Sammy Younge had grown up in the affluent, insulated environment of the Institute community. All began to reject many of the values and attitudes of the black middle class and to identify consciously with poor blacks. Younge and Burns, who had attended prep schools in the East, "had some sense of guilt for having been separated from other blacks," Patton later said. They responded to these feelings by plunging into civil rights work in the spring and summer of 1965.[27]

In April and May the students organized a protest against the hiring practices of white Tuskegee merchants. They picketed a grocery store and succeeded in preventing most blacks from shopping there. The store soon put a black on its staff. They picketed the Alabama Exchange Bank, of which Allan Parker was president. The students had singled out Parker's bank because they believed the city council president had the power to implement the changes they demanded. Parker announced that, although no blacks were now employed at the bank, all blacks would be given an equal opportunity in future hiring. When the picket did not result in immediate hirings, the students bitterly blamed their failure on Parker's power. "Parker really screwed the whole county," Wendell Paris said later. "He controlled all the Negroes." In fact, the protests did soon elicit promises of fair hiring practices from many Tuskegee merchants.[28]

Twenty-five TIAL members desegregated the formerly all-white Tuskegee city swimming pool on May 31. The next day fifty students swam in the pool, but when they returned on the third day the pool was closed because white vandals had dumped garbage into it. Acid and a baby alligator were thrown into the pool on subsequent days. City officials chose not to reopen it, citing a current water shortage. Actually, they feared the outcome of more protests. In the view of the city fathers, the picketing at the stores and the swimming pool incidents were threatening to destroy the interracial harmony engendered by the previous year's elections.[29]

Luther Foster summoned Gwen Patton to his office in early June and asked her to stop the protests in downtown Tuskegee. The town was approaching model race relations, Patton later said Foster told her, and the students' activities were threatening further progress. Patton reported Dr. Foster's request to the other student activists. "If this is such a model city," George Ware replied, "if blacks and whites get along so well, then let's go to the churches." The students then planned a series of protests designed specifically to polarize the black and white communities, which they deemed the best way to achieve more rapid change in the status of blacks. "We figured that if there was one point on which white people in [Tuskegee] would not relent, it would be the church," Ware said later. But the students did not announce their real intent. At the first desegregation effort at the Methodist Church on June 26, a church usher denied the students entry and told Ware that the presence of blacks would "break up" the congregation. "If as Christians you deny other Christians the right to enter the house of God, then your congregation is already broken up," Ware responded. The students understood that the denial of their entry into the church, whatever their own real motives, offered a powerful symbol of white bigotry.[30]

· The students returned to the Methodist Church the following Sunday, but were again turned away. On Saturday, July 10, three hundred students and several newly arrived SNCC workers met around the Confederate monument on the Tuskegee town square. They sang freedom songs and made speeches. Charles Sherrod, a SNCC field worker, told the group that there should be more black candidates for town offices. "Those white people don't believe us," Sherrod said sarcastically. "They think we want to get into office and do the same things they done to us." The students continued their church protest the next day. Approximately five hundred persons, including a few whites, went to the Methodist Church, but for the third consecutive Sunday they were denied entrance. Some protesters managed to slip inside but were quickly ejected. White bystanders attacked several protesters. Former mayor Howard Rutherford and another white resident were arrested for beating a news photographer.[31]

The scene was re-created the following Sunday, only with a larger group of unruly whites. After the students were denied entrance for the fourth straight time, the whites set upon them. Simuel Schutz, Wendell Paris, and Sammy Younge were beaten. The students later charged that the Tuskegee police had vacated the area just before the attack. Afterward several whites were arrested for the beatings. They included the proprietor of a gas station; a mechanic; the owner of a small grocery store; a bread salesman; the proprietor of a cafe; and a clerk in the local state-controlled liquor store. All were apparently part of a small group of lower-middle-class vigilantes who had coalesced during the school desegregation crisis. They now had a new cause.[32]

The students again appeared on the steps of the Methodist church on July 25, the fifth consecutive Sunday. "Your attendance here at this time will harm human relations in this city," Max Smith, a church steward, told approximately one hundred demonstrators. He denied them entrance and asked them to leave church property. "We will remain here until we are arrested or until the service is over," Sammy Younge responded. "We are aware we have no legal right to attend the church, but we will continue to demand our moral right," George Ware announced. Milling around the front of the church were dozens of blacks and whites, all apparently waiting for trouble to develop. No doubt embarrassed by the recent incidents, Tuskegee policemen patrolled the area in full force and went through the crowd collecting bottles and other weapons. The demonstration finally ended without incident.[33]

The church protests, and the resulting violence, raised the level of racial tension in Tuskegee to a new height. The students had quickly achieved the polarization they wanted. To many whites, the churches were the only institutions that blacks had not yet invaded. They were the last bastion of white power and control. Even the white liberals who believed the churches ought to be open to all took a dim view of the demonstrations, regarding them as needless, destructive incidents which undid the recent progress toward interracial harmony. The protests frightened whites already insecure about their future in Tuskegee. "The cause of civil rights, of equal opportunity," Neil Davis wrote in the *News,* "was not well served by the church integration attempts. The cause of Christian religion was not well served by the unfortunate display of ugly spiritedness which resulted." Davis posed a question to local blacks: "Would not the wiser course for civil rights proponents be to look to the proven leadership of such groups as the Tuskegee Civic Association?"[34]

Gomillion also strongly disapproved of the church demonstrations. He believed that enough distrust already existed between blacks and whites without injecting a highly emotional issue like church integration. He viewed churches as private institutions that should be controlled entirely by their members, and later suggested that if whites had been trying to force their way into his church, he would have resisted that intrusion. To him, the church protests were an immature and unfocused rebellion that damaged the already precarious race relations in Tuskegee.[35]

Still, he had not tried to stop them. He doubted that he could thwart the students' impulse to create conflict. He later observed that in 1965 many black adults in Tuskegee believed that they ought to "let the children lead." Many of the "children" involved were well known locally and no doubt had widespread support for their activities. They represented the growing national militance among young activists. Gomillion was not willing to fight for control of a community that he had led for twenty-five years. His wife was ill. At sixty-five, he recognized that younger men and women had more energy and enthusiasm for leadership. A man who had had too much pride and self-respect to suffer quietly the indignities of the Jim Crow system, Gomillion perhaps also felt that he should not have to fight to retain his power.[36]

He certainly did not want to endure the acrimony that a challenge to the students would cause. He had seen what such a fight might involve when several TIAL members appeared at a Tuskegee City Council meeting in July. Sammy Younge, who was emerging as the most militant student leader, argued with Mayor Charles Keever about the city's commitment to fairness for blacks. Younge directed several questions to Gomillion, who ignored him. Angered by Gomillion's refusal to acknowledge his questions, Younge shouted, "Gomillion, you're suppose to be the leader of the Negro people. What are you doing?" Again Gomillion made no response, but he had witnessed what might happen if he publicly denounced the students.[37]

He would acknowledge later that his unwillingness to try to counter the students' demonstrations amounted to an abdication of responsibility. He had worked for many years against seemingly more formidable opponents—Judge Varner and Sam Engelhardt, for example—to try to make Tuskegee and Macon County an interracial community. Now he failed to oppose persons who presented a different but nevertheless destructive challenge to his ideal. Coming at this time in his life, presenting opponents who should have been allies, that fight was simply too distasteful.[38]

The mood of protest among the young people continued into the fall. Institute students voted in November not to allow their annual Homecoming parade to go through downtown Tuskegee. The editor of the student newspaper, *Campus Digest,* believed that the city's invitation to have the parade come through town was "politically based." It had not been "a sincere plea for understanding and unity," the editor wrote. In making the request, Mayor Keever had said that routing the parade through town might "contribute very much to a better understanding and unity of everyone. . . . As long as people never get together, they don't know much about each other or have much interest in each other." If the city wanted to improve race relations, the editor retorted, it could prosecute the men who had beaten up the protesters at the Methodist church the previous summer. Most blacks had been angered recently when a grand jury composed largely of local whites had failed to indict any of the men charged with assaulting the demonstrators. Gwen Patton announced that she refused "to let the Tuskegee Institute student body be used as some sort of public relations group to mend differences."[39]

The students focused part of their anger on the Institute administration. School administrators had claimed that students were "not ready to assume responsibility," Patton said, but "they cannot say we are not ready if they do not give us a chance." The students wanted to sit on committees determining Institute policies. They demanded better dormitory and cafeteria services and an end to compulsory chapel. To make their sentiments felt, they marched on President Foster's home, boycotted the vesper service, walked out of a mandatory chapel meeting, and executed a "turn-over-your-plate" campaign in the Institute cafeteria.[40]

Tuskegee Institute had always been a tightly controlled school, where students were closely supervised and had relatively few personal prerogatives. Since Booker T. Washington the school administration had enforced such control because it believed that black students needed discipline to succeed in a society which put so many obstacles before them. But many Institute students in the mid-1960s—and particularly those Tuskegee natives leading the civil rights activities—had grown up in an atmosphere of relative affluence and opportunity that took away that rationale for strict discipline. Like students at the University of California at Berkeley, Columbia University, and hundreds of other American universities in the mid-1960s, they began to rebel against the administration of their school. Tuskegee Institute would become as embroiled in the generational conflict of the late 1960s as virtually any college in the country.

The student activists turned their attention to voter registration during the winter of 1965–66. Some had in mind building an all-black political organization like the Black Panther Party, which SNCC workers had formed in Lowndes County, Alabama. The students worked primarily in rural Macon County where most unregistered blacks were. The TCA had increased its efforts to register rural blacks after the 1961 court decision, but they had been only minimally successful. Illiteracy, fear of economic coercion, and poor community leadership hampered the TCA's efforts to get large numbers of rural blacks to try to register.[41]

The Tuskegee students helped many rural blacks overcome the obstacles. They sometimes lived in the rural communities and provided a daily source of assistance and leadership. Whereas the TCA had always stressed the numerous responsibilities connected with full citizenship rights, the young activists emphasized what blacks might gain by controlling county government. The Voting Rights Act of 1965, which was passed in the aftermath of the Selma march, aided the registration effort. It forbade the state to require that voters be literate. Instead of a grueling examination before harsh white registrars intent on embarrassing them, rural blacks now had to answer only a few questions, which they could do orally if they were illiterate. The number of black voters in Macon County began to increase sharply after the voting rights bill was enacted in July. The following January, when the students' registration effort reached its zenith, more than sixteen hundred blacks added their names to the voting rolls. The students, with the help of the new federal guarantee of the right to vote, were completing work that Gomillion and the TCA had begun twenty-five years earlier.[42]

The students' success would, however, be virtually overlooked because of what happened on Monday night, January 3, 1966. After working in the registration effort that day, several student activists organized a small party at the SNCC "freedom house." Sammy Younge left the party at about ten o'clock to go to a grocery store for a jar of mayonnaise. On his way Younge stopped at a Standard Oil service station in downtown Tuskegee and asked the whereabouts of "the damn bathroom." Marvin Segrest, the sixty-seven-year-old service station attendant, directed Younge to the rear of the station. Apparently believing that he was being sent to the Jim Crow toilet, Younge swore at Segrest and demanded to use the "public restroom." Segrest then drew a gun and ordered Younge off the service station property. The student left, but, according to Segrest, he made a threat. "I'm going to get you," Younge reportedly said to Segrest. The old man dared Younge to "come back on my property." Segrest would later testify that Younge had harassed him for four or five months before this night. Younge had once tried to leave the station without paying for gasoline purchased, Segrest said. Another time he had become impatient with Segrest's service and had said, "Put some goddamn gas in the car or I'll hurt you." Segrest also said Younge had "tried to run me down with the car."[43]

After Segrest pulled the gun, Younge went next door to the Greyhound bus station and asked Joseph Morris, a Tuskegee Institute student, if he had a gun. Morris replied that he did not. Facing the service station, Younge bobbed up and down behind his car and called out to Segrest, "Go ahead and shoot me." Segrest stepped toward the bus station with his gun. Younge ran to a bag of golf clubs belonging to a student waiting for a bus and took out a single club. Younge then began to run—toward Segrest, the old man later testified. Morris stated that Younge had run away from Segrest. Segrest fired a shot, missing Younge, who then ran across the street to where Morris had now moved. Younge said to Morris, "Don't leave. . . . I want you to witness this." Younge ran back across the street to the bus station and stepped on and off a parked bus. He ran around the bus into the open, still holding the golf club, when Segrest fired again. Segrest later claimed that Younge had come toward him, but Morris stated unequivocally that Younge had been moving away from Segrest. A few minutes later, Younge's body was discovered in an alley on the side of the bus terminal away from Segrest's station, a fact which supports Morris's version of the events. The second shot had hit Younge in the head, killing him instantly.[44]

The death of Sammy Younge led to an examination of the lives of two men who might otherwise have remained almost anonymous. Marvin Segrest was one of the lesser members of the large Segrest clan of Macon County. Neither well educated nor economically successful, he was known to be law-abiding. He had attended White Citizens Council meetings, but he would not have been included among Macon County's likely candidates to murder a civil rights worker. Indeed, Segrest and his supporters maintained that the incident resulted from a personal conflict, not racial hatred.[45]

Sammy Younge was descended from an old and prominent Tuskegee Institute family. His father had held administrative positions at the VA hospital and in other federal agencies. His mother was a grammar-school teacher active in social and cultural affairs in the Institute community. Sammy attended Children's House, the grammar school for the Institute children, and Cornwall Academy in Massachusetts before returning to Tuskegee to finish high school. He was a handsome boy with very light skin, blue eyes, and curly black hair who easily "passed" as white. He had good manners, many girlfriends, and a talent for singing. After high school, he joined the United States Navy, but his tour of duty was foreshortened by two serious operations, which resulted in the loss of one kidney. According to friends, he was later haunted by the memory of these operations.[46]

After the navy stint, Sammy enrolled at the Institute for the spring semester of 1965, but his civil rights activity immediately crowded out his educational interests. He went to Mississippi to work on SNCC projects after the Montgomery demonstration, but soon returned to Tuskegee to help lead the swimming pool and church protests. After the church demonstrations ended in July, Younge resigned from TIAL and withdrew from civil rights activities. He reportedly was very upset over the murder of Jonathan Daniels, a white ministerial student, in Lowndes County in the late summer of 1965. Gwen Patton also believed he was disappointed that many older blacks disapproved of the student protests. Other friends interpreted his action as an effort to conform to Tuskegee's middle-class values, of which he had recently been extremely critical. They noted that he began to drink heavily, despite doctors' orders against any alcoholic consumption. He suddenly decided to return to the movement in December, planning to form an all-black political party. His renewed civil rights involvement apparently did not change Sammy Younge's drinking habits. On the night of his death he had drunk enough to be under "the early influence of alcohol" and to experience some "impairment in judgment and reasoning," the investigating toxicologist would later testify.[47]

On Tuesday morning all that mattered in Tuskegee was the reality of Sammy Younge's death. Three thousand Tuskegee Institute students marched in the rain from the campus to downtown Tuskegee. They demanded an audience with the mayor and the City Council, who soon appeared. "You have told us this is a model city where whites and Negroes get along together," Gwen Patton said to the city fathers. "You have told us how good the Tuskegee image is. . . . You have invited us downtown for a homecoming football parade. . . . Yet, you closed the city swimming pool and barred us from your churches . . . now, we want to know what you are going to do." Mayor Charles Keever deplored the killing and promised to do all in his power to see that justice was rendered. "Regret will not bring Sammy back!" a student shouted to Keever. "That's good, but what are you going to do?" another asked. More questions followed, and then the mayor and the councilmen joined the students in prayer. They all stood in the rain and sang "We Shall Overcome," after which the students returned to the campus.[48]

One march did not vent the anger released by Sammy Younge's death. Students marched again the next day. There was no march on Thursday, the day of Younge's funeral, but President Foster called a meeting of students and faculty for that evening. Foster affirmed the right of all members of the Institute community to participate in civil rights activity and stated that he expected that "people will so involve themselves." Speaking on behalf of the just-formed Ad Hoc Committee for Justice in Macon County, Paul Puryear announced a series of demands for equal access to public accommodations in Tuskegee. Gwen Patton read a letter that she had sent to Lyndon Johnson about Younge's death. "Sir, to be honest with you," she wrote to the president, "the students of Tuskegee Institute are not planning to follow the course of nonviolence if justice is not done in this case."[49]

The students marched again on Friday morning. Patton called another meeting for that evening, but this one lacked the unity of feeling at the previous night's convocation. Luther Foster listed the actions taken in response to Younge's death. Both federal and state agents were investigating the killing. The Justice Department had filed discrimination suits against two Tuskegee restaurants. The Tuskegee City Council had already considered Puryear's proposed antidiscrimination ordinances and promised to act on them the following Tuesday. Foster ended on a cautionary note: local authorities believed that more marches would present "grave dangers" to everyone involved.[50]

Gwen Patton responded to the warning with vehemence. "Ain't no guns or rifles gonna turn us around. We realize the danger, but Sammy Younge did it by himself. So what difference does it make whether it's one or a million?" After her remarks, the group voted to march the next day. But not every one of the fifteen hundred students present agreed with the militant position. One student objected to any further marches, saying that the first one had been constructive but the others had only served to "rile people up." After this student received catcalls, P. B. Phillips, the dean of students, complained that "the rudeness tonight is certainly not civil, and if we're going to have civil rights then we have to be civil right down the line."[51]

But the militants clearly had the upper hand. If the students backed down from their demands, then they would be responsible for the next black who was murdered, George Ware warned. Wendell Paris argued against any moderation of demands by condemning Booker Washington. Referring to the famous sculpture on the Institute campus which depicts Washington lifting the veil of ignorance from a kneeling Negro, Paris said, "We got this statue out here of that man who's suppose to be lifting up the veil. Man, he's putting it back on." Here Paris was paraphrasing the author Ralph Ellison, a former Tuskegee student, who had stressed the ambiguity of the sculpture in *Invisible Man,* a novel which harshly characterized Tuskegee Institute and its leadership. Washington was a convenient and powerful symbol of gradualism on which young militants could focus their anger.[52]

Perhaps the most effective speech of the meeting was made by James Forman, who had come to Tuskegee for Younge's funeral. When will the terrorism against civil rights workers end? Forman asked. He alluded to an answer by saying that he knew his own days were numbered. He challenged the students: "What do you live for? That's the basic question, baby." He described a paradise of luxury items but asked, "Is that enough? Is that enough? Or are you going to take the education you get and give it back to the people?" Closing with a call for more action, Forman paraphrased Frederick Douglass's famous statement: "A man who won't agitate for his rights don't need no rights."[53]

One thousand students began another march toward downtown Tuskegee the next day. City policemen stopped the marchers and informed them that they could not continue without a parade permit. The marchers insisted that they would continue, and the policemen relented. When they reached the town square, the marchers sat on the sidewalk and obstructed the entry to one block of stores. Willie Ricks, a SNCC worker, pleaded with townspeople to join the protest. "When they killed Sammy, they killed all of us." Younge's death had been planned in the chambers of the Tuskegee City Council, Ricks announced to onlookers. But the inflammatory rhetoric did not spark more protest; the marchers returned peacefully to Tuskegee Institute.[54]

The City Council faced the militance on January 10 and 11 when it attempted to respond to the students' call for action. "Tuskegee is far from the model community that some insist that it is," Puryear told the councilmen. He demanded a public accommodations ordinance, the firing of the Tuskegee public safety director, and a civilian review board for the police department. Ben-Zion Wardy, an Israeli citizen teaching political science at the Institute and a participant in the church protests the previous summer, warned the council that "people will take steps to obtain these substantial demands by using other means" if the public accommodations ordinance was not passed. Wardy gave the council one day to enact the measure. He further urged it to remove the Confederate monument from the town square and rename the area "Samuel Younge, Jr., Park." Gwen Patton asked that the city boycott the service station at which Marvin Segrest was employed. Puryear told the council that Younge's death was not the result of a "personal feud," as some city officials had claimed. "We . . . do not share the view that the killing of Samuel Younge was the isolated act of one individual. . . . Mr. Younge's murder is symptomatic of much deeper and pervasive evils in our community."[55]

A small group of SNCC workers and Institute students marched every day that week. The demonstrations were peaceful until Saturday, January 15, when one of the marchers struck a deputy sheriff who was attempting to arrest him. A local merchant had charged that the demonstrator, William Scott, had bumped and kicked him as the merchant tried to enter his store. The students later said that the police had initiated the fighting. After Scott was arrested, the other demonstrators began throwing rocks and bottles at some white men who had taunted them from an automobile. Several store windows were broken.[56]

The aftermath of Younge's death worried Tuskegee whites. The liberals' regret about the killing soon gave way to concern about the impact of the protests that followed. "Those students are just a liability to this town," one liberal told a reporter. "They don't live here, they don't spend money here, they got no real stake in what happens to this town." He was frightened and pessimistic. "Tuskegee's burning down around our ears and there ain't no way out." The liberals knew that the harsh antiwhite feelings unleashed by Younge's death had damaged their efforts for interracial understanding and community peace. The dire predictions of conservative whites that racial change would result in violence, hatred, and death now seemed all too close to reality.[57]

The TCA leadership also objected to what the students were doing. Beulah Johnson, a longtime TCA activist, expressed her concerns about the effect of the student demonstrations in a letter to the *News*. "Those of us who live here and love this community have much at stake. The SNCC-type from outside and the handful who are persuaded to act outside the law do not understand this." She criticized a recent *Time* magazine article which stated that the Younge murder had removed the "façade" of racial progress. Anyone familiar with the voting situation just a few years ago knew how much progress had been made, she wrote. Councilman Buford complained to the *News* that "an idiotic climate has been created in this community by mob activities of college students and their associates which, from a behavioral point of view, cannot be differentiated from those same activities by misguided hoodlums, color notwithstanding." Another TCA member contended that "the students are downtown destroying things we worked years to get. They're emotional and immature. They don't know what they're doing."[58]

The divisions in the Tuskegee black community were dramatized at a conference on "Alabama Justice" held at the Institute in early February. Sponsored by the Ad Hoc Committee for Justice in Macon County, the conference precipitated a full public debate about civil rights strategy. Floyd McKissick, soon to become head of the Congress of Racial Equality, advanced a militant position. "If the black man is ever going to be free," McKissick said, "he's going to have to free himself. No one ever gave away power. That just ain't politics. We're going to the polls and take that power." Fred Gray, the black attorney who had represented the TCA in both the gerrymander and the school desegregation cases, agreed with McKissick and argued that blacks could best attain that power within the Democratic party. Several students roared objections to that. Referring to the Alabama Democratic party's emblem, the bantam rooster, Wendell Paris responded, "People ain't going to vote for that white rooster no more. The whole thing is corrupt."[59]

The students' vehemence evoked criticism from older black residents. "I'm disturbed by this uncontrolled hostility," Lawrence Haygood, a local minister, said. "Whites have played a magnificent role in the civil rights movement, especially in their financial support." When several TCA members defended their past record of activism, Wendell Wilkerson, a TIAL member, retorted: "I ain't interested in what you did. I'm interested in what you're going to do." The young militants accused middle-class Tuskegee blacks of not caring about poor people. One such middle-class person objected: "You're creating animosity—setting the middle class against the lower class. Where are you going to get money? How are you going to unite us?" That is not our concern, said Michele Moreland, a SNCC worker. "The question of how to unite is your problem. There are more of the poor people than of you."[60]

Deeply troubled by the open hostility of the young militants, the older activists asked for guidance from the man who had led them for twenty-five years. Gomillion's unwillingness to compete with the students for the leadership of the black community had kept him publicly silent during 1965 and through the recent weeks of turmoil. But on February 13, Race Relations Sunday, the day that he traditionally called for unity and brotherhood with white Tuskegeeans, Gomillion announced that he would make a statement. He hoped that it would not be "taken as an attempt to justify what we have done or an apology for what we have not done." He noted that the TCA as an organization had tried to refrain from telling other groups what they should do, implying that he hoped that the courtesy would be returned. "Our way is not the only way, but we have been able to accomplish many of our goals." He denied that he or the TCA had ever called Tuskegee a model community. "I have said it could become one. I still think it could. If I didn't, I wouldn't have stayed here." He defended the TCA's approach to civil rights work. "Maybe our goals haven't been high enough or comprehensive enough. But there are many of us who believe that by working together, by making necessary compromises, we can make Tuskegee a better place to live."[61]

Gomillion had accepted the fact that his leadership now seemed anachronistic to many blacks. But he was not willing to adjust his style to meet the dictates of a more militant age. If his kind of leadership was no longer popular, then he would simply step aside. Although he considered the violent, profane rhetoric of the students altogether distasteful and doubted that their militance would produce real progress, he understood that they were a young generation intent on advancing the cause of black people further than their elders had. Indeed, he had felt the same impulse in the 1930s and had begun working for change. The change he set in motion had led to greater expectations and strident demands for more change. Now, thirty years later, the mounting force of change was bringing an end to his leadership. Charles Gomillion was caught in a whirlwind that he had sown. Fortunately for him, he knew that.

12

The Grass Roots
Take Hold

THE STUDENT activists turned their full attention to politics in the spring of 1966. They resolved to nominate as many blacks as possible in the May Democratic primary. The prospects seemed excellent. Twenty-two hundred blacks had registered since January 1, raising the number of black voters to seven thousand. They outnumbered white voters by almost three to one. The students had given up the idea of forming an all-black political party. "Certainly the pace of the TCA is far from being progressive," the editor of the *Campus Digest* wrote in late February, "but it has hold of the ground roots in this county." He advised fellow students to be practical about Gomillion's influence. "The Gomillion stronghold is evident in Tuskegee and his reputation in rural areas of the county is far from being as 'tomish' as some of us purport." If the students hoped to get more blacks elected, then they had to avoid criticizing Gomillion, the editor suggested.[1]

But the primary election did reflect the divisions in the black community. Several young black men emerged to challenge the Democratic Club candidates. Thomas Reed, the proprietor of a fried-chicken restaurant, ran for state House of Representatives against Jessie P. Guzman, the veteran TCA activist. Reed aimed his campaign at lower-class blacks, many of whom would be voting for the first time. He promised to seek higher welfare payments, more public health services, and more government-sponsored employment. His emphasis on economic concerns reflected a shift in priorities among black activists and politicians, now that political rights had been secured. Arthur Scavella, a young Institute professor, challenged Frances Rush, the white liberal who had the Democratic Club's endorsement for a place on the school board. Otis Pinkard, a longtime TCA activist who, like Detroit Lee, had sometimes pushed for a more militant approach, ran for tax collector. The Democratic Club supported L. A. Locklair, a black undertaker, for that office.[2]

The race for sheriff attracted by far the greatest interest. The favorite was Harvey Sadler, whom Governor Wallace had appointed in 1964 after Preston Hornsby resigned to become probate judge. A staunch Wallace supporter, Sadler had been active in the local White Citizens Council and had helped in the building of Macon Academy. But as sheriff he had dealt fairly with blacks. A few months before the primary he appointed a black deputy. He acknowledged to a reporter that two of his children attended Macon Academy but noted that a third child went to an integrated college. Sadler understood that he had to have black votes to get elected.[3]

His main opposition came from Lucius Amerson, a thirty-two-year-old black employee of the VA hospital cafeteria and a Korean War veteran. Amerson had long aspired to be a policeman, but very few police departments in Alabama hired blacks. He had recognized that the position of sheriff of Macon County offered a good opportunity to enter the law enforcement field. The student activists received Amerson's candidacy enthusiastically, and, appealing to black unity, they campaigned for him throughout the county. The Democratic Club was cool to Amerson. He had not consulted with the club, and his student support no doubt alienated some older blacks. Gomillion and other Democratic Club leaders knew little about Amerson, who had not participated in civic affairs in the ten years he had lived in Tuskegee.[4]

Sadler might have received the club's endorsement except for an incident of brutality in March 1966. Seeking information about a crime, a white deputy sheriff forced his way into the home of a young black woman, Savannah Harvey, and whisked her to jail without allowing Harvey, who was recuperating from pneumonia, to dress. The TCA lodged a strong protest about Harvey's mistreatment with Sadler, and the sheriff promised to investigate. No report was forthcoming, however, and eventually Sadler called the Savannah Harvey incident a political trick concocted by his opponents.[5]

With Sadler no longer a viable choice, the Democratic Club hesitated to endorse a candidate in the sheriff's race. It would prove to be a serious mistake. Amerson had developed strong support among rural blacks who, to the surprise of some Democratic Club stalwarts, liked the idea of a black sheriff. Whereas many residents of the

largely insulated Institute community had never had occasion to en-
counter the sheriff, rural blacks depended entirely on him for their
protection and dealt with him in all legal infractions. They believed
that a black sheriff was more likely to serve their interests. When the
Democratic Club allowed each local precinct leader to decide whom
to endorse in the sheriff's race, almost all picked Amerson. "It never
occurred to me—until it was too late—that there was so much sentiment for a Negro sheriff," a Democratic Club member, who noted
that he had never dealt with the county sheriff, later told a *New York
Times* reporter. "If I had realized it, I would have insisted that we
pick our own candidate."[6]

Gomillion believed that the post of sheriff ought to be the last office blacks tried to capture. He knew that the idea of a black man's
exercising police power caused more white anxiety than any other
prospective change in race relations. In his view, a seat on the school
board, the City Council, the county commission, or in the state legislature offered a greater opportunity to advance black interests. But
to most blacks, the sheriff was the most important county official
because he had power over life and death. Gomillion might well
have recalled how important it had been to the TCA to rid Macon
County of Pat Evans, the brutal sheriff of the 1940s. He perhaps
should have anticipated that the student militance of 1965 would
result in a strong desire to put blacks in such key positions. He might
also have imagined that his failure to choose a good black candidate
could result in the election of a black sheriff that the TCA leaders
deemed unworthy. Indeed that was what had happened, he and
other TCA members later came to believe. This failure indicated a
degree of truth in the students' accusation that Gomillion was out of
touch with the lower class. It also reflected his retreat from leadership.[7]

Hostility between the Amerson campaign and the TCA leadership came into the open a few days before the primary runoff. Student volunteers for Amerson drove a truck equipped with a sound
amplification system down Bibb Street near the Institute campus
and loudly condemned "the middle-class niggers" who were not
supporting Amerson. Gomillion, who lived in a small white bunga-
low on the street, was offended and wounded by this tactic. He resolved not to vote for Amerson in the runoff, though he said nothing
publicly. Other TCA members did speak out against Amerson's appeal to class prejudice. Councilman Buford, vice-president of the
TCA, announced his support for Harvey Sadler three days before
the election. Tuskegee would never have interracial harmony, Buford said, if blacks "kick white moderates in the teeth." But most

black Macon Countians were no longer willing to wait for political power just to assuage white fears.[8]

Amerson won with fifty-three percent of the vote. The *New York Times* reported in a front-page story that he was likely to be the first Negro since Reconstruction to serve as sheriff of a southern county. His election was widely hailed as a triumph of the civil rights movement. Amerson credited the "masses" in Macon County for his victory. Indeed, the thousands of poor blacks had elected him. But for some of the black Macon Countians who had worked hardest for civil rights, Amerson's election was less a triumph than the end to a journey. The civil rights struggle had turned in a direction they did not choose to travel. Several persons, including Gomillion, simply got off at that point.[9]

The results in the other races showed both the successes and the limitations of the voting rights struggle in Macon County. Frances Rush, the Democratic Club's candidate for the school board, won despite strong student support for her black opponent, an indication of continued Gomillion influence in certain races.[10] Both L. A. Locklair, the black candidate for tax collector, and Harold Webb, a black candidate for the county commission, defeated white opponents for important positions. Blacks now held two of the four elected positions on the county governing body. They had the leverage to select the chairman of the commission, who, though chosen by the four commissioners, traditionally exercised the greatest authority over the county government. Since 1951 the commissioners had picked Edward Laslie for that position. The primary election put Laslie's tenure at the commission in doubt; his death in October saved him, however, from having the black commissioners remove him from office. Harry Raymon, the former school board president who had supported the desegregation effort, was subsequently chosen as the new chairman.[11]

In the two races for the state legislature, however, both black candidates lost to white opponents. Fred Gray and Thomas Reed had run for separate seats representing the same House district, which comprised Macon, Barbour, and Bullock counties. The dual representation resulted from an order in *Reynolds v. Sims,* the landmark 1964 decision against the malapportionment of the Alabama legislature. Blacks, who were easily in the majority in the new district, voted almost unanimously for Gray and Reed. But the white voter turnout, which approached one hundred percent, exceeded the black turnout. In Bullock County, the number of whites who voted was greater than the United States Bureau of the Census's count of voting-age whites. Many people who had moved from the district returned to vote, and the number of white absentee voters was extraordinarily high. Gray later charged officials in Bullock and Barbour with fraud, but the defendants were able to explain most of the white absentee voters as college students, soldiers, and shut-ins. The court found that whites maintained voting status in their "home of origin" after moving away because of "home ties, friends, property interests, nostalgia," rather than out of need to protect white political control.[12]

The defeat of Gray and Reed postponed even further the realization of a full share of political power for Tuskegee blacks. They still lacked black representation in the Alabama legislature, which, because of the concentration of political power at the state level, influenced their lives perhaps more than local government did. The state controlled the public schools and most welfare agencies. It managed the courts, the prisons, and the state troopers. It funded most colleges and contributed a significant portion of Tuskegee Institute's income. In the hands of George Wallace, state government was hostile to black interests. It promised to stay unfriendly: in the primary Wallace's wife, Lurleen, received the Democratic nomination for governor as his stand-in. The defeat of Gray, Reed, and several other black legislative candidates across the state meant that Wallace would not have the black opposition that might force him to be more sympathetic during his next administration.

The prospect of a black sheriff made the summer and fall of 1966 a nervous time in Macon County. Most whites did not willingly accept Amerson's victory. Sadler organized a write-in campaign for sheriff in the November general election, but it fell short even with enthusiastic white support. After the election Lurleen Wallace appointed several white men to serve as "constables" in Macon County, an attempt to circumvent the sheriff's office. Created in the nineteenth century to help keep the peace in rural districts, the office of constable had rarely been filled in recent times, but by law it had policing powers similar to the sheriff's. Only the most diehard segregationists, however, supported the effort to undermine Amerson's authority. Liberals like Allan Parker and Preston Hornsby promised him their full cooperation. The Tuskegee City Council announced that it backed Amerson "wholeheartedly." A reporter for the *New York Times* found that a month after Amerson assumed the office more and more whites were grudgingly accepting his presence.[13]

Tension in Tuskegee rose again in December 1966 when Marvin Segrest went on trial for the murder of Sammy Younge. Judge L. J. Tyner had moved the proceedings from Tuskegee to Opelika, twenty-five miles to the northeast, at the request of Segrest's attor-

neys. Tyner did not believe that Segrest could get a fair trial in
Macon County. Citing newspaper stories on the demonstrations
after Younge's death, he ruled that "the atmosphere created by the
repeated marchings and demonstrations of members of organizations in Macon County composed in part or promoted by professional agitators . . . is prejudicial to the accused." There was no way
of knowing whether some of the agitators might be on a Macon
County jury, Tyner said. He knew that several months earlier Judge
Johnson, ruling in a TCA suit against the local jury commission,
had issued a new jury list composed of three times more blacks than
whites. Had Segrest stood trial in Macon County, the jury would in
all likelihood have had a black majority.[14]

Segrest was tried for second-degree murder before a jury of twelve
white men. He never aimed at Younge, the defendant testified,
though he fired in that direction out of self-defense. He believed the
Negro had a gun. Younge had been advancing on Segrest when the
old man fired, defense lawyers maintained, but Joseph Morris, the
Institute student who had witnessed most of what happened, said
that Younge had been moving away from Segrest. Segrest's attorneys noted that Younge had been drinking, that he had held a golf
club in his hand, and that he had taunted and cursed Segrest. In
closing arguments, defense lawyers portrayed Segrest as a man "in
his twilight years" who had been harassed by a "husky," cursing
youth.[15]

The prosecutors presented evidence which clearly proved that Segrest had killed Younge, and then they reminded the jurors that the
case had been moved to Opelika to insure that justice was done. Although they would later be criticized for being less than energetic in
their work, the prosecutors had probably done all they could. After a
short deliberation the jury announced Segrest's acquittal. The decision demonstrated again what the trials in Lowndes County of the
men accused of killing Jonathan Daniels and Viola Liuzzo had
shown: a white jury would not convict another white of murdering a
civil rights worker. To most white men, that was inherently an act of
self-defense.[16]

Fifteen hundred Institute students marched to the Tuskegee town
square soon after the jury announced its decision. One climbed up
the Confederate statue, painted the soldier's face black, and put a
yellow stripe down his back. Inscribed on the base of the statue were
"black power" and "Sam Younge." "We're here because a year ago
Sammy Younge was killed and today they let the man who killed
our blood brother go free," one protester shouted. The Tuskegee liquor store was broken into during the demonstration, and fires were

started on the town square. When the protest began to dissolve at 4:00 A.M., 250 demonstrators threw rocks and bottles at store fronts along North Main Street.

The resentment at Segrest's acquittal did not, however, erupt again. Luther Foster announced that the jury's decision "raises again very real questions regarding the safety of Negroes in Alabama, as well as the quality of justice administered in this state." He explained the violence on the town square as aggression resulting from black insecurity. But to an Institute assembly he said that more violence could not be tolerated. Plans for a march to commemorate the first anniversary of Younge's death were opposed by both the Tuskegee City Council and Sheriff Amerson. No march took place.[17]

The protest mood among students would remain strong for the next few years. After an interracial jury failed to convict a white man charged with raping a sixteen-year-old black girl in late 1967, several SNCC activists held a mock trial in downtown Tuskegee of a dummy labeled "Cracker." The mock trial, Michael Wright of SNCC said, was intended to remind local blacks that "what happens to one black person happens to all of us." Afterwards some protesters threw bottles through two downtown store windows. One SNCC leader was unrepentant about the vandalism. "I'm only sorry it wasn't another Detroit," Scott B. Smith said, referring to the previous summer's riot in which more than forty persons had been killed.[18]

After 1967, protests were focused more and more on the Vietnam war and the absence of student participation in college policy-making. Michael Wright interrupted a speech by a State Department official in March 1968 to announce that inasmuch as "our Viet brothers don't have an air force adequate enough to do their bombing, we black brothers will help them." He then pelted the government official with eggs. A few days later, students began a boycott of classes. They demanded that the school end compulsory ROTC and give them a stronger voice in the selection of campus speakers, the hiring of faculty, and the setting of dormitory regulations. On April 6, two days after the assassination of Martin Luther King, Jr., a small group of students took the Institute Board of Trustees hostage during a trustee meeting to discuss the demands. After holding the trustees for thirteen hours, the students began to get nervous. "I've got the National Guard and the state troopers less than two miles away," Sheriff Amerson warned them. Three hundred guardsmen and seventy troopers were indeed poised to invade the campus. The students handed over their hostages.[19]

Luther Foster and the trustees immediately closed the school and

sent all three thousand students home. They were angry about what
the students had done and frightened by the presence of the state
police and the National Guard. At that moment guardsmen were on
duty in many American cities to control rioting in the aftermath of
the King assassination. Tuskegee would be no Chicago, where
twelve thousand policemen and seven thousand guardsmen had
been battling rioters for more than two days, but violence seemed
possible and the trustees had acted to prevent it. They tried to rid
the school of some protesters by requiring that all students apply for
readmission with a promise to abide by school rules. They had no
intention of readmitting the protest leaders. Judge Johnson would
later order the school to allow the expelled students to return. "You
cannot—merely by closing the Institute and reopening it two weeks
later—deprive 50 or 60 students of their status as students." But
Johnson also warned the students not to disrupt "the operation of
the Institute as an educational institution," an admonition they
subsequently heeded. In later years Institute students would con-
demn American foreign policy and criticize the school administration, but the protest spirit did not boil over again.[20]

Tuskegee whites were publicly silent about the behavior of the
Institute students, but many worried privately that the town was no
longer safe for them. Since the church demonstrations in the summer of 1965, they had viewed the students as an unpredictable
source of disorder. The bottle-throwing incidents in the aftermath of
Sammy Younge's death and Marvin Segrest's acquittal suggested to
some whites that Tuskegee might have a race riot like those that had
recently taken place in Detroit, Newark, and Los Angeles. The
trustee hostage incident must have reinforced these fears. Some
whites doubted whether the sheriff, who owed his election in part to
the students, would keep order if the young protesters challenged
him, though Amerson had treated them as lawbreakers in the hostage situation. Many whites who had predicted that the loss of white
political control would result in racial violence now regarded their
prophecy as fulfilled. The insecurity caused more whites to consider
moving from Tuskegee. No great exodus took place immediately,
but many whites sensed that leaving was inevitable.[21]

The insecurity of whites undermined the desegregation effort at
Tuskegee High. In the two school years 1964–65 and 1965–66, white
students had outnumbered blacks by about ten to one. But white
support for the school was flagging by June 1966. Joe Wilson, the
school superintendent, estimated that only eight white families were
strongly committed to the school. Most of the 250 white students
were there only because they could not afford Macon Academy's

tuition, Wilson said. He warned that if blacks came to Tuskegee High in large numbers the next fall "we will have segregation again." Should it become more than half black, Wilson predicted, all whites would withdraw, whether they could afford Macon Academy or not.[22]

Wilson was right. More than half of the students who enrolled in the fall of 1966 were black, and all whites withdrew during the next two years. Already anxious about being a small minority in an overwhelmingly black county, Tuskegee whites would not allow their children to become a minority at school. They did what most whites in predominantly black counties across the South would do in the next decade: they abandoned the public school and put their children in a private, segregated academy. By the end of the decade the public high school at Notasulga was the only integrated school in the county. Whites stayed in the Notasulga school, which served a predominantly white village, because they were able to remain in the majority. The desegregation of the Macon County public schools had largely failed. That was ironic: Judge Johnson had expanded *Lee v. Macon* in 1967 to make it a statewide school desegregation order, and the suit resulted in the generally peaceful desegregation of most public schools and junior colleges in Alabama during the next few years. The case thus fulfilled many purposes but not its original one.[23]

Other changes in race relations were made swiftly and successfully, however. Almost half of Tuskegee's white-owned businesses had implemented open-hiring practices by the end of 1967; they employed more than twenty black salespersons. The city government eliminated its discriminatory practices in employment and the distribution of services. Blacks were put into management and clerical positions in city departments. The number of black policemen rose steadily after 1964; by early 1968 eleven blacks and six whites composed the force. The City Council appointed its first black public safety director in January 1968. Unpaved streets in black areas of the city were improved, and garbage removal and sewer service were expanded. Under Allan Parker's direction, Tuskegee established an agency to acquire and administer federal antipoverty programs for Macon County. The city received a large Model Cities grant from the United States Department of Housing and Urban Development to improve housing and water service. When Parker resigned from the City Council in October 1967, he said that he was "real proud of the transition the city has made from an 18th-century philosophy to a 20th-century one."[24]

Parker left the City Council to take over as chairman of the

county commission, where progress had come more slowly. Laslie
had been a constant and effective opponent of change and his successor, Harry 'Raymon, though much more progressive, did not get
along with Sheriff Amerson. Parker accepted the chairmanship to
establish friendlier relations among county officials and to integrate
the county work force, which remained predominantly white. During the next two years he oversaw a rapid desegregation of the
county staff.[25]

Macon County blacks began to gain more control over bread-
and-butter concerns like the federal agricultural programs. The
Agricultural Stabilization and Conservation Service determined the
amount of cotton that a farmer could grow under the federal farm
subsidy programs. By projecting, on the basis of past yields, how
many pounds of cotton per acre a farmer would produce in a year, a
committee of farmers advising the ASCS could dictate how much
cotton a farmer could sell at a price held artificially high by the federal subsidy. The Department of Agriculture granted each county a
specified amount of cotton that could be protected by the subsidy.
The all-white Macon County ASCS committee had kept the projected yields of black farmers low and raised the projections for
white farmers to inordinately high levels. Hosea Guice, for example,
had produced about 500 pounds of cotton per acre for several years
but was allowed a projected yield of only 290 pounds in 1967. Some
white farmers were allowed 800 pounds, or almost two bales per
acre, which could not be reasonably projected even on Macon
County's richest land.[26]

Black farmers throughout Alabama challenged white control of
local ASCS committees in 1967. Four of the fifteen committeemen
elected in Macon County that year were black, but black farmers
charged that the election had been rigged against them. They contended that some black ballots were thrown out illegally and that
whites on the old ASCS committee had purposely added extra black
names to the ballot to split the black vote. Guice and several other
farmers were able through persistent effort to get their projected
yields raised for the next crop year, but they remained convinced
that their best strategy was to gain control of the ASCS committee.
Finally, in October 1968, after a campaign in which some blacks on
the ballot actually told people not to vote for them, nine black farmers were elected to the committee. They chose a black chairman,
who promised fair treatment to all farmers.[27]

Few political conflicts after 1966 conformed, however, to the familiar black-versus-white pattern of the ASCS challenge. Schisms
within the black community began to capture more attention than

the conflict between the races. Divisions that had long existed but had been repressed out of need to overcome white control now safely emerged.

At least six lines of conflict can be identified. Young people condemned the attitudes and actions of the older generation. Black Tuskegeeans not affiliated with the Institute accused the "La-dee-da folk" at the school of insensitivity to the "town people." A similar and related charge was made by representatives of the "grass roots," a popular euphemism for the black lower class, who claimed that middle-class blacks were ignoring the plight of the poor. Leaders in rural neighborhoods denounced the dominance of Tuskegee people in setting county policies. Self-proclaimed "pragmatists" criticized the continuing commitment of some blacks to interracialism in government and argued that it was only practical for blacks to take all political offices. Persons ambitious for political power but not part of the TCA's inner circle characterized the older leadership as unresponsive and overly cautious.

Factions often overlapped. A politician might speak for the poor, the young, and the rural, and at the same time be an "out" demanding a place in the decision-making process. Amerson had claimed to represent these groups in 1966, and subsequent officeseekers, noting his success, would attempt to put together the same coalition. But alignments sometimes were confusing. Otis Pinkard, the middle-aged VA employee who had served on the TCA executive committee since the 1940s, emerged as a leading critic of the Gomillion strategy and an ally of the young spokesmen for the "grass roots." Whites were generally ignored in the confrontations between black factions, though occasionally a spokesman for the "masses" condemned continued white "oppression" and singled out some white person—usually a liberal like Allan Parker—for special criticism.[28]

Controversy over the running of the federal antipoverty programs exposed some of the divisions. Beulah Johnson, the retired elementary-school teacher who was one of Gomillion's most outspoken supporters, became the antipoverty administrator when the Macon County Community Action program was begun in 1965. By late 1966 she had come under attack for not doing enough for the county's poor. Her primary antagonist was Consuello Harper, a public-school teacher from Tysonville, an all-black community near Shorter. Harper had tried to get Community Action funds to begin a Head Start program in Tysonville, but the Office of Economic Opportunity in Washington denied her request. OEO funded a Head Start program in Tuskegee, to which rural children would be transported. Undaunted, Harper organized a Head Start program in Tysonville, went directly to the OEO office in Washington, and came home with a separate sixteen-thousand-dollar grant to support it.[29]

Harper believed that her success had come in spite of Beulah Johnson, whom she accused of trying to obstruct her efforts in Tysonville. The Community Action office spent too much antipoverty money in Tuskegee, Harper said, and not enough in rural communities. "The masses in Macon County are not being reached," she announced at a Community Action meeting in April 1967. "Let's think about human beings, about the individual child. We should be working to improve the area where he lives—not taking him out of it—because he's coming right back there every evening." She asked Johnson whether rural community centers could be used in future antipoverty programs. "We have to find buildings that meet certain standards," Johnson replied. Harper countered sharply, "In the rurals, they are getting tired of this." When did Johnson's tenure as director expire? she asked. Others shared Harper's criticisms of Johnson; in late 1967 the Community Action board fired her because she was unable "to communicate with disadvantaged people." Johnson was replaced by a younger person who was thought to be more sensitive to the interests of the rural poor.[30]

Rural residents began to complain that the county school board favored the black public schools in Tuskegee at the expense of rural schools. Led by Harper, black residents in Shorter demanded in 1967 that teachers be transferred from Children's House, the public grammar school in the Institute community, to the Shorter school. They charged that Children's House had more equipment, a better building, and a lower teacher-pupil ratio. Significant differences did exist between Children's House and the other county schools, though some were attributable to greater parental support for the Institute school. Joe Wilson, the school superintendent, agreed to transfer teachers to equalize the teacher-pupil ratio. He told the rural parents what they wanted to hear. "In the past superintendents furnished [teachers at Children's House] with just about anything they wanted to keep them quiet." Wilson helped rural blacks fix the blame for their deprivation on middle-class blacks rather than on the conservative whites who were in fact largely responsible for the miserable conditions in rural schools.[31]

Politics elicited some of the harshest expressions of the conflict among blacks. In the 1968 race for the county commission, Wilber D. Johnston, a young black challenger, accused V. A. Edwards, the former Institute professor elected to the commission in 1964, of being insensitive to the interests of poor people. "It's time for the lit-

tle man in the county to get ahold of something besides the crumbs,"
Johnston said. Sheriff Amerson endorsed Johnston as the best choice
for the "masses." Despite the sheriff's growing political influence,
however, Edwards was reelected. In his challenge to Charles Keever
for mayor that year, Thomas Reed charged that the city government had served the middle- and upper-class residents but neglected
the poor. Reed said that city officials had not promoted federal help
for Tuskegee and that the Small Business Administration had millions of dollars simply "waiting for the asking." But Reed's appeal
did not succeed, largely because Keever had a strong following of his
own among poor blacks. The mayor beat Reed by two to one.[32]

Keever rejoiced in the fact that blacks had again chosen not to
take all city offices. "They only wanted part of the city government—they didn't want to control it, or to segregate it," he said the
night of his reelection. It was true that most blacks did not feel compelled to have complete political control in the way that most whites
had. That surprised whites who projected their own desire for total
control onto blacks. But Keever had partly misinterpreted the
sources of his victory. His personal popularity among poor blacks,
based on many years of friendly business dealings with them, was
probably more responsible for his reelection than the commitment
of some blacks to the sharing of political power. Four of the five city
councilmen elected were black; the one white councilman reelected
was L. M. Gregg, another businessman with unusually strong connections to the "grass roots." The black commitment to interracial
government was no longer strong enough to assure a liberal white's
selection; a white politician had to have a strong personal following
among lower-class blacks to be successful. Moreover, the spread of
political conflict and the rise of political ambitions among blacks
promised to make the election of whites more difficult in the future.
As more black candidates came forth and discovered issues that
united black factions, interracialism in government would become a
less relevant concern to black voters.[33]

The leading proponents of interracialism came under attack from
the grass-roots politicians. At a school board meeting in 1969, Otis
Pinkard and James Hopkins, a young black who would run for the
circuit clerkship the next year, accused Gomillion of showing favor-
itism to the few whites who remained in the public-school system.
Gomillion promptly resigned from the board. "I have enjoyed serving on the Board, but regret that I have not been able to serve effectively," he announced. He was disappointed in the failure of school
desegregation and put off by the contentious spirit among some
blacks. His hope for racial harmony and the sharing of political

power now seemed more futile than it had in the 1950s. Gomillion's resignation marked the end of his public career in Tuskegee; in a few years he would retire to Washington, D.C. Allan Parker expressed similar feelings when he resigned as chairman of the county commission in 1970. The many divisions among blacks and a bitter split between the two white commissioners had persuaded Parker that his ability to provide "functioning leadership" was gone. "I leave you with no bitterness," he announced to his constituents, "but certainly with a great deal of disillusionment."*

The spokespersons for the grass roots prevailed in the 1970 county elections. Lucius Amerson was easily reelected. He had become in effect a political boss who encouraged appeals to class and race identity. His success with that approach showed the way for other ambitious young politicians, some of whom unconsciously mimicked the attitude of the conservative whites who formerly held power. In his successful race for the circuit clerkship, James Hopkins reportedly promised to remove all white employees and all white typewriters from the clerk's office. Consuello Harper won a seat on the school board, giving the rural poor an aggressive and effective representative on that body. Thomas Reed again called for massive economic aid to the poor in his race for the state House. Both he and Fred Gray, who unified all black factions, received enough black votes to overcome another extraordinarily high white turnout. Their success was based partly on a registration effort on the Institute campus and a student campaign to turn out all rural voters. For the first time since Reconstruction, black voices would be heard in the state legislature.[34]

The rise of the grass-roots politicians culminated in the Tuskegee mayor's election in August 1972. Keever faced two black opponents in his bid for a third term. City Councilman Frank Toland, a history professor and a TCA member for more than twenty years, was the favorite of many in the Institute community to be Tuskegee's first black mayor. TCA members believed Toland had set a good example as an effective black public official. He had been instrumental in establishing the Model Cities program, which was bringing millions of federal dollars to Tuskegee. "Model Cities means money in your pocket," Toland told voters, an explanation aimed primarily at the

---

* *Southern Courier*, October 8, 1966; Tuskegee *News*, September 11, 1969; Otis Pinkard interview; Daniel Beasley interview; Gomillion interviews; Tuskegee *News*, August 27, 1970. Gomillion cited health and family concerns, not the political environment in Tuskegee, for his move from the community. Allan Parker was still living in Tuskegee in 1984.

lower-class blacks who were likely to determine the outcome of the election.[35]

The third candidate, Johnny L. Ford, was a former administrator of the Model Cities program. The twenty-nine-year-old son of a VA hospital employee, Ford had worked for Senator Robert F. Kennedy of New York and for Vice-President Hubert H. Humphrey in the 1968 presidential campaign and made much of his ties to national politicians when he returned to Tuskegee in 1969. He had ready access to the men who controlled the flow of federal money, Ford suggested. He was more reticent about a controversial relationship he began soon after his return. Handsome enough to be named to *Ebony* magazine's list of most eligible bachelors in 1970, Ford began surreptitiously dating Frances "Taz" Rainer, a young white social worker descended from an aristocratic family in Bullock County. They fell in love despite fears of violence against them. "Finally we came to the point, and said to hell with it," Ford explained later. "If I love you and you love me," he recounted saying to Taz, "we're going to do the only honest and right thing." They married in October 1970. Ford did not know at the time that interracial marriage was illegal in Alabama.[36]

Ford's marriage spiced up what already promised to be a hot race. He worried that his white wife might cost him black votes. "There ain't nothing wrong with racial pride," Ford said in campaign advertisements, "but racism is wrong whether it be by blacks or whites. . . . We are all God's children." He vowed to "close the gaps between black and white, rich and poor, young and old." He especially wanted to close the gap between Johnny Ford and poor black voters of all ages. He got help from Thomas Reed in countering the view held by some of the "grass roots" that a black mayor could not govern as effectively as Keever had. Reed assured voters that his color had not handicapped him in the state legislature. "I do not believe that you, the people of Tuskegee, will not vote for Johnny Ford because his face is black," Reed said. Lucius Amerson appealed more directly to racial solidarity in his endorsement of Ford, whom he called his "friend and brother." He asked all students at Tuskegee Institute to "come out and make it happen for our brother."[37]

The students apparently did make it happen for Ford. Keever led in the first vote with forty-three percent to Ford's thirty-three. Toland's support was confined largely to the Institute community. Ford's campaign organized hundreds of Institute students, recently returned from summer vacation, to register for the September runoff. They accounted for most of the 550-vote increase in the turnout for the runoff, nearly all of which went to Ford. He beat Keever, who received much of Toland's support, by 127 votes.[38]

The 1972 city election completed the transfer of political power from whites to blacks. Blacks now controlled both county and city government. The sheriff, the county court judge, the circuit court clerk, the school superintendent, the tax collector, and both state representatives were black. About eighty percent of local elected officials were black, which conformed closely to blacks' share of the population. The *New York Times* reported in 1973 that the county had a higher proportion of black elected officials than any other place in the United States. As was its tradition, Tuskegee led the way in black accomplishment.[39]

13

If I Forget You,
O Jerusalem

ON WEDNESDAY night, January 31, 1973, burglars broke into the home of an elderly white Tuskegee couple, Dr. and Mrs. Murray Smith. The intruders—three black men, according to Mrs. Smith—beat, choked, and raped her in the course of robbing the house. The eighty-six-year-old Dr. Smith, a retired public health physician, was unable to come to his wife's defense. That same night, the residence of another elderly white woman, who was not at home, and several Tuskegee businesses were forcibly entered. The break-ins continued on Friday night. Someone attempted to burglarize the home of still another elderly white woman but was apparently frightened away by the woman's daughter. The same man, or men, then succeeded in entering a nearby house occupied by three elderly white sisters. All three women were brutally beaten and mutilated. Evelyn Carr Page, seventy-two, was stabbed twenty-seven times and died during the attack. Josie Carr Green, seventy-eight, suffered twenty-two stab wounds and never regained consciousness; she died two weeks later. Carribec Carr, seventy-six, survived, though she was hospitalized for a long period after the attack.[1]

Tuskegee was panic-stricken on Saturday morning, February 3, as news of the violence at the Carr home spread. Mayor Ford declared a state of emergency and asked Governor George Wallace to send state troopers and the National Guard to Tuskegee. Wallace dispatched fifty troopers and alerted the guardsmen in the area. Tuskegee police put the homes of all elderly whites under surveillance. Ford ordered all stores and "juke joints" to close at 6:00 P.M.

on Saturday. "I want everyone to stay in their homes," the mayor said in a radio broadcast. "Keep your doors and windows locked and have all your outside lights turned on." He assured the citizens that everything was being done to apprehend the "maniacs" responsible for the crimes.[2]

On Sunday morning Tuskegee police arrested a man who had in his possession jewelry from the Carr home. They charged David Lee Goode, a twenty-four-year-old black who had been released from state prison only a week earlier, with murder, rape, burglary, and assault. Tensions eased and the state troopers left Tuskegee, though many white citizens worried because only one person had been arrested. Goode, they believed, had an accomplice. The break-ins ceased, however, with his arrest.[3]

These inexplicable attacks intervened in the course of history in Tuskegee. They caused a sudden outpouring of the many fears long pent up among whites. They seemed to fulfill the apocalyptic prophecy of violence that conservatives had often made about the aftermath of black political power. Coming just months after Johnny Ford was elected, they were unfairly associated in the minds of many whites with the new black government. Ford received little credit for his poised, resolute handling of the crisis. Only a few whites recognized that such criminal violence could just as easily have happened under white government. Many whites acted on their fear by moving from Tuskegee as soon as possible after the Carr murders. The town's white population had held steady during the 1960s, despite some emigration after the schools were desegregated, but it fell precipitously in the 1970s. More than half the white population left Tuskegee during the decade; fewer than 600 whites remained in the town in 1980. Other factors contributed to the exodus, but the perception of lawlessness—especially when it seemed to be vividly confirmed by the mutilation and molestation of elderly women—was clearly a primary cause.[4]

Events after the Carr murders exacerbated fears about safety in Tuskegee. David Lee Goode was tried for one of the murders, but the jury failed to reach a verdict. During the wait for a second trial, Goode apparently walked out of the unattended Macon County jail, which was run by Sheriff Amerson. He was recaptured, but in the meantime even more Tuskegeeans, black and white, had lost confidence in local law enforcement. When Tuskegee police arrested another black man for allegedly killing a white woman on the Institute campus, they refused to put him in the county jail. The suspect was placed there only after Mayor Ford received permission from Amerson to have city policemen stand guard at the jail. In early 1974 the city policemen went out on strike, leaving the citizens' safety entirely to Sheriff Amerson. To end the strike, Ford granted the policemen a large raise. He also removed the chief of police and took charge of the department himself. This sequence of events raised questions in the minds of many about whether Ford and Amerson were capable of maintaining law and order in Tuskegee.[5]

A number of indictments and accusations against public officials in the 1970s further undermined confidence in "black" government. Amerson was charged with brutality to prisoners in 1971 but was later acquitted. Several years later he was accused of embezzlement but, again, was vindicated. Both George Bulls, the chairman of the county commission, and his brother Albert, a Tuskegee city councilman, were convicted of tax evasion in 1975. Albert Bulls was also found guilty of selling food stamps illegally. An accountant with the Tuskegee Housing Authority was convicted of embezzling $250,000 in federal money in 1977. State Representative Thomas Reed and a young Tuskegee city official named Ronald Williams were convicted of trying to bribe a white legislator to get his support for a bill establishing a dog-racing track in Macon County. By no means were all charges against black officials in the 1970s sustained, and part of the attention paid to them was no doubt the result of Tuskegee's notably black government. But the steady stream of accusations suggested to some Tuskegeeans and many outsiders that corruption was rampant.[6]

Even Fred Gray, the highly respected civil rights lawyer and legislator, came in for criticism. Gray served as Tuskegee city attorney, and in that position he had some responsibility for overseeing a municipal bond issue on which the city defaulted. The default received much attention because some bondholders were recently returned prisoners of war in Vietnam who had invested their accumulated back pay. Gray said fault lay with the investment banking company selling the bonds, and he was not charged with breaking the law. Questions about the bond issue were raised, however, when Gray was nominated for a federal judgeship in 1980, and they may have been partly responsible for the eventual withdrawal of his nomination.[7]

Johnny Ford would prove to be a controversial figure throughout the 1970s. Many Tuskegee residents objected to Ford's support of Richard Nixon for president in 1972. His endorsement of George Wallace for governor in 1974 drew even more criticism. Ford explained that his alliance with conservative politicians was necessary to ensure the continued flow of federal and state money to Tuskegee—a position remarkably similar to one taken by Booker Washington three generations earlier. He pointed proudly to the large amounts of government money that his administration brought to the city—by his estimate about $50 million in the 1970s—to improve basic services like water, sewage, streets, and public housing.[8]

Ford's expediency, however, offended both the liberals of the Gomillion school and the student activists of the 1960s. He was criticized for alleged mismanagement of the city budget, especially after the city had to borrow money for operating expenses just after his 1976 reelection. Sales taxes were increased, and the municipal utilities board raised electricity rates to levels higher than those elsewhere in Alabama. Income from the utilities board was used to supplement the city budget, including the salary of the mayor. Ford was accused of maintaining a magisterial style as mayor and of keeping political cronies on the city payroll. "All of the money coming into this town from the government for help has gone in the pockets of the elected few," one citizen claimed. "We put Black[s] in office downtown and look what they have done." In 1977 the Marxist intellectual Manning Marable, then chair of political science at Tuskegee Institute, likened the situation in Tuskegee to postcolonial politics in Africa and the Caribbean in which a "black petty bourgeoisie" takes power and "popular political participation of the black masses declines, corruption is institutionalized, police and law enforcement officials increase in number, black culture becomes 'a tool for class rule,' and the history of the pre-independence movement is deliberately distorted." For Marable, who had close family ties to the Tuskegee black bourgeoisie, Tuskegee was plagued by a "politics of illusion" in the post–civil rights years, just as its earlier white supremacist politics had been based on an unreal presumption of democracy.[9]

Ford's alliance with a New York businessman, Charles Wallace, bothered some Tuskegeeans. Wallace, an oil distributor, planned to build a refinery on the site of the Tuskegee Army Air Field, land that the city of Tuskegee helped to secure for the project. For Ford's reelection effort in 1976, Wallace hosted a dinner of fried catfish for more than 3,000 people. "Stuffing their mouths with greasy fish, cold watermelon and starchy bread," Marable later wrote, "black citizens listened to Johnny Ford's mellow promises of better government. Not unlike the days of the Bourbon Democrats, when plantation owners gave a free chicken away to each black male supporter, black voters marched off to the polls two days later and gave Johnny Ford a commanding victory of 58% of the total vote. Observers noted privately that Ford's black supporters spent more money for his fish fry feast . . . than did both [his opponents] in their entire campaigns."[10]

At the root of much political controversy in Tuskegee in the 1970s was the desire for economic development. The attainment of political rights in the 1960s had raised the hopes of poor blacks for material advancement. They wanted more food, better clothing and housing, an automobile—the standard badges of American prosperity. Ford's emphasis on getting federal money for Tuskegee was largely a response to this desire for economic progress among the poor. Charles Wallace's proposed oil refinery raised hope for many new, high-paying industrial jobs. Thomas Reed's dog track was meant to make Macon County an entertainment center and, thus, to invigorate the local economy. The bond issue that damaged Fred Gray's reputation was intended to establish a new business—one producing tomatoes grown in water rather than soil—that would provide new jobs. To achieve material progress, most poor black Tuskegeeans were willing to accept Ford's consciously nonideological political posture and his self-serving relationship with Charles Wallace. The voters of Macon County so appreciated Thomas Reed's efforts for economic development in the dog-track proposal that they reelected him even after his conviction for attempted bribery.[11]

Most of the hopes for economic progress were disappointed, however. Charles Wallace's refinery had begun to seem like mere fantasy before the end of the 1970s, despite the city's generous terms for purchase of the old airfield. It would never be built. The tomato project and the dog-track proposal failed. The failures exposed a sad irony. The civil rights movement that began in Macon County in 1941 was founded on Booker Washington's assumption that political rights would follow from economic power. Thousands of poor blacks in Macon County learned in the 1970s that it would not work the other way. Political power did not lead to economic equality.[12]

The politics of the 1970s disappointed Charles Gomillion and other older blacks who had worked so hard to bring change in Tuskegee. They too had expected black political rights to bring economic uplift, though material progress had not been their primary goal. Gomillion regretted the political outcome. "It's not working out the way we initially hoped," he told the *New York Times* in 1973. The apparent corruption of some black politicians troubled him most. "We were prepared," he said later, "for some inefficiency on the part of Negro government officials during the first few years.

We were not prepared for . . . corruption." The rejection of interracial government by many blacks saddened him, because it represented a turn away from the Gomillion ideal of shared power. The
refusal of many whites to accept black political power also undermined that ideal. The failure of school desegregation deeply disappointed Gomillion, who had put much trust in the power of education to cure society's problems. When Gomillion moved from
Tuskegee to Washington, D.C., in 1974, he took with him many
doubts about the success of his almost fifty years of activism.[13]

Most white liberals shared Gomillion's disappointment in the
rejection of interracial government, the behavior of some black
politicians, and the failure of school desegregation. Their hope for
a community of racial harmony seemed futile by the mid-1970s.
Their ranks had thinned. Henry Neill Segrest died in 1974; none
of his five sons attempted to take his place in the community.
Frances Rush supported the Tuskegee public schools until her
daughter was virtually the only white child in the system. She finally gave up and moved to Auburn. No ministers arrived to continue
the tradition of outspoken racial liberalism set by Robert Miller
and Ennis Sellers. Allan Parker stayed on for many years to work for
the betterment of Tuskegee, but he took a less active part in local
politics, the character of which he often disapproved. Preston
Hornsby was the lone white liberal who seemed comfortable in the
new political climate. Reelected to the probate judgeship in 1970,
1976, and 1982, Hornsby stayed very popular among the black
lower class and with nearly all patrons of the probate office. "He
never stops campaigning," one Tuskegee resident offered in explanation for Hornsby's popularity with an overwhelmingly black
electorate. Hornsby's gregarious personality, his willingness to make
personal loans to virtually any resident of Macon County, and his
efficiency as a public official accounted for his continued success
in the volatile political environment of the 1970s.[14]

Many conservative whites believed that their dismal predictions
about the results of black political power had come to pass. Few
took consolation from feeling prescient, however. They had lost
their control over the community; they occupied none of the seats
of political power after the 1960s; and they had witnessed a rapid
decrease in their number, though many had gone not to Auburn
or Montgomery but to the Tuskegee cemetery. Ernest Bridges died
in 1965, Judge Varner and Edward Laslie in 1966. The only sons of
Bridges and Laslie died prematurely in the late 1960s. None of
Judge Varner's three sons stayed in the county. Neither did the
younger generation of Edwardses or Lightfoots. The few who

stayed—because of businesses or property or sentimental attach-ment to home—often felt isolated and threatened. In 1979 John Fletcher Segrest expressed his sympathy for white South Africans, with whose situation he closely identified. The population de-crease undermined important institutions: several civic and social clubs went out of existence. The membership in the three main Protestant churches fell steadily after the mid-1960s.[15]

When Segrest's thirty-year-old daughter Mab returned to Tuske-gee in 1979 after a long absence, she found many houses on Tuske-gee's Main Street boarded up. There were only twenty-five people at the Sunday service at the Methodist church. "Many young peo-ple in old white Tuskegee had left," Mab Segrest wrote in her auto-biographical *Memoir of a Race Traitor* in 1994. "The oldest people were dead, the old people ancient, the people my own age looking strangest of all." Now an activist against racial, religious, and sexual intolerance, Segrest had come home seeking reconciliation with her conservative parents from whom she had been alienated. As the Segrest family sang a hymn at the Methodist church, she later wrote, "I stood between my father and mother, loving them more than I had in years. Daddy on my right side making up words he didn't know, like he always had, then thundering forth on the cho-rus, Mother on the left using a large magnifying glass to find the page then singing the first verse, which she could remember, and standing in poignant dignity through the rest she could not see. I cried through the hymn, and another, and the *gloria patrae* and the doxology and silent prayer and offertory and announcements and the responsive reading.

> If I forget you, O Jerusalem
> Let my right hand wither!
> Let my tongue cleave to the roof of my mouth,
> If I do not remember you."

For Mab Segrest it was a moment of true reckoning with her past. "I was born to a town of white folks willing itself to die, a world in which love and beauty mixed inextricably with hatred and pain. How to grieve for what should not, did not, deserve to last?"[16]

At the start of the 1980s, African Americans in Tuskegee looked forward with hope for better economic prospects. A new shopping center, including a Wal-Mart store, was built on the outskirts of downtown. The city created an industrial park to lure new em-ployers. Reelected easily in 1980 and 1984, Johnny Ford continued to bring large amounts of federal and state money to Tuskegee. He even made the best of the antiwelfare policies of Ronald Reagan.

In 1982 he told *Ebony* magazine, "Look, I've been in this business long enough to be able to roll with the punches. We'll play Reaganomics for all it's worth and get as much out of it as possible. We go where the resources are." In 1984 President Reagan came to Tuskegee to announce a $9 million grant for a building to house aerospace and health-education studies, to be named for Daniel "Chappie" James, the Tuskegee Institute graduate who became a four-star general of the U.S. Air Force.

In the early 1980s many people in Tuskegee still placed their hopes for a better economic future on gambling at a proposed dog-racing track. In Greene County, Alabama, a track had been opened in 1977, and it had brought what seemed like a bonanza of jobs and taxes to a poor, predominantly black community as thousands of people from Birmingham and Mississippi traveled to "Greenetrack" to wager on the dogs. A referendum to establish a track in Macon County was held in 1980, and a spirited campaign resulted in defeat of the track. The Tuskegee Civic Association was a leader of the opposition, citing gambling's record of bringing increased indebtedness and crime to communities where it was legalized. Three years later, however, after the national recession of 1981–82 had made its impact on the community, the voters changed their minds and authorized the building of "Victoryland."[17]

The track was actually built near Shorter, about twenty miles west of Tuskegee, to accommodate the population concentrations in Montgomery and Birmingham. The city of Tuskegee then annexed the track into its limits. By law Victoryland employed many Macon Countians, and its governing authority kept a good many local politicians busy. The city utilities board accepted the cost of providing electricity and water to the track in exchange for the opportunity to generate the revenue from the utilities' sales. In addition to the strong opposition to gambling in many quarters in Alabama, there was much criticism of the city's proprietary role in Victoryland, both from within and without Macon County. Still, when the track opened in 1984, the city and county began to enjoy hundreds of thousands of new tax dollars.

Some people saw the dog-track money as a panacea for many ills. Supporters of the track imagined that it would make the community a regional center for entertainment, a kind of Las Vegas in the Black Belt. It would provide jobs for the rising number of unemployed residents and many new entrepreneurial opportunities for local businessmen. Government necessarily would have to grow to meet the new demands for services, thus creating more public employment. More immediately, some dog-track proceeds were earmarked to address the problems in the county's pubic schools. In the mid-1980s, the Macon County Board of Education hired and then fired a series of school superintendents as it tried to reverse the perception that the schools generally were not fulfilling their purposes. The system suffered a high level of truancy and drug problems. A 1989 audit of the school board's operations found much income and spending unaccounted for. Increasingly, middle-class black families transported their children forty-five miles to private schools in Montgomery rather than send them to the local schools. To improve the schools, much of the dog-track money was assigned in 1986 to underwrite a $12 million bond issue to build a new, consolidated high school to serve all Macon County students.

Consolidation of schools threatened the only successfully desegregated school in Macon County, Notasulga High School. The Notasulga school was rebuilt after the 1964 arson, but it appeared that whites were likely to abandon the school altogether when desegregation was strictly enforced in 1970–71. Many white students left for Macon Academy and other private schools. But Robert Anderson, a Notasulga graduate who had returned to teach mathematics in 1968, was determined to save his alma mater from becoming a one-race, all-black school. Made principal in 1972, Anderson began campaigning among whites in the little town to send their children back to the local high school where he thought they belonged. He endured the hostility of old friends who thought he was merely a naïve young liberal for believing that integrated education might work in Macon County. But by 1973 whites were returning, and in 1974 the Notasulga student body was exactly half black and half white. In 1974 both the *New York Times* and the British Broadcasting Corporation featured Notasulga High School as one conspicuous school desegregation success at a time when the process looked like a failure in Boston and many other places in America.[18]

In a small town like Notasulga, where school sporting events had long been the focus of much community life, in a state where college football dominated social and cultural life, winning football and basketball teams overcame many other concerns, even racial alienation. Anderson had the help of two young coaches who revitalized white interest in the school by building championship athletic teams. At his first integrated football practice in 1969, Coach Dwight Sanderson poured a cup of water, drank from it, handed it to a black player who drank from it, and then took the cup back and drank again. Sanderson then told the rest of the squad that if they wanted to play on his team they too would share the cup. In the next decade Sanderson's disciplined, biracial teams laid waste almost all their opponents among small Alabama high schools.[19]

In 1990 the Macon County Board of Education voted to close Notasulga High School and transfer its students to the new, consolidated, $12 million Booker T. Washington High School in Tuskegee. The board reasoned that one big school brought economies of scale both in instruction and building maintenance. The irony of the situation was hardly lost on Robert Anderson, who well remembered when the all-white state school board had tried to close Notasulga to prevent desegregation in 1964. Now a majority-black board was closing it, and Anderson believed the result would be to end desegregation by abolishing the one school in Macon County where it had been achieved. Notasulga whites would not send their children to the Tuskegee high school, Anderson reported after taking an informal poll of parents. "There's a big difference between the students in Tuskegee and here," one white Notasulga mother of three daughters insisted. "They're more violent. I don't want my children to go to a school that's 94 percent black." The board's lawyer noted that two other small schools, both all-black, were closing at the same time, and black students at those schools were being asked to give up no less than what whites in Notasulga were being asked to forfeit. "Macon County is 90 percent black," the chairman of the school board, a black professor at Tuskegee University, declared. "Did it get this way because blacks wanted segregation? No, because whites left." Once again, school desegregation had laid bare the deep racial alienation in Macon County.[20]

Notasulga whites organized a committee to raise money to hire a lawyer to fight the board's decision, and in 1991 they sued to stop the closure, using as their legal authority the desegregation order in *Lee v. Macon*, still in effect twenty-eight years after it was first given. At a hearing in the federal courthouse in Opelika, the ironies mounted further. Judge Robert E. Varner, the conservative Nixon appointee and son of the late probate judge of Macon County, presided during several days of testimony about whether school consolidation was good or evil and whether race played any part in the school board's decision. Robert Anderson sat at one table and his employers at another. "It was kind of like taking Mamma and Daddy to court to make them love you," he later commented. During the tense hearing, Anderson studied the notebook he always carried to remind him of important matters. On one page he had written, "Remember *Reaping the Whirlwind* and what happened to Mr. Parker," referring to the 1985 edition of this book, which recounted the failed struggle of Allan Parker and other Tuskegee liberals to desegregate Tuskegee High School. More reassuring to Anderson were the words of Martin Luther King, Jr., that he had recorded: "The ultimate measure of a man is not where he stands in moments of comfort and convenience but where he stands in times of challenge and controversy."[21]

The most persuasive testimony may have come from the state superintendent of education, who told Judge Varner that "if you believe *Lee vs. Macon* is still in place and an integrated system is worth having, the extra cost [of keeping Notasulga High open] is worth it. The effect of consolidation will be a totally segregated system." Varner soon ruled in favor of the Notasulga parents: "Here is one little town in Alabama which has been led by a black superintendent and a white principal to a belief in [integrated] education. That's what the Supreme Court believes in, and that's what Frank Johnson believes in." The board appealed the ruling, in part asserting that Varner was biased in favor of whites, but an appeals panel upheld his decision. Notasulga High School remained the county's one integrated school in 1998.[22]

By the time of the school consolidation dispute, much of the optimism in Tuskegee engendered by the dog track had been lost. Economic conditions in the town worsened in the late 1980s. Unemployment among teenagers rose to high levels, and the city experienced an epidemic of drug use. Businesses began to close, including the town's new movie theater. Automobile dealerships, one of which was owned by a black businessman, went out of business. The Wal-Mart store, opened with much celebration at the new shopping center in 1984, closed its doors in 1988. Its managers cited a problem with shoplifting, bad checks, and the high cost of utilities. "They are using utilities monies to fund [city] positions," the Wal-Mart manager told the Tuskegee *News* as he left town. Eighty-seven people lost jobs with the closure, and the big building still remained vacant a decade later. In the 1990s, there would be as many empty storefronts on the commercial streets in Tuskegee as there were businesses open. And yet the sign announcing the visitor's arrival into the town still read, "Tuskegee: Thou Pride of the Swift Growing South."[23]

When the writer V. S. Naipaul, whose Indian-immigrant father and black teachers had read to him the works of Booker Washington as a child in Trinidad, visited Tuskegee in the late 1980s, his overriding impression of the famous town was of grandeur in decay. "When black people had won the vote," he explained in *A Turn in the South*, "the white people of Tuskegee had moved away. So there had been a kind of victory here. But the town that had been taken over was small and poor, black-poor, with nothing of the life and money of the white university town of Auburn, just twenty miles away." Even Tuskegee Institute, now called Tuskegee University, reflected decay—pot-holed streets, buildings in need of paint. "Decay was melancholy enough to me, a visitor, a man passing through," Naipaul wrote, but "it wasn't a subject I felt I could raise with older people who had given their lives to Tuskegee. . . . And the subject didn't come up. Were there tennis courts? Yes, there were: just at the back of the library. But grass was growing through the asphalt surfacing of two (or three) of the courts. A kind of silence was imposed on the visitor, as in a private house; certain things were not to be seen."[24]

It was a sad sight for anyone who remembered when the town had been a lively trading center for people shopping for automobiles, clothing, food, and a variety of services. Now Tuskegee residents were more likely to travel to Auburn, Opelika, or Montgomery to purchase basic goods and services. Much of Tuskegee's economic decline was part of the overall demise of commerce in small Black Belt towns, where the closing of clothing shops, five-and-ten-cent stores, and car dealerships was commonplace, even the norm. The situation in Tuskegee was made worse, however, by the almost complete abandonment of the town by whites. According to the 1990 census, only 317 whites lived in the town of almost 12,000; Tuskegee was now 97.5 percent black. There was little reason to doubt that just a few more years would take away the last old white residents. In 1995 Macon Academy, down to sixty-two students, closed its doors and moved to Montgomery. Questions of racial conflict, or of interracial harmony for that matter, were now virtually moot in Tuskegee.[25]

In the late 1980s and the 1990s, Tuskegee citizens increasingly vented their anger at local elected officials. In 1988 Rhonda Freeman-Baraka, the young African American editor of the Tuskegee *News*, wrote critically of Thomas Reed's crusade to get the Confederate flag removed from atop the state capitol in Montgomery. "Perhaps he finds a shortage of problems about which to gripe here," Freeman-Baraka wrote sarcastically. "Well, it just so happens we have a list: Education, industry, unemployment, drug abuse, crime." Several citizens persistently criticized Mayor Ford's alleged unnecessary travel outside Tuskegee and the city's high utility rates. Others demanded to know what elected officials were going to do about providing medical care after the county's only hospital closed in 1987. The announcement of a $1.4 million shortfall in the city's budget in 1988 brought widespread complaints against city officials. Throughout the late 1980s, Macon County residents witnessed intense infighting among its public officials—the sheriff suing the county commission for failing to supply his office with funds, one racing commissioner suing another for keeping documents secret, four county commissioners demanding impeachment of their chairman. Any citizen had to wonder whether local government could work effectively in such turmoil.[26]

Officials in Macon County continued to be accused of malfeasance in office, and some were found guilty. In 1987 a Tuskegee businessman with close ties to the racing commission was indicted on many counts of misappropriating dog-track funds intended to go to Tuskegee charities. In 1988 Thomas Reed, whose conviction for attempted bribery in the mid-1970s was ultimately overturned, was convicted of bribery for influencing prison paroles. A Macon County Board of Education member was convicted of a state ethics violation for using public funds to finance his election campaign. In 1992 a state of Alabama audit of the Macon County Commission accused the commission chairman of siphoning off construction-project funds through secret ownership of equipment rented to the county. The chairman denounced the report as the "culmination of a vicious campaign by my political enemies," and other officials maintained that black Macon County officeholders were subject to character assassinations by racist white newspapers, especially the Montgomery *Advertiser*. Freeman-Baraka of the Tuskegee *News* commented that she could not "say for sure what the motives are of the white press, but I do know Macon County officials have played into their hands. . . . If there was nothing going on to report, it wouldn't be reported."[27]

In the 1990s the Macon County electorate began to rebel against their entrenched politicians. Seeking his sixth term in 1992, Mayor Ford faced a strong challenge from a political novice who emphasized Tuskegee's recent decline, citing the loss of the hospital and retail stores, unsafe streets and schools, and the big municipal deficit. Ford won but with nothing like the big margins he had enjoyed in past elections. By that year, funding for the city and for local schools was heading into a crisis. Revenues from the dog track had started to decline, the beginning of a steady downward spiral for Alabama's dog tracks that resulted from the opening of casino gambling in Mississippi and state lotteries in Florida and

Georgia. Soon Victoryland payments did not cover the interest on the bonded debt for the new high school, and the county had to raise the local sales tax. Federal funds to the city of Tuskegee were also drying up. "The days when we could go to Washington with a bushel basket," the editor of the Tuskegee *News* wrote in 1996, "and later with a wheelbarrow and then finally with an 18-wheeler to bring home those millions in federal tax dollars are gone and gone forever." The city payroll and city services were larger than the tax base could support, but city officials were not willing to cut jobs or services.[28]

In 1996 the voters made a strong statement for fiscal responsibility when in both county and city elections they turned against most incumbents. A challenger who promised "honest government and financial responsibility" defeated county commission chairman Frank Lee, whose fellow incumbents were also turned out. In the city elections, Johnny Ford faced an old political ally, Ronald Williams, who almost twenty years earlier had been convicted with Thomas Reed of trying to bribe a legislator to create the dog track. Ford reminded the voters of Williams's past legal troubles, but it seemed not to matter because Ford's long romance with the electorate clearly had ended. Williams beat him almost three-to-one. All but one incumbent city council representative fell also. "Most were simply caught up in an atmosphere of despair," the *News* explained about the defeated incumbents.[29]

By the late 1990s the Tuskegee example seemed to suggest, ever more strongly over time, that politics and public spending did not solve the problems of the post–civil rights South. And yet what the solution *could be* seemed to elude everyone. Those who came to power in 1996 knew to manage in a fiscally conservative manner, but they had yet to identify a means for overcoming the severe economic and educational problems in the community. By 1998 the Tuskegee Chamber of Commerce had begun to organize a campaign to bring more private, corporate investment into the county. No one assumed, however, that it would be an easy task.[30]

It seemed that the outcome of the civil rights movement in Macon County had disappointed everyone. No one's hopes were completely fulfilled, and some believed that their lives had been seriously harmed. White conservatives had lost the hegemony they had fought so hard to maintain, and most felt it necessary to leave the community rather than live under a predominantly black government. Poor blacks had gained political rights, but they had not significantly improved their material circumstances. To many, voting seemed an empty exercise if it did not result in economic progress. Their political power at the local level did not yield the great changes that they wanted in society. By the time blacks gained political power, local government, already weak in Alabama, had lost much of its remaining authority as a result of the rapid expansion of federal and state power in the 1950s and 1960s. Decisions about education, welfare, criminal justice, and economic development in Macon County were more likely to be made outside the county than within it. That had not been true one or two generations earlier. Poor blacks could hardly influence those more remote governments as much as they could the county commission or the city council.

The irony was inverted for white conservatives: they had fought a long, losing battle, often at great personal cost, to maintain control over the seats of local power, but what they lost was an authority diluted and weakened by the intrusion of federal and state power. It was of great symbolic importance to them, but of declining real significance in their lives. To compound the irony, the federal government—their nemesis in the 1960s and the threat that made maintenance of local control so important—became more sympathetic to conservative values in the 1970s, 1980s, and 1990s. No one could have predicted such an outcome.

The consequences of the civil rights movement disappointed black and white liberals partly because they had had unrealistic expectations. The goals of Gomillion, Allan Parker, and other liberals were democratic government, interracial cooperation, and communal harmony, the ideology Gomillion called "civic democracy." The goals of civic democracy were, however, inherently contradictory. A fundamental tension exists between harmony and democracy. Gomillion and the TCA had necessarily created disorder in the community in their effort to bring about democracy. Once democracy was implemented, its inherently contentious nature emerged. The history of Macon County after 1965 is largely the story of the development of political competition in a democracy. It seemed especially unharmonious when contrasted to the oligarchical rule of white conservatives, but the price of order and harmony in the old regime had been oppression. With freedom came competition, disagreement, and factionalism.

Gomillion and other liberals had assumed that the overthrow of the conservative elite would result in more open-minded, more sensitive public officials. In fact, democracy does not guarantee virtue in politics; it promises only that politics will reflect the society, good and bad. Most liberals expected the leadership of the community to be assumed by the people who had led the civil

rights movement—the TCA and their white allies. Many felt betrayed when young blacks challenged the older leadership. It was
inevitable, however, that the black community would cease to follow a single person after the obstacles to democracy were removed.
Soon politics in Macon County merely reflected the strengths and
weaknesses, the ideals and prejudices, of its people.

The liberals may also have misunderstood the nature of power.
They witnessed black politicians take almost all political offices
after they had spent decades fighting for the right to share power.
They believed that by appealing to black racial solidarity and ignoring the need for interracial cooperation the new officeholders
had committed the sins of white conservatives. The behavior of the
grass-roots politicians may, however, have been less a rejection of
interracial cooperation than a demonstration of the aggressive
and protective nature of political power. If people have the opportunity to acquire power, the urge to take all the power is often irre-
sistible. Once gained, power is rarely surrendered willingly. "The
people who are out of power want to get in," Fred Gray observed in
1983, and "the people who are in power want to stay in. While Dr.
Gomillion was willing to share, there are others who feel that if you
have the mechanism, and if you have the opportunity, then you
should use it to its fullest potential."[31]

Those unhappy with the aftermath of the civil rights movement
sometimes failed to see the full importance of the political changes.
For all the disorder and dissension it had wrought, democratic government gave all Macon Countians a voice in political decision-
making. It was true that political power had not imparted the control over their destiny that many had expected, but now the use
of power, whatever its limitations, was the province of all. No one
could say with certainty what political equality would mean—indeed, it was too soon to determine finally that political rights
would *not* lead to economic progress—but certainly Macon County had moved much closer to fulfilling the American ideals of
equality and individual liberty.

The events of the 1960s and afterward put Booker Washington's
historical reputation in a new light. Although he had remained a
hero all along to many blacks, to the student activists of the 1960s
Washington had represented acquiescence in white power. He
was, as they conceived him, an Uncle Tom who had postponed the
day of freedom by his willingness to accept segregation and disfranchisement. The success of the civil rights movement showed
that Washington's strategy had worked in Macon County: a group
of blacks who had acquired education and economic indepen-

dence—largely as a result of Washington's own efforts—carried out a successful movement to gain full political rights. Looking back over the twenty-five-year struggle to get the right to vote, black Macon Countians could understand Washington's public acquiescence in white political hegemony as a necessary tactic. Change usually comes one step at a time, and Washington had taken a necessary step to secure educational and economic opportunity. From the vantage point of the 1990s, it seemed clear that the attainment of political rights had followed directly from Washington's compromise, though the national movement for civil rights in the 1960s had certainly facilitated black Macon Countians' acquisition of power. Moreover, post–civil rights events appeared to vindicate the Washington strategy. The constant public quests for economic development in Macon County dramatized the fact that political rights could be unfulfilling if not accompanied by material progress. Johnny Ford's eager coalescence with Richard Nixon, George Wallace, and Ronald Reagan demonstrated that black leaders would still make controversial alliances for sound practical reasons.

The "atmosphere of despair" in Tuskegee in the late 1990s obscured from many residents the affirming, even heroic nature of their community's historical experience. Most Tuskegeans were too preoccupied with present problems to contemplate the complex meanings of their past. American popular culture and mass media tend to treat the past as either good or bad; history is often reduced to a time of triumph or one of failure. An example of how Americans remembered the "bad" of history came in 1996 when President Bill Clinton invited to the White House some of the men who had survived the infamous "Tuskegee Syphilis Experiment." A number of Macon County residents, subjects in a U.S. Public Health Service study begun in the 1930s, had been allowed to languish in disease long after penicillin was used to cure syphilis. The situation was exposed in 1972, and Fred Gray instituted a class action lawsuit that led to a $10 million settlement for the men and their families.[32] President Clinton atoned for this awful part of American history by offering a formal apology on behalf of the U.S. government. The good that was accomplished by the U.S. government's acknowledgment of its wrongs and reaffirmation of its commitment to justice must be balanced against the way that such public confessions teach that the past was unmitigated horror.

African Americans in Tuskegee owned a history that was far more useful in the present despair. Throughout the near and distant past, blacks in the community had worked courageously to improve their lives, sometimes succeeding and sometimes falling far short. The United States Park Service had advanced the appreciation of Tuskegee's history in 1974, when it made Tuskegee Institute a national historic site. The campus homes of Booker Washington and George Washington Carver were renovated and opened to the public in the late 1970s. Also refurbished was the magnificent Varner home, Grey Columns, which sits adjacent to the campus. The Park Service had enshrined the historic Tuskegee accommodation between the local black leadership and the white aristocracy. The symbolism was acceptable to most Tuskegeeans, black and white, by the late 1970s in a way that it probably would not have been in 1965. The community's new appreciation of the past also included recognition of Charles Gomillion. He had not been scorned as widely as had Booker Washington, of course, but his gradualist approach and interracial ideology had been rejected in the late 1960s. In 1977 the city named its new municipal building for him. The Gomillion Building was a monument to the civil rights movement in Macon County and a tribute to the person most responsible for bringing change to the community.

Gomillion died in October 1995, at age ninety-five, having stayed active until just days before his death and, apparently sensing that the end was near, having hurried to Tuskegee. His passing came as a surprise to some who suspected he would, quite literally, keep everlastingly at it. A memorial service at the Tuskegee University chapel brought together perhaps 200 friends, mostly elderly black people who knew of Gomillion's deeds from many years past. Very few whites attended, and the absence of whites who had shared his commitment to interracialism was conspicuous. His departure occurred at a tense time in American life—the same month that the O. J. Simpson murder trial ended and the Million Man March took place—but then most of his white friends were old or already gone themselves. Ten eulogists attempted to assess Gomillion's significance, including several politicians who reportedly never had enjoyed Gomillion's support but who were up for reelection in 1996. None of the speakers quite did justice to the character and values of the man. There were many broad generalizations about his heroic fight for the right to vote, but already Gomillion was being made into an icon, a superficial symbol for a complex human story. In truth, Gomillion represented unselfish devotion to the betterment of his race and his community. He stood for boldness, perseverance, and high personal morality. He had established a goal, civic democracy in Macon County, and worked toward it with unswerving determination for twenty-five years, accepting disappointment as an inevitable part of the struggle to realize high ideals. He never faltered in either his opposition to racial discrimination or his commitment to interracial cooperation. In their moments of disappointment about what had not changed, Macon Countians could examine the life of Gomillion and discover in it the idealism and commitment that could guide them into the future with hope and courage. In the atmosphere of despair, however, it remained to be seen who would remember the lessons of the past.

Notes

I PERFECT QUIET, PEACE, AND HARMONY

1. Testimony of James H. Alston, in United States Senate Reports, No. 22, *Testimony Taken by the Joint Select Committee to Inquire into the Condition of Affairs in the Late Insurrectionary States, Alabama,* 42nd Cong., 2nd Sess., vol. IX, 1016–22. All testimony cited in these notes is from this document.

2. Testimony of Cullen A. Battle, 1060; testimony of Alston, 1020.

3. Testimony of Alston, 1020–21.

4. *Ibid.,* 1021–22; testimony of Robert H. Abercrombie, 1104, 1106. In his testimony Alston identified a "Mr. Campbell" without giving a first name. The manuscript census for 1870 recorded only one white adult male named Campbell—George Washington Campbell—who lived in Tuskegee. Given that the other visitors were also Tuskegee residents of an economic status similar to George Washington Campbell's, I believe it is fairly safe to assume that Alston was speaking of George Washington Campbell. (*The Ninth Census of the United States: 1870,* Population Schedule, Macon County, Alabama, p. 2 [Tuskegee beat, second part].)

5. Testimony of John M. Butler, 1094–97; testimony of William Dougherty, 1026.

6. Testimony of Dougherty, 1032–34.

7. Testimony of Butler, 1092–94, 1099.

8. Testimony of Abercrombie, 1104; Battle, 1059, 1061; Butler, 1098; Dougherty, 1034.

9. Testimony of Dougherty, 1039, 1037, 1040.

10. Testimony of Butler, 1095; Alston, 1021.

11. Testimony of Abercrombie, 1112, 1111.

12. For white attitudes in Alabama during the 1850s, see J. Mills Thornton, III, *Politics and Power in a Slave Society* (Louisiana State University Press, 1978); for the 1860s, see Sarah Woolfolk Wiggins, *The Scalawag in Alabama Politics 1865–1881* (University of Alabama Press, 1977), 18–71.

13. Thomas M. Owen, *History of Alabama and Dictionary of Alabama Biography* (S. J. Clarke, 1921) III, 115.

14. *Ibid.*

15. Tuskegee *Macon Mail*, April 5, 1876.

16. Tuskegee *News*, March 4, 11, 1875.

17. Wiggins, *The Scalawag*, 91–127.

18. Tuskegee *News*, June 17, March 11, 25, April 22, June 3, 1875; August 23, 1877.

19. Jonathan M. Wiener, *Social Origins of the New South: Alabama 1860–1885* (Louisiana State University Press, 1978), 66–73; Tuskegee *News*, August 12, 1880.

20. William L. Barney, *The Secessionist Impulse: Alabama and Mississippi in 1860* (Princeton University Press, 1974), 138; Tuskegee *News*, October 21, 28, 1880.

21. *Macon Mail*, December 4, August 28, 1878; Louis R. Harlan, *Booker T. Washington: The Making of a Black Leader 1856–1901* (Oxford University Press, 1972), 112–13.

22. *Macon Mail*, October 1, 1879.

23. *Macon Mail*, July 10, 1878; July 2, 1879.

24. See especially the account in Harlan, *Booker T. Washington*, 113–14.

25. For evidence of planters establishing schools for the purpose of keeping blacks from migrating, see Wiener, *Social Origins*, 64–66.

26. Eugene D. Genovese, *Roll, Jordan, Roll: The World the Slaves Made* (Pantheon Books, 1974), 89.

27. Harlan, *Booker T. Washington*, 115–17; Louis R. Harlan, ed., *The Booker T. Washington Papers* (University of Illinois Press, 1972), II, 286–89.

28. Mrs. Lillie Wilson of Tuskegee, Alabama, has stated unequivocally that Lewis Adams, her grandfather, was the son of Jesse Adams. (Lillie Wilson Interview, January 25, 1973, Alabama Center for Higher Education interviews, Hollis Burke Frissell Library, Tuskegee Institute.)

29. Harlan, *Booker T. Washington*, 3–117.

30. Booker T. Washington, *Up from Slavery* (Doubleday, Page, 1901), 120–21; article on Tuskegee Institute's founding by George C. Wright, George Campbell's nephew, in Tuskegee *Messenger*, November, 1933; Harlan, *Washington Papers*, II, 256.

31. Harlan, *Washington Papers*, I, 39; II, 462–63, 465.

32. Harlan, *Booker T. Washington*, 286.

33. Harlan, *Washington Papers*, II, 255–62.

2   THE MODEL COMMUNITY

1. *Official Proceedings of the Constitutional Convention of the State of Alabama 1901*, II, 1437.

2. United States House Reports, No. 267, *"M. W. Whatley v. J. E. Cobb,"* January 19, 1894," 53rd Cong., 2nd Sess.; United States House Reports, No. 1122, *"Albert T. Goodwyn v. James E. Cobb,* April 4, 1896," 54th Cong., 1st Sess, 2.

3. Tuskegee *News*, September 26, 1901.

4. Thomas M. Owen, *Alabama Official and Statistical Register 1907* (Brown Printing Company, 1907), 213.

5. Montgomery *Advertiser*, June 23, 1923; Booker T. Washington, *Up from Slavery* (Doubleday, Page, 1901), 154.

6. Allen W. Jones, "The Role of Tuskegee Institute in the Education of Black

Farmers," *Journal of Negro History* LX (April 1975), 252–67; Edwin R. Embree and Julia Waxman, *Investment in People* (Harper & Brothers, 1949), 26, 42.

7. *Annual Report 1935,* State of Alabama Department of Education *Bulletin,* Number 5 (1936).

8. Charles S. Johnson, *Shadow of the Plantation* (University of Chicago Press, 1934), 103–28.

9. Theodore Rosengarten, *All God's Dangers: The Life of Nate Shaw* (Alfred A. Knopf, 1974), 288.

10. *Ibid.,* 305–19.

11. Interview with Dan Motley, Negro tenant, December 1, 1939, in Federick D. Patterson Papers, President's Vault, Tuskegee Institute.

12. For a description of Greenwood, see the Tuskegee *News,* May 24, 1934; Louis R. Harlan, *Booker T. Washington: The Wizard of Tuskegee* (Oxford University Press, 1983), 169–70.

13. Interview with W. Foy Thompson, July 11, 1978; interview with William Varner, Jr., July 18, 1978.

14. Interview with Howard R. Lamar, October 29, 1982.

15. Interview with William P. Mitchell, June 8, 1978; article on Tuskegee's founding by George C. Wright, nephew of George W. Campbell, in Tuskegee *Messenger,* November, 1933.

16. Minutes of the Tuskegee Institute Board of Trustees meeting, September 9, 1921, Moton Papers, Hollis Burke Frissell Library, Tuskegee Institute; Pete Daniel, "Black Power in the 1920s: The Case of Tuskegee Veterans Hospital," *Journal of Southern History* XXXVI (August 1970), 369; "Speech of Hon. Calvin Coolidge, then Vice President of the United States at Dedication of Government Hospital for Colored Veterans of World War, Tuskegee, Alabama, February 12, 1923," in Group I, Series C, Container 410 of the papers of the National Association for the Advancement of Colored People at the Library of Congress. (Hereinafter, citations of the NAACP papers will be abbreviated by the organization's acronym, followed by the group number in Roman numerals, the series in upper-case letter, and the container in Arabic numerals—e.g., the citation above would be NAACP, I, C, 410.)

17. Daniel, "Black Power," 369–71; Robert R. Moton to Robert H. Stanley, February 20, 1923, Moton Papers; Stanley to Moton, February 24, 1923, *ibid.;* Moton to President Warren G. Harding, February 14, 1923, *ibid.*

18. Daniel, "Black Power," 373–75; Montgomery *Advertiser,* June 23, 1923.

19. Albon L. Holsey to James Weldon Johnson, April 2, 1923, NAACP, I, C, 410; Walter White to Editor, *The Mail,* May 14, 1923, *ibid.*

20. Daniel, "Black Power," 380–83.

21. *Ibid.*

22. *Ibid.*

3 KEEP EVERLASTINGLY AT IT

1. Interview with Charles V. Hamilton, October 26, 1982; Charles Goode Gomillion, "Marriages and Family Life: 1923–1974" [autobiographical information supplied by Gomillion], August 9, 1983; FBI File Number 100-2394, "Tuskegee Civic Association, Charles G. Gomillion, President," Report on February 3, 1943.

2. Gomillion, "Marriages and Family Life."

3. Interestingly, Mary DeBardeleben was a native of Shorter, a hamlet in western Macon County.

4. Gomillion interviews; S. P. Fullinwider, *The Mind and Mood of Black America* (Dorsey Press, 1969), 103–19.

5. Interview with William P. Mitchell, June 8, 1978; interview with A. C. Bulls, Sr., July 10, 1973, Alabama Center for Higher Education interviews.

6. Ralph J. Bunche, *The Political Status of the Negro in the Age of FDR* (University of Chicago Press, 1973), 345–46.

7. Gomillion interviews.

8. *Ibid.*

9. Gomillion interviews; interview with Frederick D. Patterson, October 26, 1982; interview with Luther Foster, May 17, 1983; interview with Paul Puryear, May 19, 1983; Gomillion, "Marriages and Family Life."

10. Patterson interview; Gomillion interviews.

11. Mitchell interview.

12. Gomillion interviews.

13. Bunche, *Political Status,* 283, 392. The black voter quoted here may have been Archie Yates, a florist, whom Bunche cites elsewhere.

14. *Ibid.,* 395, 392, 396.

15. *Ibid.,* 281–82.

16. Interview with William Varner, Jr., July 18, 1978; Bunche, *Political Status,* 281.

17. William Varner, Jr., states that his father had heard stories of blacks being herded to the polls, Varner interview; Bunche, *Political Status,* 394.

18. Tuskegee *News,* April 17, 1941; Gomillion to "Citizen," December 9, 1941, Tuskegee Civic Association Files, TCA office, Tuskegee, Alabama (hereinafter cited as TCAF); Gomillion, "The Responsibilities of Social Scientists as Citizens in the Crusade for Civic Democracy in the South," n.d., TCAF.

19. This influential civics textbook was written by the socialist economist Scott Nearing, though Gomillion does not remember its title. Gomillion interviews; Gomillion to "Citizen," December 9, 1941, TCAF.

20. Gomillion to "Citizen," December 9, 1941.

21. FBI File, "Gomillion," Reports on December 21, 1942; February 3, 1943.

22. Interview with Lewis Jones, August 10, 1978.

4 THE VOICE OF JACOB, THE HAND OF ESAU

1. "Experiences of T. Rupert Broady with the Macon County Board of Registrars," affidavit by Broady given December 3, 1941, in TCAF (hereinafter cited as "Broady Affidavit"); Gomillion interviews.

2. Broady Affidavit.

3. *Ibid.*

4. *Ibid;* Affidavit by William A. Shields, December 1941, TCA.

5. Broady Affidavit; Shields Affidavit; Gomillion interviews.

6. Broady Affidavit; Shields Affidavit; Affidavit of M. D. Sprague, November 25, 1941, TCA.

7. Richard M. Dalfiume, *Desegregation of the Armed Forces: Fighting on Two Fronts* (University of Missouri Press, 1969), 25–43; Dalfiume, "The 'Forgotten Years' of the Negro Revolution," *Journal of American History* LV (June 1968), 90–97; New Jersey *Herald News,* July 19, 1941; interview with Frederick D. Patterson, October 26, 1982.

8. Frederick D. Patterson to Robert Patterson, May 6, 1941, Frederick Patterson Papers.

9. Telegram from Walter White to Frederick Patterson, January 4, 1941, NAACP, II, B, 194; New Jersey *Herald News*, July 19, 1941; William H. Hastie, *On Clipped Wings: The Story of Jim Crow in the Army Air Corps* (National Association for the Advancement of Colored People, 1943), 12.

10. Roy Wilkins to the Editor of the Pittsburgh *Courier*, March 19, 1942, NAACP, II, B, 194; Patterson interview.

11. Interview with Noel F. Parrish, December 7, 1982; Patterson to Brigadier General Benjamin O. Davis, Sr., August 15, 1941, Patterson Papers. A former military science instructor at the Institute, Davis had been made the Army's first black general in October 1940. His son of the same name was a flying instructor at the Tuskegee Army Air Field.

12. Hastie, *Clipped Wings,* 20; Hastie memorandum to the Provost Marshal General of the War Department, May 7, 1942, in Frank Dixon Official Papers, Civil Archives, Alabama Department of Archives and History; memorandum from Truman K. Gibson, Jr., Assistant Civilian Aide to the Secretary of War, to the Provost Marshal General, April 4, 1942, Dixon Official Papers; Parrish interview; memorandum from Major General Virgil L. Peterson, the Inspector General, to the Commanding General, Services and Supply, April 24, 1942, Dixon Official Papers.

13. Memorandum from Colonel Philip Doddridge to Office of the Provost Marshall, War Department, May 18, 1942, Dixon Official Papers.

14. R. H. Powell to Frank M. Dixon, November 30, 1942, Dixon Official Papers; Dixon to Powell, December 1, 1942, *ibid.*

15. George Brown Tindall, *The Emergence of the New South, 1913–1945* (Louisiana State University Press, 1967), 713–15; Dixon to Powell, October 13, 1942, Dixon Official Papers.

16. Kimble to Commanding General, Maxwell Field, Alabama, May 13, 1942, Dixon Official Papers; Baltimore *Afro-American*, December 26, 1942; Oklahoma City *Black Dispatch*, December 27, 1942; Chicago *Defender*, January 2, 1943; Pittsburgh *Courier*, January 2, February 20, 1943.

17. Pittsburgh *Courier*, January 2, February 20, 1943; October 7, 1944. It should be noted that many black officers also lived off base. (Parrish interview.)

18. Case files for *United States of America v. Edwin Eugene Evans and Henry Franklin Faucett*, Case Number 1297, Eastern Division, Middle District of Alabama, deposited at Federal Records Center, Atlanta, Georgia; *U.S.A. v. Edwin Eugene Evans*, Case Number 1299, Eastern Division, Middle District of Alabama, deposited at Federal Records Center.

19. *U.S. v. Evans.*

20. Gomillion interviews; interview with William P. Mitchell, June 8, 1978.

21. FBI File, "Gomillion," Report on December 21, 1942; Montgomery *Advertiser*, April 23, 1943. The TCA's action against Evans apparently sparked the FBI investigation of Gomillion.

22. Interview with Florida Broward Segrest, June 14, 1978; FBI File Number 44-668, "Edwin Eugene Evans," Report on June 1, 1943.

23. Montgomery *Advertiser*, June 22, 23, 1943.

24. *Advertiser*, June 23, 24, 25, 1943.

25. Tuskegee *News*, July 1, 1943.

26. Florida Segrest interview.

27. *Advertiser*, December 12, 1942.

28. *Alabama: The News Magazine of the Deep South,* April 7, 1944.

29. McCorvey quoted in Stephen F. Lawson, *Black Ballots: Voting Rights in the South 1944–1969* (Columbia University Press, 1976), 90.

30. *Alabama,* January 15, 1943; Powell to Dixon, December 23, 1942, Dixon Personal Papers, Manuscripts Division, Alabama Department of Archives and History; William Logan Martin to Dixon, October 21, 1942, Dixon Official Papers.

31. Detroit Lee to Walter White, June 2, 1944, NAACP, II, C, 4; Robert A. Spiceley to [NAACP], August 1, 1944, *ibid.;* Ella J. Baker to Spiceley, August 4, 1944, *ibid.*

5 SOMETHING GOOD FROM NAZARETH

1. Case files for *William P. Mitchell v. Mrs. George C. Wright and Virgil W. Guthrie,* Case Number 102, Eastern Division, Middle District of Alabama (1945), deposited at the Federal Records Center, Atlanta, Georgia, hereinafter cited as *"Mitchell v. Wright* files"; Pittsburgh *Courier,* August 11, 1945. Wright's reputation for kindness to black friends and employees was recounted by Mrs. Florida Segrest. (Florida Broward Segrest interview.) Descriptions of Wright were provided by William Varner, Jr., her great-nephew, and William P. Mitchell. (William Varner, Jr., interview; William P. Mitchell interview.)

2. *Mitchell v. Wright* files.

3. Gomillion interviews; Mitchell interview; Pittsburgh *Courier,* August 11, 1945; Montgomery *Advertiser,* August 23, 26, 30, 1945.

4. *Mitchell v. Wright* files; Mitchell interview; interview with Daniel L. Beasley, August 3, 1978; interview with Otis Pinkard, July 31, 1978.

5. Mitchell interview; Gomillion interviews.

6. *The Sixteenth Census of the United States: 1940, Census of the Population, Alabama; The Seventeenth Census of the United States: 1950, Census of the Population, Alabama.* Partly as a result of the decision in *Missouri ex rel. Gaines v. Canada,* which required states to provide equal graduate education opportunities for blacks, the state of Alabama funded several graduate programs at Tuskegee Institute beginning in the mid-1940s. (Frederick D. Patterson, *Tuskegee Institute and the State of Alabama,* pamphlet published by the Institute in July, 1943; Frederick Patterson interview, May 29, 1973, Alabama Center for Higher Education interviews.) The VA hospital administrator in 1951 stated that more than fifteen hundred people worked at the hospital. (Program for Dedication Ceremony, New Clinical Building, Veterans Hospital, April 10, 1951, Tuskegee Institute Archives.)

7. Opinion, Alabama Supreme Court, *Williams v. Wright,* 249 Ala. 9; Montgomery *Advertiser,* February 14, 1947; October 13, 1945; Alabama *Journal,* April 25, 1946.

8. Montgomery *Advertiser,* August 26, 1945.

9. Ellis is quoted in William D. Barnard, *Dixiecrats and Democrats: Alabama Politics 1942–1950* (University of Alabama Press, 1974), 40–41.

10. *Ibid.,* 46, 33.

11. Tuskegee *News,* May 30, June 6, May 9, 1946. Florida Segrest stated that her husband's testimony against Evans and his support of Tuskegee Institute were used against him in all subsequent political races. (Florida Segrest interview.)

12. Birmingham *News,* September 6, 1946.

13. Montgomery *Advertiser,* September 6, October 4, 1946; *Mitchell v. Wright* files; Birmingham *News,* November 3, 1946; Barnard, *Dixiecrats,* 70–71.

14. *Mitchell v. Wright* files; Mitchell interview.

15. *Mitchell v. Wright* files.

16. *Ibid;* Mitchell interview.

17. *Mitchell v. Wright* files; Booker T. Washington. *Up from Slavery* (Doubleday, Page, 1901), 120–21; article on Tuskegee Institute's founding by George C. Wright in Tuskegee *Messenger,* November, 1933.

18. *Mitchell v. Wright* files; *Advertiser,* December 18, 1946; "Decision of William P. Mitchell *vs.* Mrs. George C. Wright and Virgil W. Guthrie, January 8, 1947," in TCAF; Mitchell interview; Gomillion interviews.

19. Arthur Shores to Robert L. Carter, May 23, 1947, NAACP, II, B, 194; Carter to Shores, May 29, 1947, *ibid.;* Marian Wynn Perry to Shores, September 12, 1947, *ibid.;* Richard Rives to Shores, September 24, 1947, *ibid.;* Shores to Gomillion, October 17, 1947, TCAF.

20. Gomillion interviews; Gomillion, "Report of the Political Action Committee," November 9, 1947, TCAF.

21. Patterson interview; Patterson interview, Alabama Center for Higher Education interviews; Patterson, *Tuskegee Institute and the State of Alabama;* Edwin R. Embree to Patterson, May 10, 1943, NAACP, II, A, 621; Alexander B. Siegel to Walter White, April 7, 1943, *ibid.;* White to William H. Hastie, April 15, 1943, *ibid.*

22. Patterson interview.

23. *Ibid.*

24. *Advertiser,* December 18, 1947; *Alabama Journal,* December 10, 1947.

25. Tuskegee Civic Association to Folsom, October 14, 1947, TCAF; *Advertiser,* December 18, 1947; April 14, 1948.

26. Gomillion to Folsom, April 19, 1948, TCAF; Gomillion to C. A. Walwyn, April 19, 1948, TCAF.

27. Daniel L. Beasley, "Report on Macon County Voting Situation," July 20, 1948, NAACP, II, B, 210. For personal information on Tommie and Rodgers, *Advertiser,* January 4, 1949; Florida Segrest interview; Tuskegee *News,* April 22, 1948.

28. Gomillion, "Report of the Political Action Committee"; Gomillion to Mitchell, April 3, 1948, TCAF; Gomillion interviews; Birmingham *World,* December 24, 1948; Minutes of TCA executive committee meetings, May 26, July 23, 1950, TCAF.

29. Gomillion to A. Abbot Rosen, April 19, 1948, TCAF; Gomillion to Mitchell, May 8, 1948, TCAF; Mitchell to George F. Friedman, September 19, 1950, TCAF; Beasley to Friedman, September 25, 1950, Papers of Daniel L. Beasley, in Beasley's possession (hereinafter cited as Beasley Papers).

30. Mitchell to Folsom, September 30, 1948, Beasley Papers; *Advertiser,* October 14, 1948; Gomillion to Ira B. Thompson, October 27, 1948, TCAF.

31. Tuskegee *News,* December 16, 1948; *Advertiser,* December 17, 1948.

32. Barnard, *Dixiecrats,* 32; Gomillion interviews; *Alabama Journal,* December 22, 1948.

33. Beasley interview; Mitchell interview; interview with Robert Bentley, August 10, 1978; Tuskegee *News,* June 20, 1946; December 20, 1945.

34. Robert Bentley interview.

35. Gomillion interviews; Beasley interview; Mitchell interview; "Registration of Voters" file, TCAF. William Mitchell kept a record of every black who made a voter application from January 1949 to the mid-1960s.

36. Beasley interview.

37. Robert Bentley interview.

38. "Registration of Voters" file, TCAF; Minutes, TCA executive meeting, July 1, 1950, TCAF; Mitchell to George F. Friedman, September 19, 1950, TCAF; Beasley to Friedman, September 25, 1950, Beasley Papers.

39. Mitchell interview; Gomillion interviews.

40. Gomillion interviews.

41. Interview with Samuel M. Engelhardt, June 26, 1978.

42. Gomillion interviews; Patterson interview.

43. J. Mills Thornton III, *Politics and Power in a Slave Society: Alabama, 1800–1860* (Louisiana State University Press, 1978), 267–342.

44. For a provocative and instructive discussion of alienation, see David M. Potter's essay "The Roots of American Alienation" in Don E. Fehrenbacher, ed., *History and American Society: Essays of David M. Potter* (Oxford University Press, 1973), 306–33.

45. Suzanne Keller, *Beyond the Ruling Class: Strategic Elites in Modern Society* (Random House, 1963), 233.

46. Mitchell interview. Judge Varner subsequently removed the courtesy titles from the names of white women on the voter list.

6 MORE WAYS THAN ONE TO KILL A SNAKE

1. Engelhardt interview; John Bartlow Martin, *The Deep South Says "Never"* (Ballantine Books, 1957), 105–6.

2. Engelhardt interview; Martin, *Deep South,* 106.

3. My interpretation of Engelhardt's personality is based on my interview with him and an examination of his personal papers deposited at the Alabama Department of Archives and History.

4. Engelhardt interview; on Joe Edwards's relationship with Persons, interview with Neil O. Davis, August 21, 1978; on Grady Rogers's kindness, Florida Segrest interview.

5. *Alabama: The News Magazine of the Deep South,* June 6, 1951.

6. Elnora Williams to B. L. Balch, January 2, 1951, TCAF; Balch to Williams, January 9, 1951, TCAF; petition of parents and infants to County School Board of Macon County, Alabama, February 1, 1951, TCAF; Annual Report of Secretary, Tuskegee Branch NAACP, 1951, in NAACP, II, B, 210; Birmingham *News*, February 10, 11, 1951.

7. "Selected Aspects of Public Education in Macon County Alabama 1945–46 and 1949–50," Tuskegee Civic Association report, p. 7, TCAF.

8. *Alabama,* August 17, 1951.

9. Montgomery *Advertiser,* August 29, 1951; *Alabama,* August 17, 1951. The single-shot strategy could not be used in cities like Tuskegee where councilmen represented specific wards.

10. Donald S. Strong, *Registration of Voters in Alabama* (University, Alabama: Bureau of Public Administration, 1956), 25–34.

11. "Registration of Voters" file, TCAF; "Eight-year Summary of Registration Efforts of Negroes in Macon County: Reactions of the Macon County Boards of Registrars" (1958), TCAF; "An Observation made by Beulah C.

Johnson on August 3, 1953," TCAF; "Observations," signed by Beulah C. Johnson, December 22, 1953, TCAF.

12. Tuskegee *News,* May 24, 1951; Montgomery *Advertiser,* May 27, 1951; Minutes, TCA meeting, July 29, 1951, TCAF; William P. Mitchell to James P. McGranery, Attorney General of the United States, June 20, 1952, TCAF; Thurgood Marshall to James M. McInerney, July 16, 1952, TCAF; Minutes, executive meeting, September 14, 1952, TCAF; Arthur Shores to Vernon McDaniel [president, Tuskegee NAACP chapter], April 7, 1953, TCAF; Warren Olney, Assistant United States Attorney General, to William P. Mitchell, June 1, 1953, TCAF; Montgomery *Advertiser,* November 7, 1953; Arthur Shores to Daniel L. Beasley, October 10, 1953, TCAF; Birmingham *World,* February 2, 1954; Shores to Mitchell, February 17, 1954, TCAF; Mitchell to Shores, February 18, 1954, TCAF; File memorandum, March 1954, TCAF; "Registration of Voters" file, TCAF.

13. Gomillion to Dr. P. M. Lightfoot, January 11, 1952, TCAF.

14. Press release, February 9, 1954, TCAF; Guzman quoted her 1954 campaign speech in a talk entitled "Is the Negro the White South's Problem?" given at a TCA meeting on February 10, 1959. (TCAF.)

15. The results of the Democratic primary in Macon County were analyzed by Frank D. Toland, a political scientist at the Institute, at the TCA meeting on May 9, 1954. (Minutes, regular meeting, May 9, 1954, TCAF.)

16. Union Springs (Alabama) *Herald,* April 1, 1954.

17. Thomas J. Gilliam, "The Second Folsom Administration: The Destruction of Alabama Liberalism 1954–1958" (Ph.D. diss., Auburn University, 1975), 101, 70.

18. *Ibid.,* 29, 27.

19. *Ibid.,* 108–9.

20. Montgomery *Advertiser,* February 13, 1955; Gilliam, "Second Folsom," 142–45.

21. Engelhardt interview; Gilliam, "Second Folsom," 84–85, 142–45; Montgomery *Advertiser,* April 3, 1955; Birmingham *News,* July 10, 1955.

22. Montgomery *Advertiser,* July 21, September 4, 1955; Engelhardt interview.

23. "Registration of Voters" File, TCAF.

24. Montgomery *Advertiser,* January 19, 1956.

25. "Registration of Voters" File, TCAF; Montgomery *Advertiser,* March 18, 1956; Birmingham *News,* July 10, 1955.

26. Bernard D. Cohn to Folsom, June 19, 1956, TCAF; Charles M. Keever to Folsom, July 24, 1956, TCAF; Gomillion to Folsom, August 15, 1956, TCAF; Montgomery *Advertiser,* September 21, 1956; Gomillion to Folsom, October 26, 1956, TCAF; Tuskegee *News,* December 6, 1956.

27. Montgomery *Advertiser,* March 7, 1957; Gomillion to Arthur Burns, March 11, 1957, TCAF.

28. My source on Folsom's drinking and absenteeism is a high official in his administration, who, because of the nature of the information, wishes to remain anonymous. Folsom's alcoholism was, however, well known. See Marshall Frady, *Wallace* (World, 1968), 107–8; Robert Sherrill, *Gothic Politics in the Deep South* (Ballantine Books, 1969), 319–20.

29. Engelhardt interview; Foy Thompson interview, July 11, 1978; interview with J. Allan Parker, June 27, 1978.

30. Bernard Taper, *Gomillion Versus Lightfoot: The Tuskegee Gerrymander Case* (McGraw-Hill, 1962), 14, 114.

7   SOP IN YOUR OWN DAMNED GRAVY

1. Gomillion interviews.
2. *Ibid.;* Baltimore *Afro-American,* July 6, 1957; tape recording of TCA mass meeting, June 25, 1957, TCAF.
3. Recording, mass meeting, June 25, 1957.
4. *Ibid.*
5. *Ibid.;* Baltimore *Afro-American,* July 6, 1957; "What the Tuskegee Civic Association Has Attempted to Do," August 19, 1957, TCAF; Atlanta *Constitution,* October 14, 1957.
6. Gomillion interviews; Mitchell interview; Montgomery *Advertiser,* February 14, 1956; minutes, TCA executive committee meeting, May 22, 1957, TCAF; Gomillion interviews.
7. Gomillion interviews; Mitchell interview; TCA executive committee minutes, May 22, 1957, TCAF; Tuskegee Minister's Association to Gomillion, June 18, 1957, TCAF; minutes, TCA executive cabinet, June 27, 1957, TCAF.
8. Birmingham *News,* January 22, 1958; Baltimore *Afro-American,* April 19, 1958; *Advertiser,* August 17, 1957; Lewis Jones and Stanley Smith, *Voting Rights and Economic Pressure* (New York: Anti-Defamation League of B'nai B'rith, 1958), 26; Baltimore *Afro-American,* July 13, 1957.
9. *Advertiser,* June 30, 1957.
10. *Advertiser,* July 25, 1957.
11. *Ibid.; Advertiser,* September 7, 8, 1957.
12. *Advertiser,* July 25, 27, 30, 1957; interview with George Busby, November 5, 1973, Alabama Center for Higher Education interviews.
13. *Southern School News,* July 1956.
14. *Advertiser,* July 30, 1957; interview with John Patterson, May 22, 1973, Alabama Center for Higher Education interviews.
15. Birmingham *World,* August 21, 1957; *Advertiser,* September 7, 1957; January 22, June 22, 1958.
16. *Advertiser,* July 3, 1957; Baltimore *Afro-American,* July 20, 1957; *Southern School News,* August 1957; Gomillion interviews.
17. Bernard Taper, *Gomillion Versus Lightfoot: The Tuskegee Gerrymander Case* (McGraw-Hill, 1962), 34.
18. New York *Post,* August 7, 1957.
19. *Life,* July 22, 1957; *Newsweek,* July 29, 1957; *Time,* July 8, 1957; *U.S. News,* July 12, 1957; Gomillion interviews.
20. *Time,* November 25, 1957; *The Nation,* October 12, 1957.
21. *The Nation,* October 12, 1957.
22. *Advertiser,* November 14, 1957; *The Reporter,* October 31, 1957.
23. Baltimore *Afro-American,* April 19, 1958; Birmingham *News,* January 22, 1958; Atlanta *Constitution,* October 15, 1957; *The Reporter,* October 31, 1957; Atlanta *Constitution,* October 14, 1957; *Advertiser,* November 14, 1957.
24. W. J. Cash, *The Mind of the South* (Alfred A. Knopf, 1941); Baltimore *Afro-American,* August 17, 1957; *Advertiser,* December 12, 1957; Baltimore *Afro-American,* September 14, 1957; *Advertiser,* November 14, 1957.
25. I base my analysis of the conservative elite partly on Robert E. Hughes, "First Report on Tuskegee," July 9, 1957, in Fellowship of Reconciliation Papers, Peace Collection, Swarthmore College Library. Hughes was executive director of the Alabama Council on Human Relations, a statewide interracial

group. Hughes's perception of the elite was substantially confirmed by Sam Engelhardt and J. Allan Parker, a liberal Tuskegee banker. (Parker interview.) The extent of Laslie's power was suggested by Neil O. Davis, editor of the *Lee County Bulletin* and, later, the Tuskegee *News*. (Interview with Davis, August 21, 1978).

26. Hughes, "Report on Tuskegee."

27. Engelhardt interview; Hughes, "Report on Tuskegee."

28. Hughes, "Report on Tuskegee."

29. Interview with Lewis W. Jones, August 10, 1978; "The Tuskegee Crisis Study," files deposited at the Hollis Burke Frissell Library, Tuskegee Institute. The Crisis Study also examined black attitudes, but few of the black survey forms were saved.

30. Tuskegee Crisis Study, white respondent questionnaires 5, 23, 80, and 9. All respondents cited below are white.

31. Respondents 30, 45, 26.

32. Respondents 20, 23, 29, 34, 45, 63, 76, 91, 36, 80, 18, 25, 26, 66, 88, 91, 24.

33. Respondents 53, 47, 75.

34. Respondents 57, 59, 67.

35. Respondents 94, 83, 57, 67, 86, 43, 46, 17, 88. Apparently, Gomillion did reject the initial overtures for interracial discussion precisely for the reason the editor cited. Robert E. Hughes to Glenn Smiley, July 10, 1957, Fellowship of Reconciliation Papers.

36. Respondents 23, 21.

37. Respondents 31, 77, 23.

38. Respondents 15, 10, 16, 51, 86, 90.

39. Respondents 9, 13, 15, 19, 32, 45, 46, 48, 49, 55, 60, 66, 86, 31.

40. Respondents 2, 5, 7, 9, 13, 15, 19, 22, 23, 31.

41. Tuskegee *News,* May 1, 1958.

42. Gomillion interviews; Mitchell interview; Gomillion, Statement to the Macon County Committee, February 14, 1958, TCAF; *Advertiser,* February 15, 1958.

43. *Advertiser,* February 15, 1958.

8   THE INVASION OF INJUSTICE

1. Charles G. Gomillion to S. W. Boynton, February 15, 1957, TCAF; Washington *Post,* July 31, 1957; Steven F. Lawson, *Black Ballots: Voting Rights in the South, 1944–1969* (Columbia University Press, 1976), 192–93.

2. Arthur Shores to Charles Gomillion, September 3, 1958, TCAF; *Advertiser,* September 11, 1958; William P. Mitchell to Gomillion, September 28, 1958, TCAF; Gomillion to Mitchell, October 27, 1958, TCAF.

3. Mitchell interview; *Hearings before the United States Commission on Civil Rights. Voting* (Washington: Government Printing Office, 1959), 1–30 (hereinafter cited as *Voting*).

4. *Voting,* 30–50.

5. *Ibid.,* 75, 108.

6. Interview with Hosea Guice, July 20, 1978.

7. *Voting,* 77.

8. *Ibid.,* 79.

9. *Ibid.,* 127–52.

10. *Ibid.,* 153–60; Marshall Frady, *Wallace* (World, 1968), 127.

11. *Advertiser,* December 9, 10, 1958; *Voting,* 206–7.

12. *Voting,* 206–7.

13. Lawson, *Black Ballots,* 216.

14. *Advertiser,* December 12, 1958.

15. Tinsley E. Yarbrough, *Judge Frank Johnson and Human Rights in Alabama* (University of Alabama Press, 1981), 62–72; *Advertiser,* January 27, 1959.

16. *Voting,* 285–322.

17. Montgomery *Alabama Journal,* February 6, 1959; Lawson, *Black Ballots,* 210, 399.

18. Lawson, *Black Ballots,* 399, 210.

19. Memorandum Opinion, *Gomillion v. Lightfoot,* 167 F. Supp. 405 (1958); Gomillion to William P. Mitchell, November 22, 1958.

20. *Advertiser,* July 21, 22, 23, December 7, 1959; May 3, 1960.

21. William P. Mitchell to Clarence Mitchell, June 10, 1959, TCAF.

22. Mitchell interview; interview with Charles V. Hamilton, October 26, 1982; Mitchell to Paul Douglas, June 16, 1959, TCAF; Minutes of Conference Regarding H. R. 7957, August 23, 1959, TCAF; *Advertiser,* September 9, 1959; Lawson, *Black Ballots,* 227.

23. "Statement of Governor John Patterson of Alabama Before the Rules and Administration Committee of the United States Senate, Washington, D.C., February 2, 1960," John Patterson Official Papers, Alabama Department of Archives and History.

24. Grady Rogers to George Andrews, March 28, 1960, George Andrews Papers, Auburn University Archives, Auburn, Alabama.

25. "Senator Douglas Reports" [n.d.], TCAF.

26. *Alabama Journal,* May 17, 1960; Birmingham *News,* April 10, 1960.

27. Affidavit of Willie Turner, Jr., August 1960, TCAF.

28. *Alabama Journal,* June 6, 1960; Charles G. Gomillion to Martin Luther King, Jr., September 1, 1960, TCAF.

29. Affidavit of Mrs. Annie E. Walker, November 28, 1960, TCAF; Gomillion to King, September 1, 1960, TCAF.

30. Affidavit of Ben Williams, [July 1960], TCAF; affidavit of Herbert Fort, [n.d.], TCAF.

31. *Advertiser,* October 11, 12, November 21, 1960.

32. Bernard Taper, *Gomillion Versus Lightfoot* (McGraw-Hill, 1962), 86–87.

33. *Ibid.,* 92–93.

34. *Ibid.,* 103–6.

35. *Gomillion v. Lightfoot,* 364 U.S. 344–47 (1960).

36. Joel William Friedman, "The Burger Court and the Prima Facie Case in Employment Discrimination Litigation: A Critique," *Cornell Law Review* 65 (November 1965), 18; *Baker v. Carr,* 369 U.S. 186 (1962); *Reynolds v. Sims,* 377 U.S. 533 (1964).

37. This account of the Kennedy Justice Department's involvement in the Macon County suit is based on Doar's introduction in Robert F. Kennedy, Jr., *Judge Frank M. Johnson Jr.* (Putnam's, 1978), 12–13.

38. John Doar and Dorothy Landsberg, "The Performance of the FBI in Investigating Violations of Federal Laws Protecting the Right to Vote" (typed manuscript in the possession of Carl M. Brauer), 12–13.

39. *Advertiser,* February 21, 23, 1961.

40. *United States v. Alabama,* 192 F. Supp. 677 (1961).

41. *Ibid.*

42. Kennedy, *Johnson,* 256.

43. William Mitchell to John Doar, April 10, 1961, TCAF; *Advertiser,* March 18, 1961.

44. *Advertiser,* March 19, 1961.

9 HARDBOY PREPARES

1. Engelhardt interview.

2. *Advertiser,* September 21, 1960; Montgomery *Alabama Journal,* October 20, 1960; *Advertiser,* November 23, 1960; Tuskegee *News,* August 11, 1960. Lightfoot was quoted in Bernard Taper, *Gomillion Versus Lightfoot* (McGraw-Hill, 1962), 47.

3. Minutes, TCA executive committee meeting, April 5, 1961, TCAF; Thompson interview; minutes, TCA executive meeting, March 1, 1961, TCAF.

4. Parker interview; Mitchell interview; Gomillion interviews; minutes, biracial meeting, May 13, 1963; TCAF.

5. Gomillion interviews.

6. Tuskegee *News,* January 8, 1959; September 19, April 25, 1963.

7. Interview with Robert D. Miller, July 25, 1978; Davis interview.

8. Parker interview.

9. *Ibid.*

10. Interview with Howard R. Lamar, October 29, 1982.

11. Parker interview.

12. Mitchell interview; Gomillion interviews; Parker interview.

13. Parker to Norman C. Jimerson, June 1, 1963, in files of the Alabama Council on Human Relations, stored at the council's former offices in Auburn, Alabama. Jimerson was then executive director of the council.

14. Florida Segrest interview; Miller interview.

15. Mitchell interview; interview with Preston Hornsby, August 25, 1978.

16. Miller interview.

17. Interview with Frances Hodnett Rush, July 30, 1978.

18. *Ibid.;* Gomillion interviews.

19. William P. Mitchell to John Doar, June 5, 20; July 10, 23; August 7, 1961, TCAF; *Advertiser,* August 19, September 9, 27, 1961; Mitchell to Doar, February 12, 19, March 9, 20, April 3, 18, June 6, 1962, TCAF; "Summary of Voter Applicants," TCAF; tabulated election results, May 1, 1962, Democratic primary, with designation of Macon County Democratic Club endorsement, TCAF.

20. Mitchell to Doar, July 6, 19, December 26, 1962; January 8, July 8, 17, 1963, TCAF; Mitchell to Wiley A. Branton, January 11, 1964, TCAF. Branton was director of the Southern Regional Council's Voter Education Project.

21. Detroit Lee to Gomillion, September 6, 1962, TCAF; *Advertiser,* July 17, 1955; Gomillion to Lee, November 20, 1956, TCAF; interview with Detroit Lee, April 17, 1983; Gomillion to Lee, October 9, 1962, TCAF.

22. Writ of Injunction, *Lee v. Macon,* CA 604-E [M.D. Ala., 1964].

23. Carl M. Brauer, *John F. Kennedy and the Second Reconstruction* (Columbia University Press, 1977), 252–59, 293–95; *Alabama Journal,* August 28, 1963.

24. Brauer, *John F. Kennedy,* 253; *Advertiser,* January 15, 1963.

25. Erwing W. Wadsworth, "A Historical Perspective of Education in Macon County, Alabama: 1836–1967" (Ph.D. diss., Auburn University, 1968), 344.

26. Miller interview; interview with Ennis G. Sellers, April 18, 1983; deposition of C. A. Pruitt, January 7, 1964, in case files, *Lee v. Macon*, in Clerk's Office, Montgomery Federal Courthouse (hereinafter cited as "Pruitt deposition").

27. *Southern School News,* August 1955; Pruitt deposition; Wadsworth, "Education in Macon County," 351.

28. Pruitt deposition; *Advertiser,* August 30, 1963; *Alabama Journal,* August 28, 1963.

29. Wadsworth, "Education in Macon County," 353; memorandum, Captain R. W. Godwin and Lieutenant E. J. Dixon to Major W. R. Jones, August 30, 1963, George C. Wallace Official Files, Alabama Department of Archives and History (hereinafter cited as "Godwin memorandum"). Godwin and Dixon were Alabama state troopers who attended the meeting and filed a long report on it to their superiors.

30. Godwin memorandum; Sellers interview.

31. Godwin memorandum.

32. *Ibid.*

33. *Ibid.*

34. *Ibid.*

35. *Ibid.*

36. Pruitt deposition.

10   THE END AND THE BEGINNING

1. Pruitt deposition; *Lee v. Macon* case files; Writ of Injunction, *Lee v. Macon,* CA 604-E [M.D. Ala., 1964].

2. Ennis G. Sellers, "Tuskegee, the Methodist Church and School Integration," 1964, unpublished manuscript in author's possession (hereinafter cited as "Sellers, 'The Methodist Church' "); Montgomery *Advertiser,* September 3, 1963; Birmingham *News,* September 3, 1963.

3. Sellers, "The Methodist Church"; interview with Alice Lee Wadsworth, August 24, 1978. Alice Lee Wadsworth was not related to Erwing Wadsworth, the principal of Tuskegee High.

4. Birmingham *News,* September 3, 1963; *Advertiser,* September 4, 1963.

5. Pruitt deposition; Birmingham *News,* September 3, 1963; Montgomery *Alabama Journal,* September 3, 1963.

6. Flowers was quoted in Marshall Frady, *Wallace* (World, 1968), 141; Carl M. Brauer, *John F. Kennedy and the Second Reconstruction* (Columbia University Press, 1977), 294.

7. Godwin memorandum.

8. Sellers, "The Methodist Church"; interview with Perry Motley Wadsworth, August 24, 1978.

9. *Advertiser,* September 4, 1963.

10. Brauer, *John F. Kennedy,* 293–94.

11. *Ibid.*

12. Tuskegee *News,* September 5, 1963.

13. *Advertiser,* September 10, 11, 13, 1963; Erwing W. Wadsworth, "A Historical Perspective of Education in Macon County, Alabama: 1836–1967" (Ph.D. diss., Auburn University, 1968), 371.

14. Florida Segrest interview.

15. *Ibid.;* Pruitt deposition; *Advertiser,* September 17, 1963.

16. *Advertiser,* September 13, 1963; interview with John Fletcher Segrest, July 8, 1978.

17. *Advertiser,* September 13, 1963.

18. *Advertiser,* September 20, 1963.

19. *Advertiser,* September 10, 1963; *Alabama Journal,* September 27, 1963; testimony of Martha Culbertson Oliver, in case files of *Lee v. Macon,* deposited at the Clerk's Office, Montgomery Federal Courthouse; *Advertiser,* September 17, October 9, 1963; Tuskegee *News,* March 26, 1964.

20. *Advertiser,* September 17, 1963.

21. Tuskegee *News,* September 12, 1963.

22. Parker interview.

23. Varner interview; Miller interview; Parker interview; Pruitt deposition; Wadsworth, "Education in Macon County," 378; John Fletcher Segrest interview.

24. Parker interview; Florida Segrest interview; John Fletcher Segrest interview; Rush interview.

25. Alice Lee and Perry Motley Wadsworth interviews.

26. *Ibid.*

27. *Ibid.;* Alice Lee Howard Wadsworth, autobiographical essay, in author's possession.

28. Alice Lee Wadsworth interview and autobiographical essay.

29. Alice Lee Wadsworth interview.

30. *Ibid.;* Mott Wadsworth interview; Florida Segrest interview.

31. Sellers interview; Sellers, "The Methodist Church."

32. Sellers interview.

33. *Ibid.*

34. Sellers, "The Methodist Church."

35. Miller interview.

36. *Ibid.*

37. *Ibid.*

38. *Ibid.*

39. Robert D. Miller, "The End and the Beginning," sermon delivered at the Tuskegee Presbyterian Church, July 17, 1964.

40. Miller interview.

41. *Ibid.*

42. Interview with Anthony Lee, April 18, 1983; Wadsworth, "Education in Macon County," 374. For analysis of the impact of desegregation on the children involved, see Robert Coles, *Children of Crisis: A Study of Courage and Fear* (Little, Brown, 1964).

43. Writ of Injunction, *Lee v. Macon,* CA 604-E [M.D. Ala., 1964]; *Advertiser,* January 10, February 1, 1964.

44. *Advertiser,* February 2, 4, 1964.

45. *Advertiser,* February 3, 4, 5, 6, 7, 9, 11, 12, 1964.

46. *Advertiser,* February 14, 1964; John Fletcher Segrest interview.

47. *Advertiser,* April 18, 24, 1964: *Alabama Journal,* April 30, 1964; Tuskegee *News,* April 23, 1964.

48. Birmingham *News,* March 11, 1964; *Alabama Journal,* February 5, 1964. The editor stated what would become the conventional wisdom about the effectiveness of Wallace's obstructionism: that his defiance resulted in more rapid and more all-encompassing desegregation decrees. In Macon County, however, Wallace was largely responsible for keeping education segregated in 1963–64 and in-

strumental in building Macon Academy, the institution that would insure segregated education for at least the next two decades.

49. Alice Lee Wadsworth, autobiographical essay.

11 LET THE CHILDREN LEAD

1. "The Macon County Democratic Club," statement of activities, 1964, TCAF.

2. *Ibid.*

3. Bernard Taper, "A Break with Tradition," *The New Yorker,* July 24, 1965, p. 68.

4. "Results of the Municipal Election held August 11, 1964," TCAF.

5. *Ibid.*

6. "Meet the Candidates of the Non-Partisan Voters League of Macon County," campaign brochure, TCAF.

7. *Advertiser,* August 21, 1964; Detroit Lee interview; Puryear interview.

8. Gomillion to Davis, August 20, 1964, TCAF.

9. W. P. Mitchell to Wiley Branton, October 3, 1964, TCAF.

10. Taper, "A Break," 61–62.

11. Parker to Gomillion, November 5, December 8, 1964, TCAF; Tuskegee *News,* April 29, 1965.

12. Taper, "A Break," 82; Writ of Injunction, *Lee v. Macon,* CA 604-E [M.D. Ala., 1964].

13. "Macon Academy: A Report to You," 1965, TCAF.

14. Detroit Lee interview.

15. Gomillion interviews; Gomillion to Macon County Democratic Club Precinct Leaders, October 28, 1964, TCAF.

16. Rev. O. C. Bryant to Citizens Council Member, October 9, 1964, TCAF.

17. *Advertiser,* November 15, 1964.

18. Taper, "A Break," 69.

19. Mitchell interview.

20. Hamilton interview; Mitchell interview; Gomillion interviews; Hamilton, *Minority Politics in Black Belt Alabama* (McGraw-Hill, 1960), 24–32.

21. Gomillion interviews; Hamilton interview.

22. *Campus Digest,* March 1, 1960; *Advertiser,* April 7, 8, 1960; Hamilton interview.

23. Hamilton interview.

24. Interview with Gwen Patton, April 18, 1983; Clayborne Carson, *In Struggle: SNCC and the Black Awakening of the 1960s* (Harvard University Press, 1981), 160.

25. Patton interview; James Forman, *Sammy Younge, Jr.: The First Black College Student to Die in the Black Liberation Movement* (Grove Press, 1968), 79–81.

26. Forman, *Sammy Younge,* 81–101; Patton interview.

27. Forman, *Sammy Younge,* 109; *Campus Digest,* March 20, April 10, 1965; Patton interview.

28. Forman, *Sammy Younge,* 126–29, 143; Patton interview; *Campus Digest,* May 24, 1965; Tuskegee *News,* June 3, 1965.

29. Tuskegee *News,* June 10, 1965; Forman, *Sammy Younge,* 142–43.

30. Patton interview; Forman, *Sammy Younge,* 154; *Southern Courier,* July 16, 1965.

31. *Courier*, July 16, 1965.
32. Tuskegee *News*, July 22, 29, 1965.
33. *Courier*, July 25, 1965.
34. Tuskegee *News*, July 25, 1965.
35. Gomillion interviews.
36. *Ibid.*
37. Forman, *Sammy Younge*, 153.
38. Gomillion interviews.
39. *Courier*, November 6, 1965.
40. *Campus Digest*, November 20, December 4, 1965.
41. Forman, *Sammy Younge*, 182–84: William P. Mitchell to Wiley A. Branton, January 11, 1964, TCAF.
42. Mitchell interview; Mitchell to John Doar, February 2, 1966, TCAF.
43. Patton interview; *Courier*, December 24, 1966.
44. *Courier*, December 24, 1966.
45. *Ibid.;* interview with William M. Russell, August 24, 1978. Russell represented Segrest in his subsequent trial for murder.
46. Forman, *Sammy Younge*, 13, 35, 70–71; Patton interview.
47. Forman, *Sammy Younge*, 109–27, 174–77; Patton interview; *Courier*, December 24, 1966.
48. *Campus Digest*, January 8, 1966.
49. Arnold S. Kaufman, "Day of Wrath in the Model Town," *The Nation*, January 31, 1966, 122.
50. *Ibid.*, 121–22.
51. *Ibid.*
52. *Ibid.*
53. *Ibid.*
54. *Ibid.*
55. *Courier*, January 15, 1966; Tuskegee *News*, January 13, 1966.
56. Tuskegee *News*, January 20, 1966.
57. *Courier*, February 5, 1966.
58. Tuskegee *News*, January 20, 27, 1966; *Courier*, February 5, 1966.
59. *Courier*, February 12, 1966.
60. *Ibid.*
61. *Courier*, February 19, 1966.

12   THE GRASS ROOTS TAKE HOLD

1. William P. Mitchell to Marvin Wall, June 27, 1966, TCAF; *Campus Digest*, February 19, 1966.
2. *Southern Courier*, March 26, 1966.
3. *Courier*, April 12, 1966.
4. *New York Times*, June 1, 2, 1966; Gwen Patton interview; Gomillion interviews; Mitchell interview; Beasley interview.
5. Affidavit of Savannah Harvey, March 21, 1966, TCAF; William P. Mitchell to Sheriff Harvey Sadler, April 15, 1966, TCAF; *Courier*, April 30, 1966.
6. *New York Times Magazine*, February 26, 1967.
7. Gomillion interviews.
8. Gomillion interviews; *New York Times*, June 1, 1966.
9. *Times*, June 1, 1966.

10. *Courier*, May 7, 1966. Rush had won in the first primary, four weeks before the runoff.

11. *Courier*, June 4, 1966.

12. Mitchell to Wall, June 27, 1966, TCAF; Detroit Lee interview; Perry Motley Wadsworth interview; *New York Times*, June 1, 1966: *Gray v. Main*, 309 F. Supp. 207 (1968).

13. *Courier*, November 12, 1966; January 28, 1967; Tuskegee *News*, January 19, 1967; *New York Times*, February 26, 1967.

14. *Courier*, November 12, 1966.

15. *Courier*, December 17, 1966.

16. *Ibid*. The men who killed Liuzzo were later convicted of a federal charge of violating her civil rights.

17. *Ibid*.

18. *Courier*, November 11, 1967.

19. *Courier*, March 9, 1968; Tuskegee *News*, March 28, April 11, 1968; Birmingham *News*, April 7, 8, 1968.

20. Birmingham *News*, April 8–10, 1968; *Courier*, April 27, 1968.

21. Varner interview; Florida Segrest interview; John Fletcher Segrest interview.

22. *Courier*, June 4, 1966.

23. *Courier*, September 10, 1966; *Annual Reports, 1969–70* and *1975–76*, State of Alabama Department of Education.

24. *Courier*, October 14, 1967; January 27, 1968.

25. *Courier*, October 14, 1967; Parker interview.

26. *Courier*, November 18, 1967; January 27, 1968.

27. *Courier, February* 24, October 5, 1968.

28. Parker interview; Patton interview; Beasley interview; Gomillion interviews; interview with Fred D. Gray, December 30, 1983.

29. *Courier*, November 19, December 10, 1966.

30. *Courier*, April 29, September 2, November 25, December 2, 9, 1967; February 10, 1968.

31. *Courier*, May 5, December 9, 1967.

32. *Courier*, May 4, July 20, 1968.

33. *Courier*, August 17, 1968.

34. Tuskegee *News*, May 7, June 4, 1970; Florida Segrest interview; Gray interview.

35. Tuskegee *News*, May 18, 1972.

36. Montgomery *Advertiser*, November 10, 1972.

37. Tuskegee *News*, June 29, May 4, 18, August 10, September 7, 1972.

38. Tuskegee *News*, September 14, 1972.

39. *New York Times*, June 27, 1973.

13 IF I FORGET YOU, O JERUSALEM

1. Birmingham *News*, February 4, 5, 1973.

2. *Ibid*.

3. *Ibid*.

4. *The Nineteenth Census of the Population: 1970, Census of the Population, Alabama; The Twentieth Census of the Population: 1980, Census of the Population, Alabama*; Florida Broward Segrest interview; John Fletcher Segrest interview.

5. Birmingham *Post-Herald*, May 21, 1973; *New York Times*, June 27, 1973; *Christian Science Monitor*, October 28, 1974; Birmingham *News*, January 21, 1974.

6. Manning Marable, "Tuskegee and the Politics of Illusion in the New South," *The Black Scholar* IX (May 1977), 15–24; Marable, *From the Grass Roots: Essays Toward Afro-American Liberation* (South End Press, 1980), 175; Tuskegee *News*, September 8, 1975.

7. Birmingham *News*, October 20, 1974; February 2, 1975. Gray himself remains perplexed about why Senator Howell Heflin withdrew his support for Gray's nomination to a federal judgeship. See Fred D. Gray, *Bus Ride to Justice: Changing the System by the System: The Life and Works of Fred D. Gray* (Black Belt Press, 1995), 291–306.

8. *Ebony*, July 1982, 52–58.

9. Montgomery *Advertiser–Alabama Journal*, January 30, 1977; Marable, "Politics of Illusion," 19, 24.

10. Marable, "Politics of Illusion," 20.

11. Gomillion interviews.

12. Birmingham *News*, June 26, 1976; July 11, 1977; Mitchell interview.

13. Mitchell interview; *New York Times*, June 27, 1973; Gomillion interviews.

14. Florida Broward Segrest interview; Rush interview; Parker interview; Hornsby interview; Gray interview; Mitchell interview.

15. Florida Broward Segrest interview; John Fletcher Segrest interview.

16. Mab Segrest, *Memoir of a Race Traitor* (South End Press, 1994), 136–37. The responsive reading was taken from Psalm 137.

17. Tuskegee *News*, February 14, April 3, 10, 1980.

18. Melinda Bogardus, "The History of Notasulga High School," unpublished report by the Student Coalition for Community Health, University of Alabama, Summer 1990, in author's possession.

19. *Ibid.*

20. Atlanta *Journal-Constitution*, June 30, 1991.

21. Judy Sheppard, "The Measure of a Man," *Alabama* (November–December, 1992), 41.

22. *Ibid.*, 40.

23. Tuskegee *News*, October 13, 1988.

24. V. S. Naipaul, *A Turn in the South* (Alfred A. Knopf, 1989), 148–49.

25. *1990 Census of Population and Housing. Summary Population and Housing Characteristics. Alabama*; Tuskegee *News*, June 1, 1995.

26. Tuskegee *News*, January 21, March 10, April 14, August 18, September 29, October 27, 1988; April 6, 1989.

27. Tuskegee *News*, May 26, 1988; November 12, 1992; Montgomery *Advertiser and Alabama Journal*, May 30, 1987.

28. Tuskegee *News*, July 25, August 1, 1996; Paul Davis interview, March 27, 1998.

29. Tuskegee *News*, June 27, August 29, September 12, 19, 26, 1996.

30. Paul Davis interview.

31. Gray interview.

32. James H. Jones, *Bad Blood: The Tuskegee Syphilis Experiment* (The Free Press, 1981).

Bibliography

I   MANUSCRIPT COLLECTIONS

Alabama Council on Human Relations Files, Auburn, Alabama.
George Andrews Papers, Auburn University Archives, Auburn, Alabama.
Daniel L. Beasley Papers, in Mr. Beasley's possession, Tuskegee, Alabama.
Frank Dixon Official Papers, Alabama Department of Archives and History.
Frank Dixon Personal Papers, Alabama Department of Archives and History.
Samuel M. Engelhardt, Jr., Personal Papers, Alabama Department of Archives
    and History.
Edwin Eugene Evans Files, Federal Bureau of Investigation, Washington, D.C.
Fellowship of Reconciliation Papers, Peace Collection, Swarthmore College
    Library.
James E. Folsom Official Papers, Alabama Department of Archives and
    History.
Charles Goode Gomillion Files, Federal Bureau of Investigation, Washington,
    D.C.
Case Files, *Lee v. Macon* (1963), Montgomery Federal Courthouse.
Case Files, *William P. Mitchell v. Mrs. George C. Wright and Virgil W. Guthrie*
    (1945), Federal Records Center, Atlanta, Georgia.
Robert R. Moton Papers, Hollis Burke Frissell Library, Tuskegee Institute.
National Association for the Advancement of Colored People Papers, Library
    of Congress.
Frederick D. Patterson Papers, President's Vault, Tuskegee Institute.
John Patterson Official Papers, Alabama Department of Archives and History.
Tuskegee Civic Association Files, Tuskegee, Alabama.
The Tuskegee Crisis Study Files, Hollis Burke Frissell Library, Tuskegee
    Institute.
Case Files, *United States of America v. Edwin Eugene Evans and Henry Franklin
    Faucett* (1943), Federal Records Center, Atlanta, Georgia.

Alice Lee Howard Wadsworth Personal Papers, in Mrs. Wadsworth's possession, Auburn, Alabama.
George C. Wallace Official Files, Alabama Department of Archives and History.

II   ORAL HISTORY

Alabama Center for Higher Education Interviews, Hollis Burke Frissell Library, Tuskegee Institute
    Buford, Kenneth L.
    Bulls, A. C.
    Busby, George
    Gomillion, Charles G.
    Patterson, Frederick D.
    Patterson, John
    Toland, Frank

III   GOVERNMENT PUBLICATIONS

"*Albert T. Goodwyn v. James E. Cobb*, April 4, 1896," 54th Cong., 1st Sess. United States House Reports, No. 1122.
Annual Report 1935. State of Alabama Department of Education.
Hearings before the United States Commission on Civil Rights. Voting. (Government Printing Office, 1959).
"*M. W. Whatley v. J. E. Cobb*, January 19, 1894," 53rd Cong., 2nd Sess. United States House Reports, No. 267.
Official Proceedings of the Constitutional Convention of the State of Alabama, 1901.
Testimony Taken by the Joint Select Committee to Inquire into the Condition of Affairs in the Late Insurrectionary States, Alabama, 1871. 42nd Cong., 2nd Sess. United States Senate Reports, No. 22.
1990 Census of Population and Housing. Summary Population and Housing Characteristics. Alabama.
The Nineteenth Census of the Population: 1970, Census of the Population, Alabama.
The Ninth Census of the United States: 1870, Population Schedule, Macon County, Alabama.
The Seventeenth Census of the United States: 1950, Census of the Population, Alabama.
The Sixteenth Census of the United States: 1940, Census of the Population, Alabama.
The Twentieth Census of the Population: 1980, Census of the Population, Alabama.

IV   JUDICIAL DECISIONS

Baker v. Carr, 369 U.S. 186 (1962).
Gomillion v. Lightfoot, 167 F. Supp. 405 [M.D. Ala., 1958].

Gomillion v. Lightfoot, 364 U.S. 339 (1960).
Gray v. Main, 309 F. Supp. 207 (1968).
Lee v. Macon, CA 604-E [M.D. Ala., 1964].
Mitchell v. Wright, 62 F. Supp. 580 [M.D. Ala., 1945].
Mitchell v. Wright, 154 F. 2d 924 (5th Cir., 1946).
Reynolds v. Sims, 377 U.S. 533 (1964).
United States v. Alabama, 192 F. Supp. 677 [M.D. Ala., 1961].
Williams v. Wright, 249 Ala. 9.

V BOOKS AND ARTICLES

Barnard, William D., *Dixiecrats and Democrats: Alabama Politics 1942–1950*. University of Alabama Press, 1974.
Barney, William L., *The Secessionist Impulse: Alabama and Mississippi in 1860*. Princeton University Press, 1974.
Brauer, Carl M., *John F. Kennedy and the Second Reconstruction*. Columbia University Press, 1977.
Bunche, Ralph J., *The Political Status of the Negro in the Age of FDR*. University of Chicago Press, 1973.
Carson, Clayborne, *In Struggle: SNCC and the Black Awakening of the 1960s*. Harvard University Press, 1981.
Cash, W. J., *The Mind of the South*. Alfred A. Knopf, 1941.
Dalfiume, Richard M., "The 'Forgotten Years' of the Negro Revolution," *Journal of American History* LV (June 1968).
———, *Desegregation of the Armed Forces: Fighting on Two Fronts*. University of Missouri Press, 1969.
Daniel, Pete, "Black Power in the 1920s: The Case of Tuskegee Veterans Hospital," *Journal of Southern History* XXXVI (August 1970).
Embree, Edwin R., and Waxman, Julia, *Investment in People*. Harper & Brothers, 1949.
Forman, James, *Sammy Younge, Jr.: The First Black College Student to Die in the Black Liberation Movement*. Grove Press, 1968.
Frady, Marshall, *Wallace*. World, 1968.
Friedman, Joel William, "The Burger Court and the Prima Facie Case in Employment Discrimination Litigation: A Critique," *Cornell Law Review* 65 (November 1965).
Fullinwider, S. P., *The Mind and Mood of Black America*. Dorsey Press, 1969.
Genovese, Eugene D., *Roll, Jordan, Roll: The World the Slaves Made*. Pantheon Books, 1974.
Gray, Fred D., *Bus Ride to Justice: Changing the System by the System: The Life and Works of Fred D. Gray*. Black Belt Press, 1995.
Hamilton, Charles V., *Minority Politics in Black Belt Alabama*. McGraw-Hill, 1960.
Harlan, Louis R., *Booker T. Washington: The Making of a Black Leader 1856–1901*. Oxford University Press, 1972.
———, *Booker T. Washington: The Wizard of Tuskegee 1901–1915*. Oxford University Press, 1983.
———, ed., *The Booker T. Washington Papers*. University of Illinois Press, 1972. Vols. I–III.
Hastie, William H., *On Clipped Wings: The Story of Jim Crow in the Army Air*

Corps. National Association for the Advancement of Colored People, 1943.

Johnson, Charles S., *Shadow of the Plantation.* University of Chicago Press, 1934.

Jones, Allen W., "The Role of Tuskegee Institute in the Education of Black Farmers," *Journal of Negro History* LX (April 1975).

Jones, James H., *Bad Blood: The Tuskegee Syphilis Experiment.* The Free Press, 1981.

Jones, Lewis, and Smith, Stanley, *Voting Rights and Economic Pressure.* Anti-Defamation League of B'nai B'rith, 1958.

Kennedy, Robert F., Jr., *Judge Frank M. Johnson, Jr.* G. P. Putnam's Sons, 1978.

Lawson, Steven F., *Black Ballots: Voting Rights in the South 1944–1969.* Columbia University Press, 1976.

Marable, Manning, "Tuskegee and the Politics of Illusion in the New South," *The Black Scholar* IX (May 1977).

———, *From the Grass Roots: Essays Toward Afro-American Liberation.* South End Press, 1980.

Martin, John Bartlow, *The Deep South Says "Never."* Ballantine Books, 1957.

McMillan, Malcolm C., *Constitutional Development in Alabama, 1798–1901.* University of North Carolina Press, 1955.

McMurry, Linda O., *George Washington Carver: Scientist and Symbol.* Oxford University Press, 1981.

Naipaul, V. S., *A Turn in the South.* Alfred A. Knopf, 1989.

Owen, Thomas M., *Alabama Official and Statistical Register 1907.* Montgomery: Brown Printing Company, 1907.

———, *History of Alabama and Dictionary of Alabama Biography.* S. J. Clarke, 1921.

Potter, David M., "The Roots of American Alienation," in Don E. Fehrenbacher, ed., *History and American Society: Essays of David M. Potter.* Oxford University Press, 1973.

Rosengarten, Theodore, *All God's Dangers: The Life of Nate Shaw.* Alfred A. Knopf, 1974.

Segrest, Mab, *Memoir of a Race Traitor.* South End Press, 1994.

Sheppard, Judy, "The Measure of a Man," *Alabama* (November–December, 1992).

Strong, Donald S., *Registration of Voters in Alabama.* University, Alabama: Bureau of Public Administration, 1956.

Taper, Bernard, *Gomillion versus Lightfoot: The Tuskegee Gerrymander Case.* McGraw-Hill, 1962.

Thornton, J. Mills, III, *Politics and Power in a Slave Society.* Louisiana State University Press, 1978.

———, "Challenge and Response in the Montgomery Bus Boycott of 1955–1956," *The Alabama Review* XXXIII (July 1980).

Tindall, George Brown, *The Emergence of the New South, 1913–1945.* Louisiana State University Press, 1967.

Washington, Booker T., *Up From Slavery.* Doubleday, Page, 1901.

Wiener, Jonathan M., *Social Origins of the New South: Alabama 1860–1885.* Louisiana State University Press, 1978.

Wiggins, Sarah Woolfolk, *The Scalawag in Alabama Politics 1865–1881.* University of Alabama Press, 1977.

Yarbrough, Tinsley E., *Judge Frank Johnson and Human Rights in Alabama.* University of Alabama Press, 1981.

VI DISSERTATIONS AND THESES

Gilliam, Thomas J., "The Second Folsom Administration: The Destruction of Alabama Liberalism 1954–1958," Ph.D. diss., Auburn University, 1975.
Parrish, Noel F., "The Segregation of Negroes in the Army Air Forces," thesis, Air University at Maxwell Air Base, May 1947.
Wadsworth, Erwing W., "A Historical Perspective of Education in Macon County, Alabama: 1836–1967," Ph.D. diss., Auburn University, 1968.

VII NEWSPAPERS

Birmingham *News*, 1942, 1955, 1958, 1961–78.
Birmingham *World*, 1954, 1957.
Campus Digest, 1960, 1965–68.
Montgomery *Advertiser*, 1923, 1942–47, 1953–66.
Montgomery *Alabama Journal*, 1954, 1963–64.
New York Times, 1966–67, 1973.
Pittsburgh *Courier*, 1942–43, 1945.
Southern Courier, 1965–68.
Southern School News, 1955–57.
Tuskegee *Macon Mail*, 1876, 1878–79.
Tuskegee *Messenger*, 1933.
Tuskegee *News*, 1875, 1880, 1901, 1934, 1941–98.

VIII PERIODICALS

Alabama: The News Magazine of the Deep South, 1943–44, 1951, 1992.
Life, 1957.
The Nation, 1957, 1966.
Newsweek, 1957.
The New Yorker, 1965.
The Reporter, 1957.
Southern Patriot, 1960.
Time, 1942, 1957.

IX PERSONAL INTERVIEWS

Daniel L. Beasley, Tuskegee, Alabama, August 3, 1978.
Robert Bentley, Tallassee, Alabama, August 10, 1978.
Neil O. Davis, Auburn, Alabama, August 21, 1978.
Paul Davis, Auburn, Alabama, March 27, 1998
Samuel M. Engelhardt, Jr., Montgomery, Alabama, June 26, 1978.
Luther Foster, Washington, D.C., May 17, 1983.
Charles G. Gomillion, Washington, D.C., March 13, 1978, and December 6, 1979.
Fred D. Gray, Tuskegee, Alabama, December 30, 1983.
Hosea Guice, Shorter, Alabama, August 15, 1978.
Charles V. Hamilton, New York, N.Y., October 26, 1982.

Preston Hornsby, Tuskegee, Alabama, August 25, 1978.
Lewis W. Jones, Tuskegee, Alabama, August 10, 1978.
Howard R. Lamar, New Haven, Connecticut, October 30, 1982.
Anthony Lee, Montgomery, Alabama, April 18, 1983.
Detroit Lee, Tuskegee, Alabama, April 17, 1983.
Robert D. Miller, Atlanta, Georgia, July 25, 1978.
William P. Mitchell, Tuskegee, Alabama, June 8, 1978.
J. Allan Parker, Tuskegee, Alabama, June 27, 1978.
Noel F. Parrish, telephone interview, December 7, 1982.
Frederick D. Patterson, New York, N.Y., October 26, 1982.
Gwendolyn Patton, Montgomery, Alabama, April 28, 1983.
Otis Pinkard, Tuskegee, Alabama, July 31, 1978.
Paul Puryear, Charlottesville, Virginia, May 19, 1983.
Frances Hodnett Rush, Auburn, Alabama, July 30, 1978.
William M. Russell, Tuskegee, Alabama, August 24, 1978.
Florida Broward Segrest, Tuskegee, Alabama, June 14, 1978.
John Fletcher Segrest, Tuskegee, Alabama, July 8, 1978.
Ennis G. Sellers, Montgomery, Alabama, April 18, 1983.
W. Foy Thompson, Auburn, Alabama, July 11, 1978.
William Varner, Jr., Auburn, Alabama, July 18, 1978.
Alice Lee Wadsworth, Auburn, Alabama, August 24, 1978.
Perry Motley Wadsworth, Auburn, Alabama, August 24, 1978.

X   MISCELLANEOUS

Bogardus, Melinda, "The History of Notasulga High School," unpublished
    report by the Student Coalition for Community Health, University of
    Alabama, Summer 1990, in author's possession.
Doar, Joan, and Landsberg, Dorothy, "The Performance of the FBI in
    Investigating Violations of Federal Laws Protecting the Right to Vote,"
    typed manuscript in possession of Carl M. Brauer.
Miller, Robert D., "The End and the Beginning," sermon in Miller's
    possession.
Program for Dedication Ceremony, New Clinical Building, Veterans Hospital,
    April 10, 1951, Tuskegee Institute Archives.
Sellers, Ennis G., "Tuskegee, the Methodist Church and School Integration,"
    1964, unpublished manuscript in Seller's possession.

Index